Th

Secr

Ad

About the Author

Jane Allen learnt about addiction the hard way. For twenty years, she juggled marriage, three daughters and a job with chronic alcoholism. Jane has been through extensive therapy and stayed in the best treatment centres money can buy – both in and outside the UK. However, her true recovery began only when she met John Gillen, himself a recovering alcoholic and now an addiction specialist. Together, they have built a new life and turned their knowledge and years of experience into a unique and extraordinarily successful recovery programme. Their rehabilitation centre, Affinity Lodge, is located near Radlett, Hertfordshire.

Their work has received extensive coverage on television and in the national press.

Anna Moore
Journalist

This book is dedicated to all those who seek 'the truth of the matter'.

The Secret Disease of Addiction

The Dis-ease which tells you it isn't a Disease

Jane Allen

First published in the United Kingdom in 2008 by
Affinity Lodge
105–107 Gloucester Place
London W1U 6BY

ISBN 978-0-9558391-0-8

Printed and bound in Great Britain

Contents

Acknowledgements

Any good book or film needs a storyline, main characters and a cast. Intellectually stimulating, emotionally inspiring, this tells the story, a journey of the secrets behind the scenes of addiction. The main characters, without whom I could not have written this, are:

The inspiration – John Gillen BSc

His own journey demands a book in its own right. Wisdom gained on his personal New Path from professional race-horse trainer to chronic alcoholic to therapist extraordinaire opened my eyes to life itself. His passionate yet explicit explanations of the cold hard facts and profound insight compelled me to examine every aspect of this disease and myself. His acute observations demanded honesty from my addictive nature. His loving guidance brought me back to my own true spiritual self. I am his scribe. This book contains all I have internalised from his words and actions. We lead by example. John performs the leading role in my new story. I trust our joint discovery of Hope, Faith and Love in recovery lifts off these pages to enter the script of your new life story.

Thank you for watching over me, guiding, teaching all the while as the seasons came and went with my continual writing, researching, brain-talk and protestations: 'I've nearly finished!'

The Referring Addictionologist – Dr Paul M. D'Amico

Dr D'Amico's lifetime's work (70+ years to date) has been passed on to us for continued exploration and a constant source of reference. With revolutionary vision and intense perception of the 'undercurrents' of addiction he formulated a 'prescription' for the 'arrest' of the destructive disorder. He was medical director of two Biochemical Dependency programmes in New York, a consultant to various clinics and rehabilitation centres, a dynamic lecturer, a prolific writer whose insights surpass 'theories' and whose videos transfix the mind with his penetrating personality, awareness and acumen. Now in retirement (but still writing), the greatest addictionologist I will ever possibly meet and have the privilege to know.

His vast experience has been brought into the twenty-first century by the use of computer technology and relevant scientific findings. But the innate truth of his understanding: 'Distorted information, when acted upon as if it were the truth, corrupts human behaviour, enslaves him'; that it is only the 'truth of the matter' which can 'make us free' from the Prison of Addiction, stands as firm today as it did over 40 years ago, and will forever remain so. Thank you Dr D'Amico for the gift of your works. You know we sing from the same sheet!

The Soul Provider – The Divine Source of Love and Guidance

My source of creativity and comfort 24/7. Whether or not People, Places, Things fill my life with their own confusions, I always have Him in my heart. If I get stuck, I simply 'plug in'. With Divine Light it's amazing how easily we can find our way!

The Cast

Everyone and Everything, life experiences, good or not so good. To all other authors whose works I have learnt from, thank you (and sorry for not writing a complete list of references/citations). To Lee Gerdes – grateful thanks for permission to reproduce material on Brain State Conditioning™. To clients for sharing their personal life scripts, all similar to our own, thank you. To my parents for bringing me into this existence, thank you. To three extra special creations of life in the form of my daughters whom I love unconditionally, please accept my simple thank you with all its heartfelt meaning. (The Reward Circuit herein will explain perceived lack of responsible love for other parents.)

To all those who participated in the production:

Action Publishing, including Miles Bailey for support and knowledge, Rachel Woodman for diligently typing my hand-written manuscript (with several alterations) and Fiona Thornton for editing expertise.

Dr Peter Willis: Having gained insight for his own recovery from this unique programme, his restored enthusiasm and changed perspectives propelled his return to medical practice. He is currently a consultant for Complementary Nutritional Therapy and a highly regarded member of the team at Affinity Lodge.

Barry Welch at Digitex for continuous out-of-hours commitment.

Martin Clabby at Shake for translating my humble sketches ino amazing presentations.

Paul Airy at Four-Nine-Zero for the perfect book cover and creative skill to transform my drawings into 'finished' labelled diagrams.

Sean Gillen (SeanGillen60@hotmail.com) for the unique and atmospheric sound track on the DVD.

Last, but not least, Jade Saffer (contact through Affinity Lodge) for the back cover photograph: may your life's journey, as those of others, be filled with naturally occurring good experiences. I have one heart-felt word to all: Gratitude.

www.actiontechnology.co.uk
Digitexvideo.co.uk
ShakeStudios.com
fourninezerodesign.co.uk
www.affinitylodge.com
www.thesecretdiseaseofaddiction.com

Illustrations

Using the *DVD* in conjunction with this book:
Initially view the information to start the process of absorption!
As you read you may wish to refer to specific sections or plates, which are *slides* taken from the *DVD*.

Note: My illustrations are interpretations as well as scientific representations.

Enjoy this book!

Jane Allen

Introduction

Destructive addiction: 'A primary, chronic, neuroendocrine disorder of the brain and Autonomic (mainly Sympathetic – adrenergic) Nervous System having correlates that are behavioural in nature (structural or biological definition). The disease begins when the threat of perceived psychobiological tension reaches intolerable levels (functional or physiological definition).' As defined by leading Addictionist Dr Paul M. D'Amico.

'A living nightmare: for our self, others, and the world in which we live – **sad years** – that often starts in our teens by **happy hours** "just having fun".' As defined by author/alcoholic/addict Jane Allen.

'What is wrong with me?'

'Why can't I just stop?'

'Where can I turn for help?'

Three simple questions answered in this book.

For everyone, directly and indirectly affected, this book tells the truth. In simple words with the empathy which can only arise from personal understanding. It will take you on an incredible journey into the workings of addiction on body, mind and spirit.

Discovering the psycho (mind)-biology (body) of the Secret Disease of Addiction is an exciting, inspiring experience. It will be comforting if you feel you're 'going mad' – for there is nothing baffling about truthful information.

Exploring the essential part of us which exists (even in our darkest times) is the key by which we find freedom from the Prison of Addiction; enabling us to take a 'trip' on nothing more than life itself and take control of our life.

This education, this adventure of spirit, can change your life.

There are many misconceptions surrounding this well-documented, media-feeding, promoted pastime of changing our perception. When does 'feeling good' become 'I need it to feel normal'? What makes it so hard to stop and stay stopped? What can we do to help the process of recovery? All these questions and many more are answered in a way you will understand.

This book is written with the sole purpose of enlightenment for all those experiencing addiction. Even in this age of information overload, there remain secrets of addiction, which cause confusion and stigmatic labelling.

For those 'in the field of treatment' this book gives extra tools of efficacy. In an ideal world less attention would be placed on the consumption of substance units; which places the emphasis on the physical symptoms of addiction (liver damage etc.). In contrast, correct information on the creation of distorted perceptions, proper acknowledgement of units of disinformation in our brain (our control centre for thoughts and feelings) could change the way this ever-increasing disorder is understood, allowing knowledge to be the cornerstone on which to build a better viewpoint. 'An alcoholic does not have a drink problem.' 'A drug addict does not use to get high.' 'Abandon the substance – focus on the disease.' Discover the meaning behind these statements in this book.

A complex mix of social, psychological and spiritual aspects contribute to this disorder of disinformation, denial, internal tension and much more ...

A disease that tells us it's not a disease

This book will illuminate the multiple myths surrounding addiction, giving simple solutions with which to rebuild your life. 'I didn't know' becomes 'I understand'. Knowledge + Action = Success.

Take this book and read it. Cover to cover. This astounding insight may at worst 'make you think differently about addiction', at best save your life. Any bits you don't 'get' immediately will simply require extra attention. Something which seems impossible to grasp is often actually right under your nose ... recovery is an 'inside job'. Like addiction itself: what you put in is what you get out.

We so often get swept along by the Party Effect of mood-altering substances, unaware of the geometric progression of this disorder. This is an opportunity, a life raft to help you swim against the tide leading to the shore of destructive addiction.

Immerse yourself in this information. Digest and absorb this with the same prioritisation as you do/did your D.O.C. (Drug of Choice). Only recognition of certain truths will precipitate a sea of change against the tsunami and ripple-effect addiction assimilates on society and us in general.

In the words of a song, 'If you don't give up and don't give in, you just may be OK ... you can listen as well as you hear ...' You can read this: you can change your life!

Models of Treatment

Generally speaking addiction is treated as a psychiatric/psychological problem.

Psychiatry is the branch of medicine concerned with the diagnosis and treatment of mental disorders.

Psychology is the study of human behaviour and personality.

Whilst some people do get well from treatment this way the general overall ratio of stable recovery/treatment is a mere 1 in 3.

When you are treated in a psychiatric hospital you are with other psychiatric patients. Sometimes you are locked in.

The majority of us are neither 'mad' or 'bad' but hospitals and centres do provide a safe, secure environment in which to take 'time out' and learn a little on the psychology of addiction.

The use of *biomedical* treatment has its place for some in recovery. However, allopathic medicine will often treat the symptom of a problem and not its source. Whilst on medication symptoms may disappear and there is relief. It doesn't mean that the pathology won't recur, since the source isn't always treated.

Psychological knowledge of personal cognitive function and the use (short-term) of medication can be most effective:

Once there is complete understanding of the psychobiology of addiction.

Some say this is a strictly *spiritual* problem: that we compromised our morals, 'injured' our self and our families, left the spiritual order of life and 'broke down' by misusing a good substance.

AA (Alcoholics Anonymous) and NA (Narcotics Anonymous) etc. were founded on twelve steps which lay out in detail this 'off-track' behaviour and 'character defects' with 'steps' to follow to 'correct' or 'amend' our behaviour. Their programmes consist of 'turning over a new leaf' to enter into a spiritual order for the rest of your life (i.e. continued attendance at meetings). Whilst this is the most successful programme available to date for recovery, offering friendship, support and 'identification', there are some who just don't 'get it'.

Mentioned as an 'illness' only, many are unable to find 'similarities' with reference to behaviour weakness, deficiency, inadequacy or deficiency. This is quite tragic. Because the underlying message of AA, that we need our Higher Power to help us recover, to bring spirit back to matter, will forever remain the truth of the matter.

There are those who see this primarly as a 'social problem'. Indeed, the chaos and Ripple Effect Destructive Addition brings in its wake *is* of the highest social concern. The United States of America attempted to 'take away' the 'problem' with Prohibition. No alcohol – no alcoholics! However, like many theories put into practice, though there *was* a dramatic decrease in 'medical cases', this option proved flawed and fruitless (possibly due to human nature – we often want, even more, what we are told we can't have!). As humans we are subject to any biopsychosocial Neural Communication (see Cause and Effect, Chapter 2). Social systems, etc., influence our use of mood-altering substances. Today, many countries have social 'workers' or 'intervention' to bridge the gap between someone 'using', their environment, and 'harm reduction' (not primarily, abstinence) or 'recovery' and maintenance of sobriety. The magnitude of this *social problem* demands recognition of all the above, and more.

The missing link between these models of treatment is the Knowledge of the Truth:

Destructive Addiction is a Disease.

When we know 'why' and 'how', we are able to see 'what' we can do to maintain sobriety. Recovery from a disorder and maladaption to stress (external and internal) begins with Information:

Addiction begins and ends in the brain.

This book explains clearly the psychobiology (i.e. the biological model) of addiction.

A Note on Spirituality

As we go through life, developing our concepts of People, Places and Things, we can easily lose our conscious awareness as an observer; limiting our perceptions with Rigid Thinking, becoming trapped by our own boundaries of thought, ego, and the 'I'. Awarenes, sense of True Self, is limitless. To look 'outside the box' or 'observe'; to realise we are *spirit* and *matter*, not merely our mind, frees us from set perceptions. Words are pointers, not descriptions. The word 'God' is only a word, a concept; but one which can immediately cause the reader to react with set opinions, prejudices, or judgements, creating instant rejection, argument, or just plain protest and aversion to continue reading! To many, however, God just IS; neither form nor concept: an awareness to help define our very existence. Perhaps, for those who struggle with the abstract idea of a Higher Power in any way, shape or form, asking oneself 'Who am I?' with the conscious imagination and understanding of Self as an observer can ultimately bring us closer to a conscious contact with 'something' other than ourself. For it is our 'self' we need to concentrate on if we are to survive, overcome addiction and maintain sobriety. As Anthony De Mello (in *Awareness*) puts it so beautifully:

Awareness releases reality to change you

Synonymous with Good, G–d has been printed with a gap in the middle (sometimes) for your own intepretation. A 'barrier' or a 'blessing', personal understanding is just that: personal. Going above and beyond how we usually perceive People, Places and Things is vitally necessary if we are to change.

Section One

‘Look to this day . . .’

Look to this day
for it is life
the very life of life.
In its brief course lie all
the realities and truths of existence
the joy of growth
the splendour of action
the glory of power.
For yesterday is but a memory
And tomorrow is only a vision.
But today well lived
makes every yesterday a memory
of happiness
and every tomorrow a vision of hope.
Look well, therefore, to this day ...

Ancient Sanskrit poem

1 What Science Knows

'The capacity of the mind is as great as that of space ...'
Sutra of Hui Neng

The adventure begins: A 'trip' to discover the 'why?' of destructive addiction and the 'how' to transcend its devastating consequences ...

And so today let's start out with what we know in science. Let's start out with what we know in psychobiology and let's start out with a drug that's mood-altering.

When we take any mood-altering substance, whatever it is, in whatever form, it must enter into our brain.

All mood-altering drugs act in our brain.

But how?

How does our brain work or function?

From all the information it receives!

Just as we act on all the information it feeds back to us.

In fact, some may say human beings are just a mass of information – right down to a tiny strand of DNA – that we are nothing more than flesh and blood, with coded cells – run by a series of electrical impulses governed by a master unit we call the brain: the body's communication system.

And some feel we are made up of far more – that spirit and soul come with our bodily form – that consciousness includes information from 'another' source, other than our five senses.

For now let's concentrate on bringing our conscious awareness to 'the matter in hand' – our 'problem'.

The truth of the matter lies in the 'matter' of our mind.

Brain and Behaviour

So let's see how our brain functions. How we receive our 'information' and how our brain processes its 'messages' to ultimately create our thoughts, which in turn, affects our behaviour.

Our Nervous System monitors and controls almost every organ system in our body through a series of positive and negative feedback loops. On a basic level you may relate your 'nerves' to stress, anxiety, and tension, or 'I need a drink, my drug of choice (D.O.C.), to help me cope!'

Understanding a little of how our brain works will explain this often acute 'liking' or 'desire for' a mood-altering substance. For whatever reasons we decide to 'pick up' – positive or negative – we need to understand 'why?'.

You might now be protesting: 'I don't *need* my D.O.C., what's all this got to do with my liking the odd one or two? I just *feel* like one, that's all!'

OK, that's accepted. For now just keep in the back of your mind these questions:

How much?

How often?

How does 'it' change my behaviour?

How do my thoughts reflect my feelings, and vice versa?

Do they alter my quality of life when I'm 'best mates' with my D.O.C.?

Am I controlling 'it' or is 'it' controlling me?

Should I, can I, STOP?

Read this book then answer your own questions.

The Truth Shall Set Us Free

We use mood-altering substances to change our mood: how we are thinking or feeling.

We may drink or use our D.O.C. *because* of thoughts and feelings.

Thoughts and feelings are 'manufactured' by our entire being. Our physiological and psychological 'factory' is governed by a controlling unit: our brain.

This incredibly distinguished, though often distressing 'boss', becomes confused by distorted information from any D.O.C.!

It is a simple truth: we can't 'fix' something until we know exactly what is wrong. We need the right information . . .

Truthful information which you can use to transform your life
To create a 'miracle' within your self
The miracle of change.
The miracle of *transformation* comes from a
Renewal of the mind.
And a renewal of the mind starts with imagination!

Close your eyes for a minute and think.

- What is it you really want? To continue living: thinking, doing and feeling as you do now?
- Or do you want to make changes, to feel better – without the use of a mood-altering substance?

By opening our eyes to the truth we can change our 'reality'.

For those of us stuck in the Prison of Addiction, life can seem a living hell: an isolated world of

- Old destructive thoughts
- Old destructive behaviour

We become increasingly 'alone' when no one understands . . . When we don't understand our self. This book can help you, if you look, listen and learn.

To create something new.

A re **NEW** al of your life

A better 'quality' of life. Freedom from the Prison of Additcion.

To achieve this renewal of our mind we need more information. Information on:

- How our mind works
- How it processes information

Creating Change: knowledge – The Power Within

- Nothing happens unless first a dream ...
- Changes are not as hard as they may seem ...
- Once we Know and Accept the Truth

And the acceptance that the truth comes from within.

So, let's start making those life changes – *by defining this 'problem'*.

Our 'definition' of the truth regarding Destructive Addiction to mood-altering drugs:

A primary, chronic neuroendocrine disorder of the brain and Autonomic, mainly Sympathetic, Nervous System which has behavioural consequences

A 'Brainy Bit' – The Nervous System

Our communication system consists of the Central Nervous System (CNS), the Peripheral Nervous System (PNS) and other sub-systems connected to these.

The Central Nervous System (CNS) includes the brain and spinal cord. The Peripheral Nervous System (PNS) connects the CNS to other parts of the body, and is composed of nerves (bundles of neurons). As you will discover, mood-altering drugs – basically chemicals – alter the chemicals which alter activity or function of these neurons.

You don't know, yet, exactly how these chemicals are altered, but you do know the effect this has on your Central Nervous System.

The brain has many different departments: vision, speech, balance, etc., all of which we affect when we use our D.O.C. too much. Think of all the times you haven't been able to walk, talk, think properly.

The spinal cord is related to our behaviour by a reflex arc: the simplest behavioural pattern when a stimulus provokes an automatic response such as 'Ouch, that's hot!'

Different 'tracks' or 'patterns' of all our nerves connected to our spinal cord contain our sensory neurons.

(Incidentally, when the brain stem – the part of our spinal cord that attaches our brain – is affected, we pass out or have a 'blackout', which is actually one step away from our body's total shut-down or dysfunction – death!)

Most sensory input carried in the PNS remains below the level of conscious awareness. Input that does reach the conscious level contributes to perception of our external environment. There are two main components of the PNS:

1. Sensory Pathways (tracks and patterns) provide 'information' for the CNS
2. Motor Pathways, that carry signals or 'messages' to muscles and glands

There are two major subdivisions of the PNS motor pathways:

1. The Somatic – which includes all nerves controlling the muscular system and external sensory receptors: i.e. touch, taste, smell, sound, sight and skin.
2. The Autonomic – consisting of motor neurons that control internal organs. Divided into two systems: The Sympathetic and The Parasympathetic. These two are responsible for maintaining bodily homeostasis – our physiological equilibrium, i.e. how we 'feel' internally!

Cranial nerves in the PNS take impulses to and from the brain (CNS). Spinal nerves take impulses to and from the spinal cord. PNS sensory input is processed by the CNS (brain). Responses are sent by the CNS via the PNS to organs of the body.

The Endocrine System is a collection of glands that produce hormones. Hormones influence almost every cell, organ and function of our bodies, transferring information and instructions from one set of cells to another.

The Endocrine System broadcasts its hormonal messages to essentially all cells by secretion into blood and extra-cellular fluid. Like a radio broadcast, it requires a receiver to get the message.

In the case of endocrine messages, cells must bear a receptor for the hormone being broadcast, in order to respond. And how we respond! Later we will discuss the effects of 'messages of stress' in Attack of the Adrenals (the adrenal gland being just one of many included in the Endocrine System).

Even though the Nervous System and Endocrine System are separate systems, they often work together to help our body function properly. Indeed, some neurons function as endocrine cells.

The bottom line: mood-altering drugs affect all bodily functions, to a lesser or greater degree depending upon how much, how often, we feel the need to change our internal homeostasis.

So. What's all this got to do with a drink or drug 'problem'? – **Everything!**

Only by understanding

- The link between our brain and behaviour
- The biological and physiological consequences of taking mood-altering drugs

can we conclude our definition:

Our behaviour is secondary to this disorder: the dis-ease of addiction

Dis-ease Creating Disease

Because we can't possibly make changes or 'complete the jigsaw' without all the right pieces, let's explain briefly why

We don't have the control we think we have
once in the grips of addiction ...

To explain to others, when they say: '*Why can't they just stop?*'

There are Two Divisions of our Autonomic Nervous System (as mentioned):

1. The Sympathetic Nervous System
2. The Parasympathetic Nervous System

What are these two divisions responsible for and what does that mean to us?

- SYMPATHETIC: arouses body emergency system
  - To us that means Tension: 'I need a drink!'
- PARASYMPATHETIC: quietens body, most active after an emotional event
  - To us that means RELIEF!

Now we have explained a little why we define this as a primary, chronic, neuroendocrine disorder of the brain and Autonomic, mainly Sympathetic, Nervous System, which has behavioural consequences, let's go to the heart of the matter: how our D.O.C. distorts all sensory information.

Nifty Neurons – Gaps in our Brain

Addiction begins and ends in the brain: it's all in the gap.

The 'Nitty-gritty'

There are several different types of neuron: most of those in the brain and spinal cord are 'multipolar' neurons.

A neuron consists of:

- Dendrites – filaments branching from the cell body receive impulses from other neurons.
- Axons – also known as nerve fibres, axons conduct impulses away from the cell body. Some are more than 1m (3ft) long!
- The cell body – contains a nucleus (which does not multiply as most other cells do); damage to the cell body may result in degeneration of the entire neuron. Within the cell body are nissl 'granules' which synthesise proteins, and mitochondrion, which are involved in cellular respiration and the production of energy.
- The myelin sheath – helps insulate and protect the axons and increases the speed of the impulse transmission. Formed by support cells. (Tiny 'breaks' between the sheath are called nodes of Ranvier.)

No glial, no glory – several types of support cells, or glial cells, make up the majority of cells inside the brain. They do not carry electrochemical impulses; instead they do the 'housework' for

Neuron

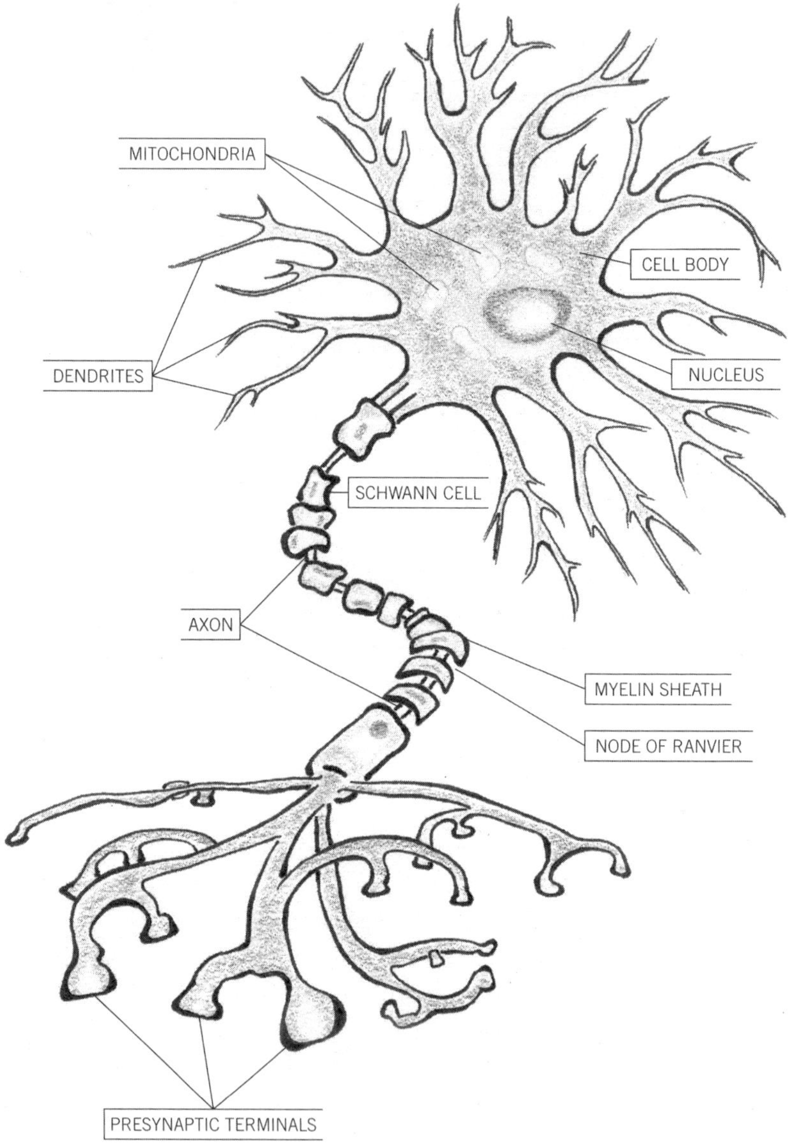
MITOCHONDRIA
CELL BODY
DENDRITES
NUCLEUS
SCHWANN CELL
AXON
MYELIN SHEATH
NODE OF RANVIER
PRESYNAPTIC TERMINALS

Communication Connection

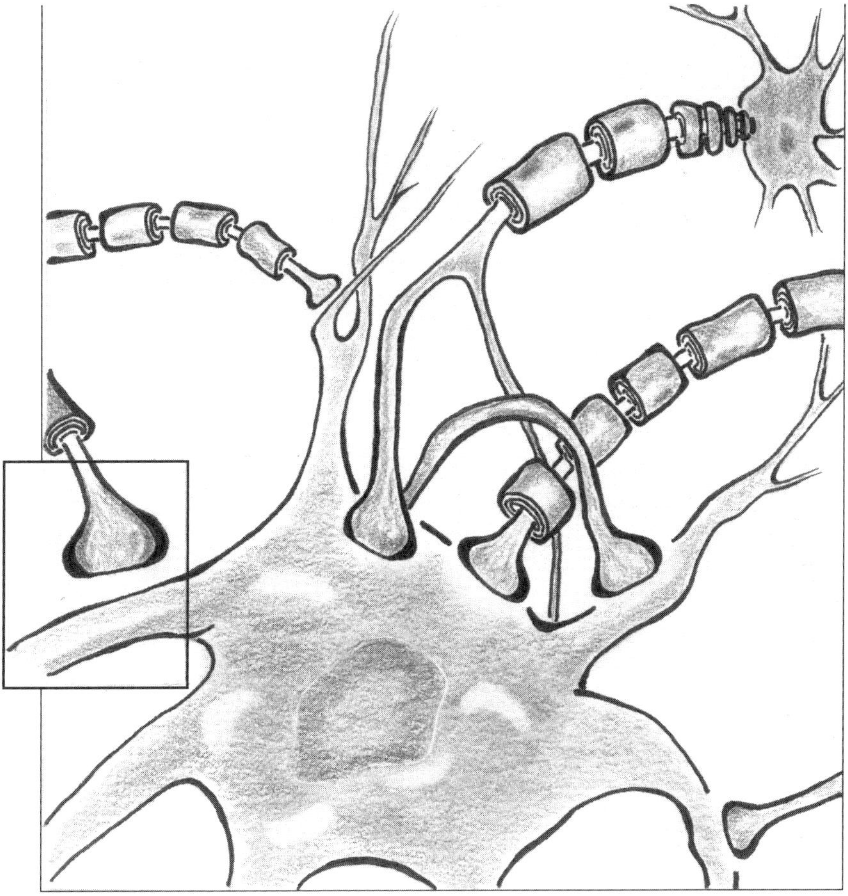

Dendrites and Axons, part of a neural net, reaching out to communicate information across the gap.

neurons by providing structural and nutritional support, cell maintenance, and by removing dead cells.

A single neuron contains between 1,000 and 10,000 connections with other neurons, releasing messages into the synaptic gap 1,000 times a second!

Synapse

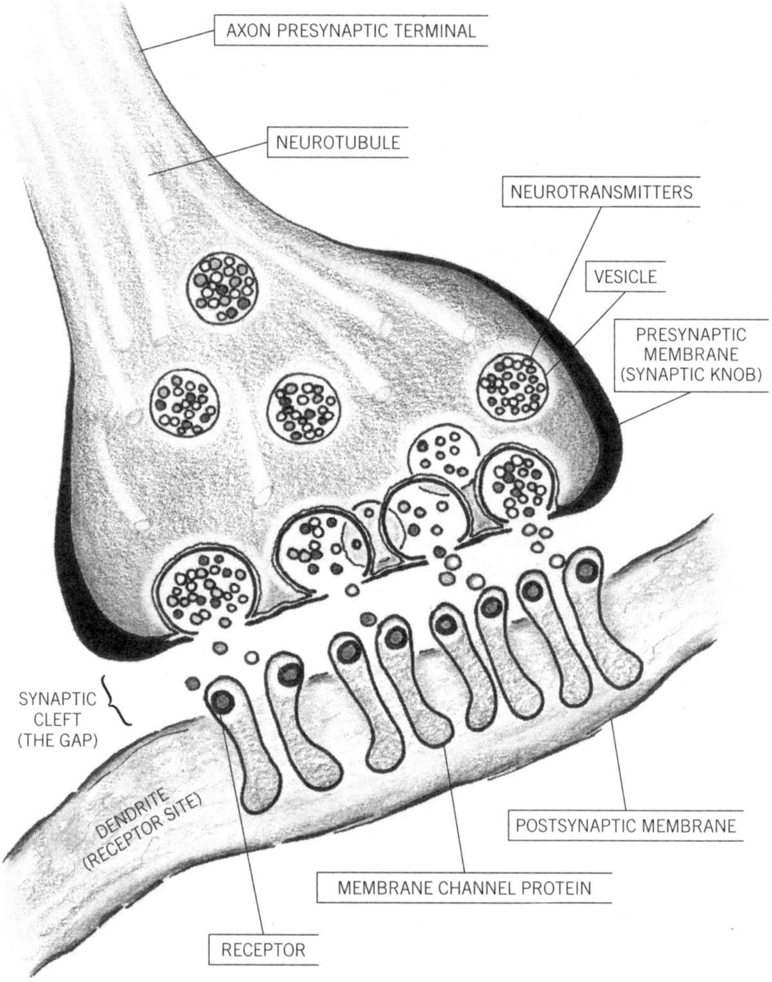
AXON PRESYNAPTIC TERMINAL
NEUROTUBULE
NEUROTRANSMITTERS
VESICLE
PRESYNAPTIC MEMBRANE (SYNAPTIC KNOB)
SYNAPTIC CLEFT (THE GAP)
DENDRITE (RECEPTOR SITE)
POSTSYNAPTIC MEMBRANE
MEMBRANE CHANNEL PROTEIN
RECEPTOR

The Connection: The Gap

As a signal passes down the axon to the presynaptic terminal, it reaches a series of small sacs called vesicles, which contain molecules of information, i.e. neurotransmitters. (Microtubules along the terminal nerve fibre help transport molecules to synaptic membrane.

Neurons must be triggered by a stimulus to produce nerve impulses, which are waves of electrical charge moving along the nerve fibres.

A stimulus changes the electrical charge on the inside of the cell membrane from negative to positive (remember that when we talk about Putting Good in the Gap!).

This nerve impulse travelling down the axon is known as the action potential.

At the end of the synaptic 'knob' of the axon, chemical 'messenger' molecules are released from the vesicles into the synaptic cleft – The Gap – where mood-altering mischief takes place!

Neurotransmitters cross the gap between neurons: the brain's way of talking and listening.

On the receiving dendrite side of the gap are receptor sites. The target cell membrane has channels which make the charge inside the membrane change from negative to positive and 'hold' the receptor sites. If this process is interrupted the response in the target cell is compromised. The action is a potential of distorted information!

Our D.O.C.'s false chemical messages can inhibit nerve signals as well as stimulate them, or simply block the channels. If false molecules of information force their way in by 'mimicking' natural neurotransmitters the outcome is disastrous – we are receiving the *wrong message*!

The conclusion is simple: Our brain will not be 'firing on all cylinders'!

Sabotage at the Synapse

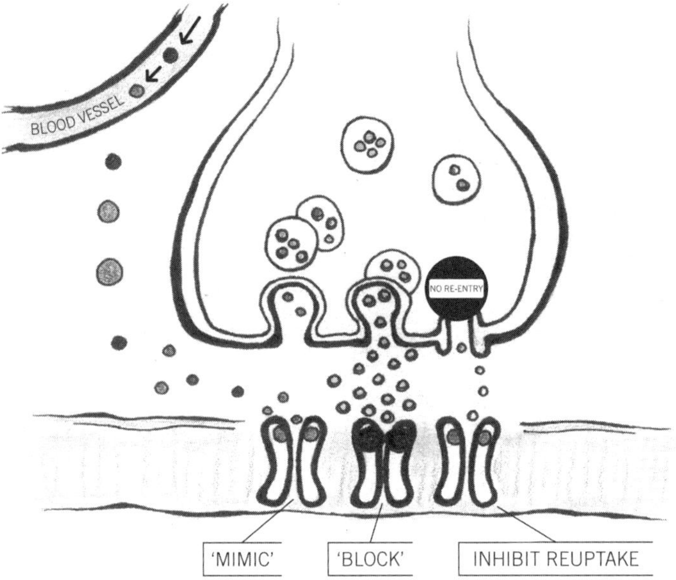

All mood-altering drugs cause 'grief in the gap'!

Various drugs disrupt the synapse to make the user feel 'high'. False chemical messages will block, mimic or prevent re-uptake of normal pleasure chemicals such as dopamine (more about this in the Reward Circuit). Neurons outside of the reward pathway may structurally change with use of mood-altering substances.

All 'Methed-up'

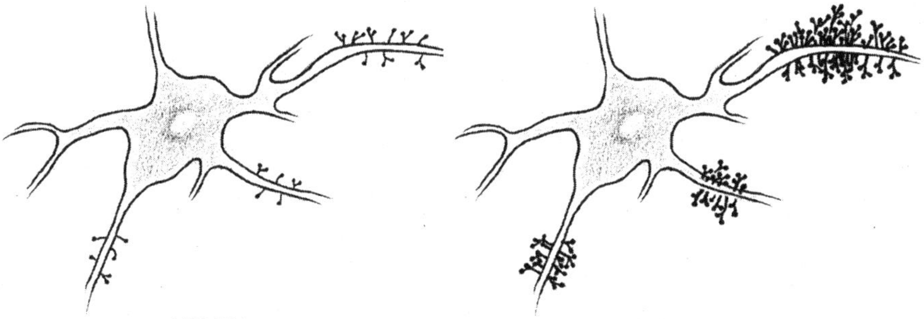

NORMAL METH ADDICT

Processing Sensory Information

Everything we see, hear, smell, touch and taste is information.

Because it enters our systems via our five senses we call it sensory information.

All sensory information is transported by nerve cells to various departments in the brain to be processed.

These departments are affected by alcohol and other psychotropic drugs. Speech, movement, sight, etc. are affected – but also the Limbic System (the emotions network), while the brain stem is the last, and most dangerous, area to be affected.

Just remember all those areas you affected when you took a drink!

To understand fully how drugs act let's go inside our brain and discover more about this transmission of information.

Discovery

Years ago, before the electron microscope was invented, we used to think information, entering our brain, did so on a series of different circuits, which were modulated by exchange systems, just like a telephone system with exchanges.

But, with the microscope, we discovered something which surprised us.

Between every single nerve cell along the system was a space or a gap. Now, if there's a space or a gap between every single nerve cell, how does the information go from cell to cell and distribute itself throughout our Nervous Systems?

By what they called neurotransmitters. Neuro because they're chemicals in the brain and transmitters because they transmit information from cell to cell across the gap. Just as we communicate with words, our brain communicates with neurotransmitters. Think of them as messengers of information.

Now, if there's a gap, of any kind – a gap in a conversation, a gap in a parking lot, a gap in daily routine – there becomes a space to let something in.

And that's exactly what mood-altering drugs do. All mood-altering drugs get in and interfere with neurotransmitters. So what? you might be thinking. Well, these chemical messengers are the foundations of our thoughts and feelings.

2 Perceptions of Reality

'Who looks outside dreams. Who looks inside, awakens.'
Carl Jung

We form our perceptions – our ideas, thoughts and feelings, from all the information our brain processes.

This sensory information is processed to become our reality.

But if drugs chemically interfere with the transmission of information then it becomes clear:

all mood-altering drugs interfere with our perception of reality!

Now, ask yourself, if someone gives you wrong directions, wrong information, will you end up in the right place, where you really thought you were going? No! You will end up lost, with no idea where you are, confused, not knowing where to go next.

That confusion, that distortion of information, happens to our thoughts when we take our drug of choice!

You must 'take this in' and understand, for this is vitally important to our recovery from this disease:

All mood-altering drugs distort information. Information forms our perception of reality.

And as perceptions form our ideas, our thoughts, our feelings, what do you think happens to those? Yes, they become distorted!

Now, those basic components are the building blocks for our *behaviour*.

We act on our ideas, thoughts and feelings, and just as neurotransmitters act with false chemical information in the gap, so we act or behave with false ideas, thoughts and feelings in our lives!

Just remember all those times you've 'acted', that you've said 'sorry' once 'the drink' has worn off – even those of us stuck in denial secretly admit our behaviour does change.

But we won't give out that information! Instead, our attitude, the way we view or perceive things, changes to match our altered moods.

Has anyone ever said to you 'You're a different person when you drink – you change, you're like Jekyll and Hyde!'?

When we change our views, our behaviour, the information we send out changes, so other people's views on us change.

When we change, things change.

Cause and Effect

Basic laws in science dictate every *action* has a *re-action*. We are no different! Our actions, i.e. behaviour and attitude, have an effect on others and vice versa.

Many of us may have said: 'You made me do that! You made me feel and think like that!'

Consider the cycle of cause and effect:

Cause and Effect

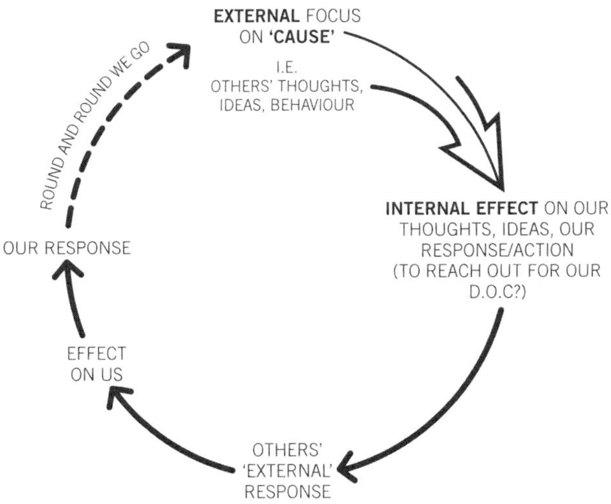

Remember:

> All mood-altering substances **distort our perception of reality,** affecting the CAUSE–EFFECT cycle.

Now consider changing the cycle, by creating a GAP:

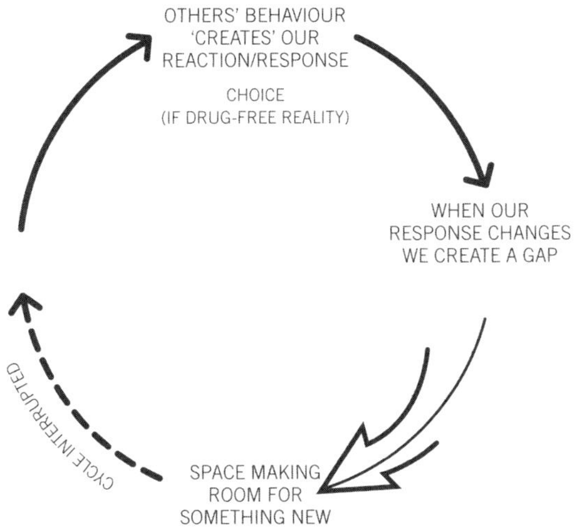

Then let's put something new in the GAP: a changed attitude, an alteration in our behaviour, i.e. actions:

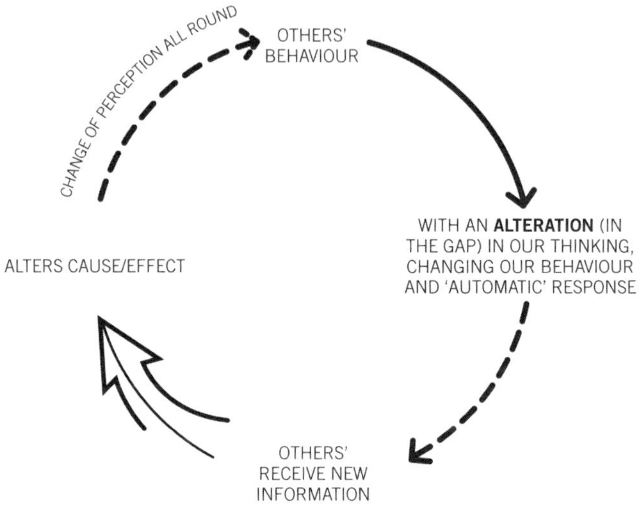

This obviously requires initial self-awareness on our part and the willingness of ourselves and others to initiate change.

This change in cause and effect may take many 'attempts' to achieve, particularly if the emotional and memory content of thought is hard-wired.

But, if we continually put something new in our gap the likelihood increases of others eventually changing their perceptions (of us!).

Consider an everyday exchange of perceptions: the cause–effect of OTHERS–OUR behaviour, attitude, thoughts and feelings, which ultimately create our 'reality'.

Take, for example, an exchange of perceptions between two people: in this case, a man and a woman.

The 'conversation' or 'exchange of information' help form our *internal* and *external reality*, i.e. how each *responds* (internal thoughts/feelings) can have a direct effect on how they react, what they do (external reality).

Wheel of 'Perceptions'

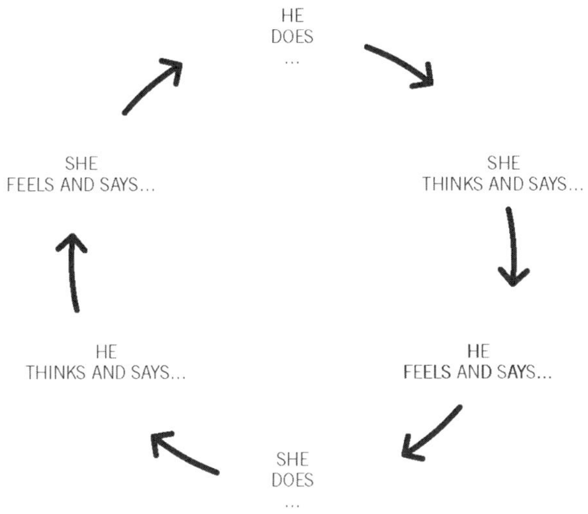

The ever-turning wheel of perceptions by which we ultimately communicate is a perfectly natural part of real life: if – and it's a big if – what we're feeling, and thinking, and doing is coming from reality, in the true sense of the word – not just how we're perceiving things through the distortion of a mood-altering chemical.

If our messengers of communication have been misinformed then it becomes a wheel of misinformation and misconceptions and misunderstandings, all of which can lead to anxiety and stress (basically fear). (More on those later.)

Now, let's recap:

- Distorted perception
- Distorted ideas
- Distorted behaviour
- Conflict!

Conflicts with others and conflict within ourselves.

Because substances work secretly, this becomes a secret disease, a disease which tells us it isn't one!

Addiction is a disease of denial. Because we don't understand, we haven't had the right information!

The truth is: our sense of well-being starts with the action of our neurotransmitters.

The state of increasing psychobiological dysfunction from over-use of any mood-altering substance creates a decreasing quality of life – mentally and physically.

This affects not only our self, but others. We are a biopsychosocial system. Or, in simple terms: how we function on a biological and psychological basis ultimately determines our social function. Our neural communication (internal reality) dramatically influences our social communication (external reality).

Neural Communication

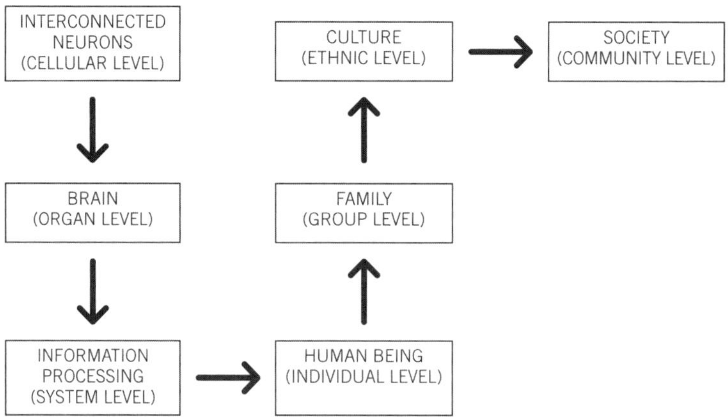

As our substance use increases, so too, more often than not, does the conflict – external and internal – in our lives.

And as this experience unfolds you will see alterations – mental and physical – in the structure of your thoughts and certain functions in your brain.

The Definition of Disease

Disease can be defined as any impairment of normal physiological function affecting any organism, especially any change caused by stress, etc., producing characteristic symptoms, illness or sickness in general.

Anything 'psycho' is to do with the mind or mental process; 'biological' is to do with the study of living organisms.

Therefore, it is essential to study both aspects to understand the disease of addiction.

'Psycho' comes from the Greek for spirit. We know we lose our spirit for life when we are trapped in the Prison of Addiction, and we go into hospital with physical symptoms to 'get our head together'.

And since it is a disease which tells us it isn't one, and if we don't realise we have it when we're sober:

How are we going to follow a prescription for a disease that we don't think we have?

By getting the right information – right now!

Our behaviour is secondary to the disease of addiction.

Mood-altering drugs neuroanatomically interfere with sensory information, which our brain receives to process as more information: our thoughts and feelings:

This interference ultimately distorts our perception of reality.

Creating an alteration in the way we think and feel.

Molecules of Emotion: the Gap Within.

It must be made clear, however, that although all mood-altering substances change or distort our perception of what is really going on – externally or internally – those emotions we experience are real, at that moment.

You see, the action of psychotropic drugs may vary – depending upon which one you take – but all are basic chemicals. And so are human emotions! In fact, there is a chemical to match every emotion we experience.

They're called neuropeptides. Neuro – in the brain, and peptides which are part of proteins. (More on neurotransmitters, neuropeptides and neuromodulators at the end of the book.)

Neuropeptides affect emotions and emotion affects the number and type of neuropeptides. These chemicals are involved in a whole array of different bodily functions, including hormone regulation in our Endocrine System and memory storage. That's one reason we call this a neuro-endocrine disorder (more about memory, the storage of thoughts, later).

The information to perceive here is that alcohol, cocaine, heroin, puff, etc., don't *give* us anything; that this experience or change of mood comes from within our own bodily chemical structures; that those 'outsiders' or 'pretenders' we take change the structure or function of what we already possess in our own brain! That we have the potential to experience a natural 'fix' or 'high'.

Let's meet some neuropeptides and neurotransmitters on the page opposite.

Emotions may be technically mere molecular messengers, chemicals of information, but don't they just hurt sometimes! In fact, as you will discover, non-material thoughts and feelings become real manifestations of physical symptoms and behaviour.

Craving, needing more of something, is one emotion we all experience in life! We all search, at some time in our existence, for that transient, often elusive, something called 'happiness'. We have a 'Gap' within which craves to find a substance of satisfaction.

Filling the Gap Within

Have you ever felt you were searching for something outside yourself to make you feel at peace within?

Shopping, drugs, sex, food, work: lots and lots of things to fill that empty gap in your life.

We call it the 'bigger, better, more' syndrome: trying to 'fix' or 'fill' the emptiness inside.

But we often forget that the 'things' we really need are not

Emotions Colour our Thoughts

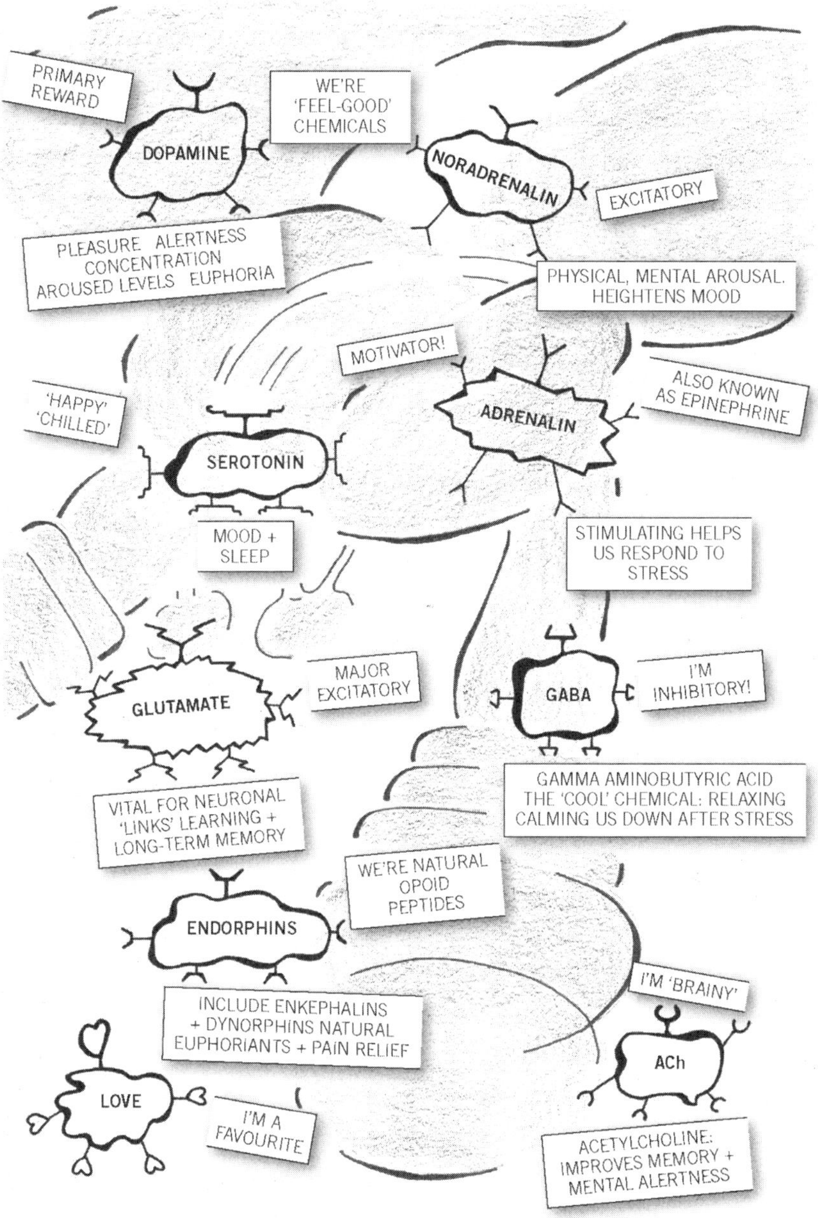

Key Intentions

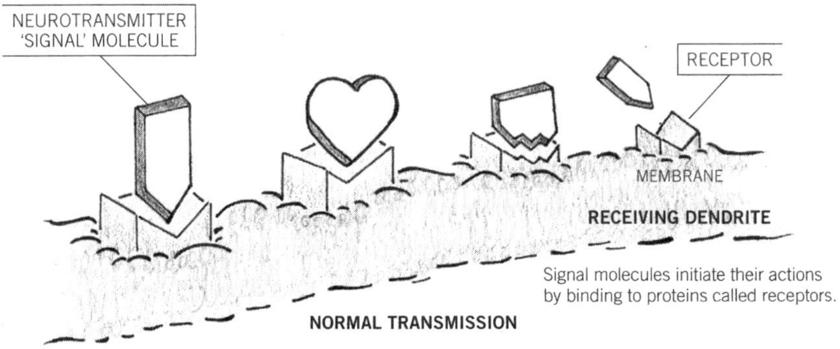

Neurotransmitters 'fit' into their appropriate receptor.

IF THE KEY FITS: THE 'CONVERSATION'

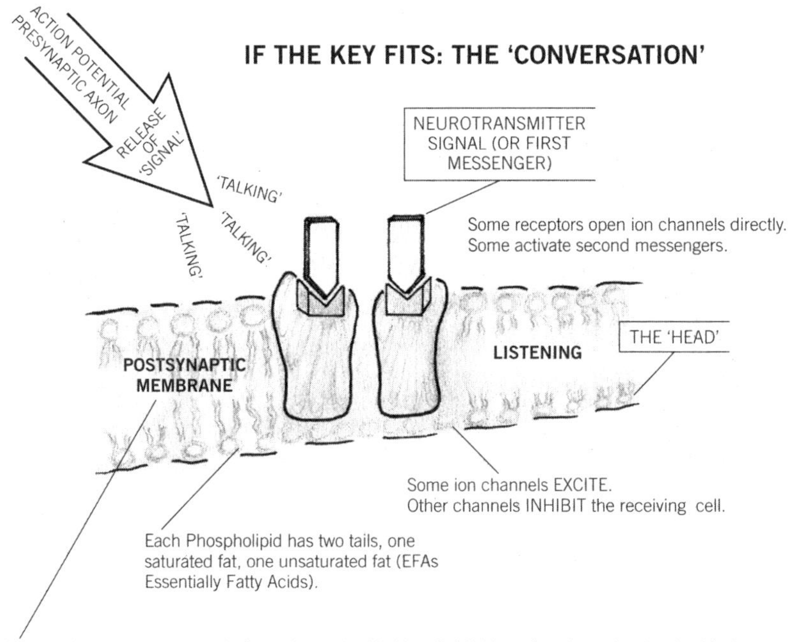

Cell membranes are composed of proteins embedded in a fluid bi layer (two layers back to back) of fatty (Lipid) molecules, interspersed with carbohydrate chains and cholestrerol.
Most membrane lipids are phospholipid one end, the 'Head' is attracted to water.

THE 'GOOD' CONVERSATION

'TALKING' REQUIRES A GOOD SUPPLY OF NUTRIENTS (E.G. AMINO ACIDS) FOR THE BUILDING BLOCKS OF THE NEUROTRANSMITTER. 'LISTENING' TO ENSURE OPTIMAL RECEPTION TO KEEP BRAINS' RECEPTORS IN GOOD CONDITION WE NEED THE RIGHT NUTRIENTS.

(SEE **FOOD FOR THOUGHT** FOR MORE INFORMATION ON 'BRAIN FOOD' FOR 'WELL TUNED' COMMUNICATION.

necessarily the things we want or desire – but are possibly on the products of advertising, media and peer pressure to make us perceive or believe we can't do without them!

We think you'd agree: sex, drugs and rock and roll were only a temporary fix.

It is natural to want more of anything which makes us feel good – that's part of our basic biological human instinct, our survival mechanisms.

All of us at some point may feel we are ruled by our thoughts and emotions: never more so than when we are in the grips of a destructive addiction. Whether it be to People, Places or Things.

So many of us say: 'Never again' ... yet again!

And yet again all our promises, our best intentions, disintegrate into thin air ...

Why? Lack of will-power, because we don't care?

If you study the next section, 'craving', that 'need' which consumes our rational thought process, is explained in the 'desire' for basic REWARDS for 'feeling good'.

The Reward Circuit

The Reward Circuit in the brain exists so we can recognise the basic needs

- Survival
- Safety
- Security

as being good (the Limbic System contains the brain's Reward Circuit).

The reward pathway reinforces behaviour – its central job is to make us feel good when we engage in behaviours that are necessary for our survival. These beneficial behaviours include eating, drinking and sex.

All mood-altering drugs directly or indirectly target the brain's reward system by flooding the circuit with dopamine.

Dopamine is a neurotransmitter present in regions of the brain that regulate movement, emotion, cognition, motivation and feelings of pleasure. Over-stimulation of this system, by the use of False chemicals, produces 'fake' euphoric effects and damages our entire 'communication' system.

At first we may use our D.O.C. to feel good (pleasure-seeking).

Then we use it to feel better (self-medicating).

The time between voluntary periodic drug use – to compulsive behaviour motivated by craving – is the difference between the non-addicted state and the addicted state of being: The Invisible Line.

Drugs which are mood-altering alter the brain's natural reward pathway over time – causing tolerance – to change other pathways and affect our entire brain, resulting in addiction.

Included in our brain circuits is the serotonin pathway.

Serotonin is a neurotransmitter that is affected by many D.O.C.s we misuse including cocaine, amphetamines, LSD and alcohol. Serotonin plays a role in many brain processes, including regulation of body temperature, sleep, mood, appetite and pain. Problems with the serotonin pathway can cause Obsessive Compulsive Disorder, anxiety disorders and depression. (Most of the drugs used to treat depression today work by increasing the levels of serotonin in the brain.)

Study the next few diagrams carefully.

If you have ever wondered *why* it is *so hard to stop*, the reward system explains: because we *think we need it* for our very *survival*!

1. This first illustration shows a simplified way of looking at the brain's normal reward system. We see the various drives and needs of the body such as hunger, sex, thirst and friendship. When these drives are satisfied a signal is sent out within the brain to make us feel good.
2. This diagram shows the effects that alcohol and drugs have on the brain's Reward Circuit. The normal chemical messengers are hijacked and bypassed which short-circuit the survival mechanisms. The result is dependence on the immediate, fast 'fix', reducing the body's interest in and motivation to make life's normal rewards work.

THE NORMAL REWARD SYSTEM

Satisfying survival and pleasure needs causes the brain's monitor cells to send chemical signals to the reward centre, and this pleasure/reward is recorded in the memory.

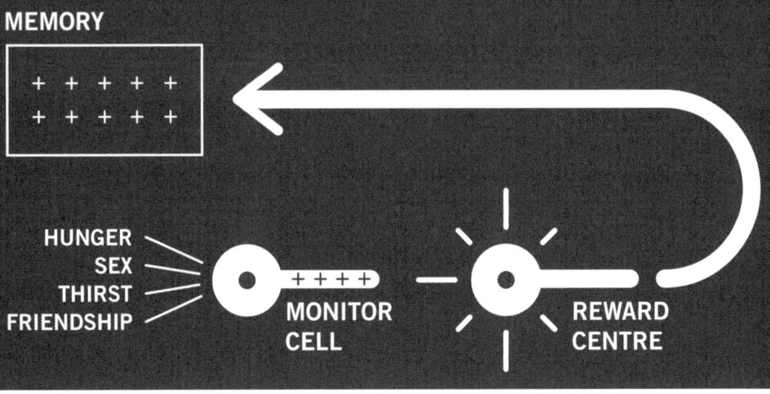

THE DRUG / ALCOHOL 'REWARD' SYSTEM

Drugs / alcohol provide artificial feelings of pleasure, and the true survival / pleasure signals can be completely ignored. The subconscious memory records this as a 'reward'.

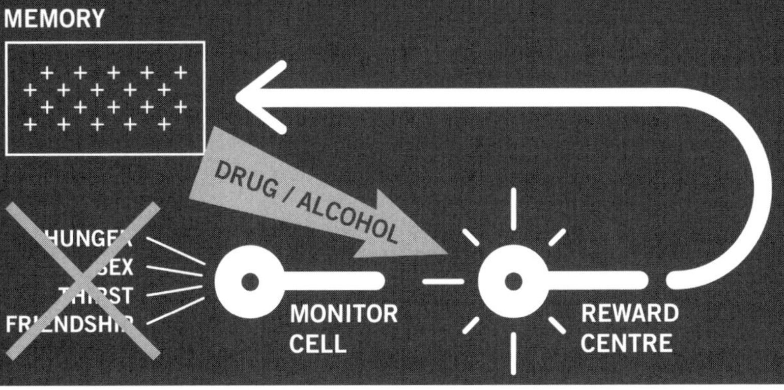

Why are drugs more addictive than natural rewards?

They can release two to ten times the amount of dopamine. In some cases this occurs almost immediately (as when drugs are smoked or injected) and the effect can last much longer than those produced by natural rewards (or so we think!).

But what happens if we keep taking an 'instant fix'? Just as we turn down the volume on a radio that is too loud, the brain adjusts to the overwhelming surges in dopamine (and other neurotransmitters) by producing less dopamine or by reducing the number of receptors that can receive and transmit signals (for more on this see 'Why One is Never Enough' in Chapter 7).

As a result, dopamine's impact on the Reward Circuit of anyone who misuses drugs can become abnormally low, and the ability to experience any 'normal', natural pleasure is reduced.

We eventually feel flat, lifeless and depressed, unable to enjoy things that previously brought us pleasure.

Now we need to take 'it' just to feel 'normal'.

Once our dopamine function is up to par (normal level), we need to take more to create a dopamine 'high' – an effect known as tolerance.

Physical Dependency

As the brain continues to adapt to the presence of our D.O.C. – tolerance – we may become physically *dependent* as the *disease* progresses. Though we still have hangovers when we 'binge', we may stop feeling 'ill' once we've had our 'top-up' amount: relief for our Reward Circuit. Regions outside of the reward pathway are also affected.

Brain regions responsible for judgement, learning and memory begin to physically change or become 'hard-wired'.

Our brains are wired to ensure that we will repeat life-sustaining activities by associating those activities with pleasure or reward – the brain teaches us to use our D.O.C. again and again, without thinking about 'it' consciously!

But as our physical tolerance increases our psychological

confidence in ‘it’ increases; we begin to think of ‘it’ consciously as a means for ‘survival’ – i.e. any time we are under ‘threat’ we reach out to our D.O.C. for help! (See Chapter 8 on stress.)

Physical dependency becomes apparent when we feel the effects of withdrawal.

WITHDRAWAL = ABSENCE OF REWARDS

If the drugs / alcohol are taken away after the body’s natural chemistry is suppressed, there will be strong feelings of panic. The subconscious memory records this as something to avoid.

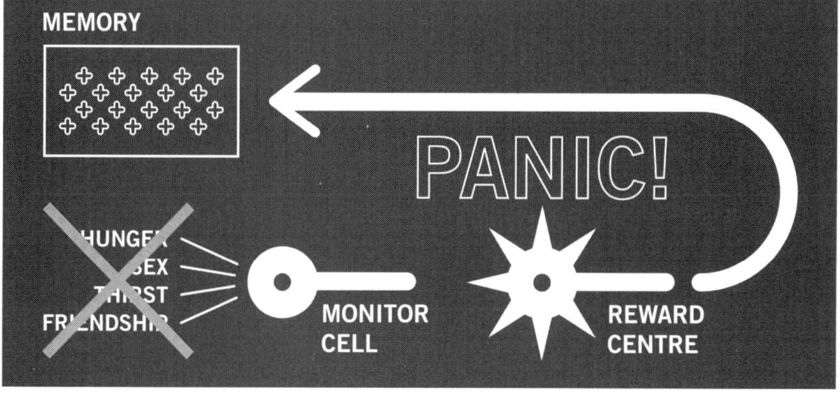

Biochemical Withdrawal

When we stop taking our D.O.C. our neurons have to cope with a new biochemical environment which they are no longer ‘used to’ or adapted to. Our Reward Circuit quite simply misses ‘it’. Crying out for their usual ‘medicine’ for ‘survival’ our systems experience discomfort and cravings. To overcome dependency we must initially go through a period of withdrawal until our neurons have re-learned how to function without false chemicals. This re-adjustment is commonly known as ‘detox’.

Pleasure Centres affected by drugs

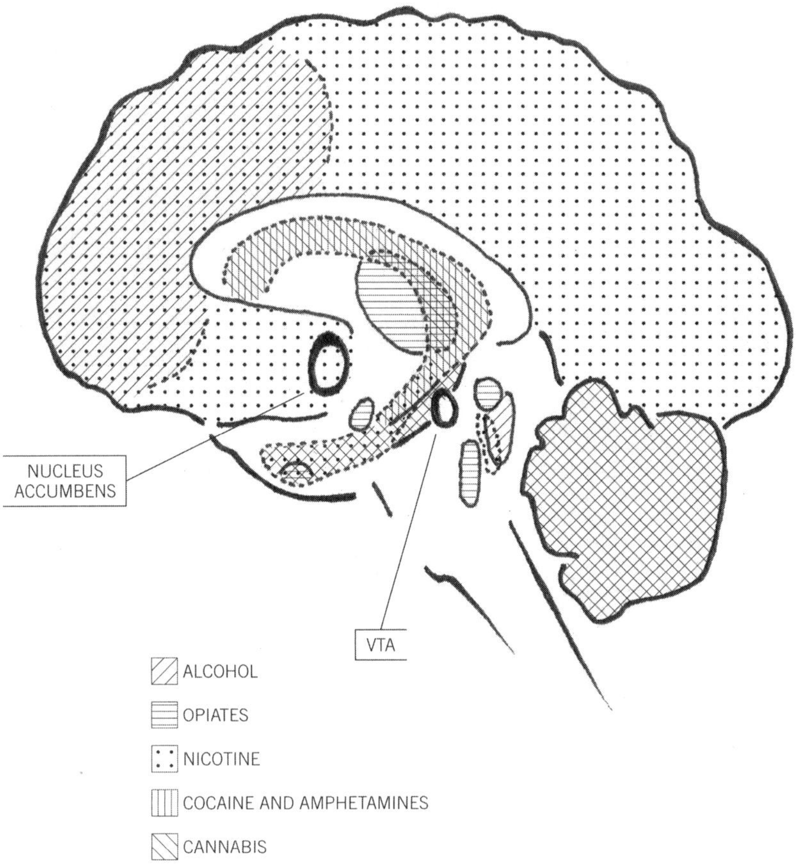

ALCOHOL affects not only the basic structures of the reward circuit, but also several other structures that use GABA as a neurotransmitter.

COCAINE AND AMPHETAMINES concentrate in the central link of the reward circuit (the VTA and the nucleus accumbens). These areas contain especially high concentrations of dopaminergic synapses.

OPIATES act not only on the central structures of the reward circuit, but also on other structures that are naturally modulated by endorphins.

CANNABIS The active ingredient in cannabis is THC, which concentrates chiefly in the VTA areas and the nucleus accumbens, but also in the hippocampus, the caudate nucleus and the cerebellum.

THE NICOTINE in tobacco stimulates several parts of the reward circuit including the hippocampus and the cortex.

Psychological Dependency and Withdrawal

At all times we must remember: *This is a disease which tells us it's not a disease.*

We cannot 'think' our way out of addiction to any mood-altering drug, primarily because destructive addictions are rooted in the Reward Circuit – our sense of survival.

The psychobiology of the disease of addiction is a primary biological need which overrides psychological 'common sense'.

In recovery, automatic responses to craving thoughts (the hard-wiring) can be re-wired by a New Way of Thinking.

Alcohol and other addictive drugs are able to hijack our survival system by artificially stimulating the reward pathway, or pleasure areas, in our brain without anything beneficial happening to our body.

At the same time our thinking patterns or pathways became distorted.

We may initially use our D.O.C. to increase our confidence.

In the beginning, the pleasure impressions in the memory were quite small. But as the natural chemistry in our brain becomes more and more suppressed and altered, the survival mechanism receives a greater and greater feeling of pleasure through the use of false chemicals.

And when we don't use 'it' we biologically feel the withdrawal.

Psychologically our cognitive functions deteriorate. What once gave us confidence, ultimately feeds our insecurities. The yo-yo effect on our brain's chemistry (drink/no drink), results in mood-swings, anxiety, paranoia, depression, palpitations and panic attacks (look at the diagram again).

As this dis-ease progresses this 'panic' is felt every time we feel 'stressed'. Increasingly, the solution to any problem becomes our D.O.C.

Psychologically we prioritise 'its' use over other activities: because biologically we 'need' our D.O.C. Using 'it' relieves the biological withdrawal symptoms, reinforcing our Reward Circuit: 'I needed that!' The subconscious memory is learning through the body that our D.O.C. is not only something that is pleasurable, but something that is needed to make us feel 'normal'.

Conclusion

What began as a pleasurable experience, through continued misuse and the effects on our Reward Circuit, becomes a biological need. As this happens it leads to increased confidence in alcohol and less confidence in the normal rewards in life.

Survival feelings are ignored and bypassed

The result is lack of confidence for and confidence in, other areas in life. People, places and activities involved with using our D.O.C. become more important (prioritisation). People, Places and Things (activities and lifestyles) that worked through our normal reward system before using become less important. In fact after a while, we will actually resent anything which interrupts or takes us away from the 'love' of our life!

In recovery, our Reward Circuit needs to be re-wired by a new ideology: People, Places and Things which *are* conducive to our basic survival. When we 'shift' our perceptions, living in 'reality' (acknowledging this dis-ease exists primarily in SOBRIETY), we can move onto our New Pathway in life, finding pleasures which are infinitely more rewarding than a quick 'fix'.

The Limbic System

Before we looked at the Reward Circuit we stated: 'It is natural to want more of anything which makes us feel good.' Having looked at the Reward Circuit we can conclude that wanting more – addiction – of our drug of choice becomes a quite 'natural' feeling – in a biological sense, because *we have created a real biological need which demands relief.*

This disease causes a change in our basic behaviour patterns, in our thinking, so we feel we need it for our very survival! This demand for relief takes over all other instinctive needs, wants and desires. We lose interest in food, our family, our non-drinking friends – if we have any! Work – we may have lost or struggle to keep up with that anyway. The love of our life – our drug of choice – continues to become everything to us. We even lose

Location of Reward Circuit

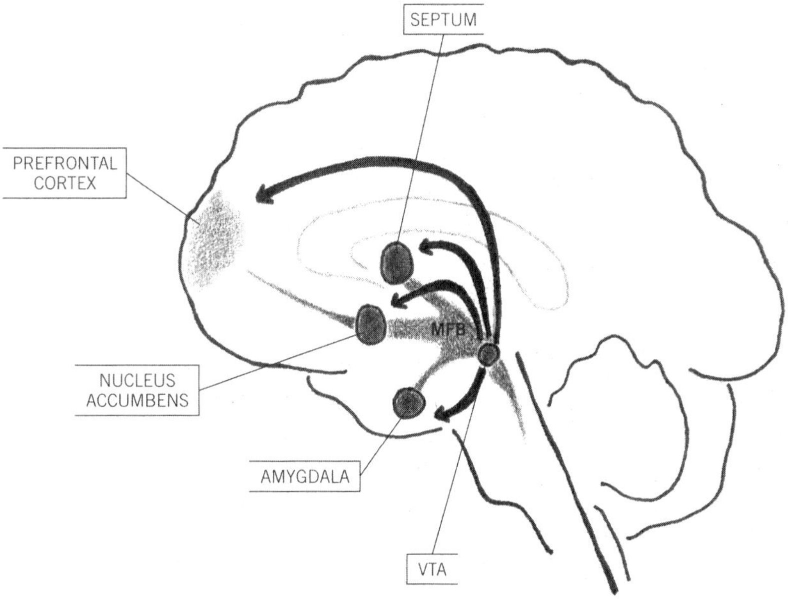

The main centres of the brains' REWARD CIRCUIT are located along the Medial Forebrain Bundle (MFB).

NOTE: The nucleus accumbens or vental striatum, which is located in the septal region, innervated by the Ventral Tegmental Area (VTA), serves as an interface between the LIMBIC SYSTEM and the motor system, and the prefrontal cortex, whose role in the process of attention and motivation is well established.

LIMBIC SYSTEM

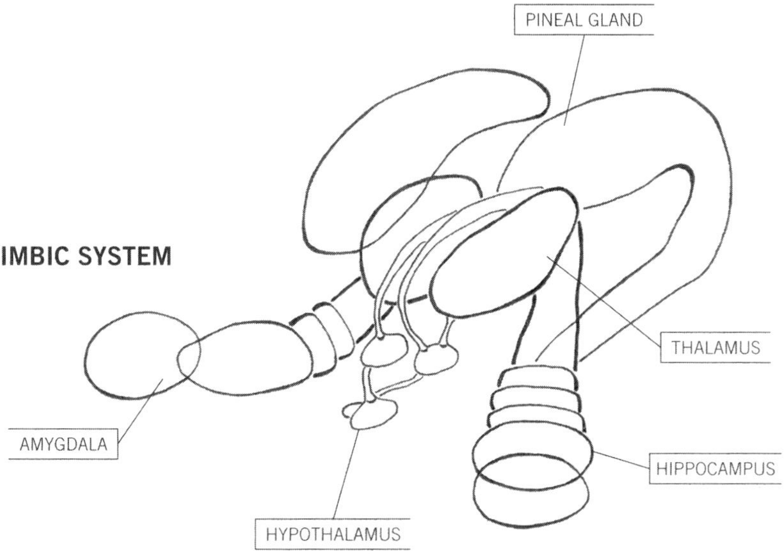

The Limbic System within the anatomy of the brain

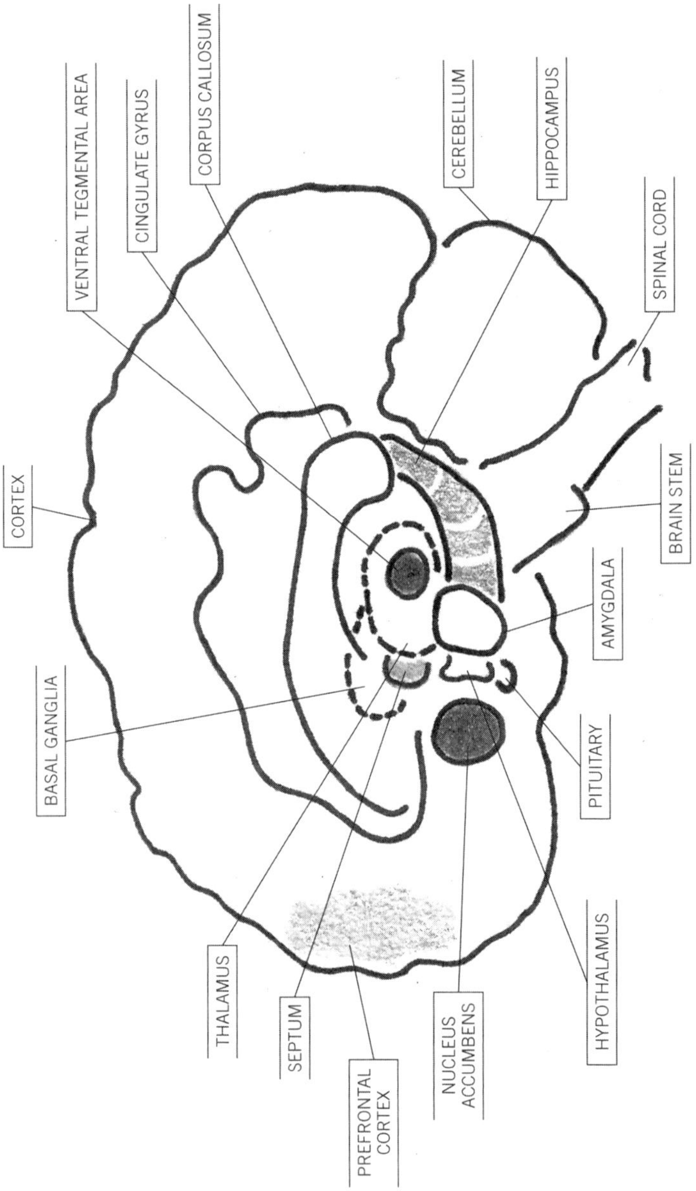

interest in sex – possibly the most basic survival instinct.

Basically, we become our need. We feel we cannot survive without it!

And on a deeper level of consciousness, this takes away another very basic human need – to have a purpose for our existence, our reason for being, which is one reason why suicide may seem preferable to the seemingly never-ending nightmare and hell of addiction.

Just think, we can reach a point we no longer see a point in living, all because we initially wanted to change a mood because we weren't satisfied with what feeling we had – we wanted more!

And so, in the bigger picture, it is when we confuse what we want or desire with what we really need and become continually dissatisfied with what we get that our lives can ultimately become unmanageable, as any stressed-out, hard-pressed soul living in the twenty-first-century civilisation will confirm!

The 'Home' of our Emotions

Emotion involves the entire Nervous System, of course. But there are two parts of the Nervous System that are especially significant: the Limbic System and the Autonomic Nervous System.

The Limbic System is sometimes called the 'emotional brain' or 'old mammalian brain' as it evolved in the more primitive mammals about 150 million years ago. This is where our emotions reside, where memory begins and where these two functions combine together to mark behaviours with positive or negative feeling i.e. reward. It's where mostly unconscious value judgements are made. Information going through the Limbic System are filed under 'agreeable or disagreeable'. It also plays a role in salience (what grabs our attention), spontaneity and creativity.

Located in the Limbic System are:

The Amygdala

Helps in storing and classifying emotionally-charged memories. Plays a large role in producing our emotions, especially fear. Triggers responses to strong emotion i.e. sweaty palms, feeling cold, increased heart-beat/respiration and stress hormone release.

Interestingly, animal studies have found that when the amygdala was stimulated electrically animals responded with aggression, and if the amygdala was removed the animals got very tame and no longer responded to things that would have caused rage before. But there is more to it than just anger: when it was removed animals also became indifferent to stimuli that would otherwise have caused fear and even sexual responses. (Just a bit like our aggression or apathy?)

The Hippocampus

Primary role is in memory formation, classifying information, long-term memory. Like the RAM in a computer it processes and stores new and temporary memory for long-term storage. Also involved in interpreting incoming nerve signals. Damage results in the inability to convert things that are 'in our mind' at one moment (in short-term memory) into things we remember (long-term memory). Have you ever said: 'Can't remember last night!' Or do you have to make continual lists to remember anything?

Hypothalamus

Linked closely with the pituitary gland to control many of the body's functions (the pituitary gland is our hormone 'factory'). Monitors and controls our circadian rhythms (our daily sleep/wake cycle). Responsible for homeostasis (making sure our body is running smoothly). Receiving inputs from various sources, the hypothalamus is one of the busiest parts of the brain, regulating hunger, thirst, response to pain, levels of pleasure, sexual satisfaction, anger and aggressive behaviour, and more. It also regulates the functioning of the Parasympathetic and Sympathetic Nervous System. By sending instructions to the Autonomic Nervous System the hypothalamus has ultimate control of things like blood pressure, heart rate, breathing, digestion, sweating, and all the sympathetic and parasympathetic functions.

Such a role in emotions, autonomic functions and motor functions demands great fortitude to return us to homeostasis after a night or day's 'binge'!

The Thalamus

The relay station in the brain.

Most sensory signals – auditory (sound), visual and somatosensory (from our skin and internal organs) – go through this organ (gland) on their way to other parts of the brain for processing.

Also plays a function in motor control.

Pineal Gland

While little is known about this gland in relation to addiction, studies in rodents suggest the pineal gland may influence the actions of the drugs of abuse, such as cocaine etc., antidepressants (such as Prozac), and contribute to the regulation of neuronal vulnerability.

Melatonin is a neurohormone present in the highest concentrations in the pineal gland. Production is stimulated by darkness and inhibited by light.

Melatonin's primary function is as the synchroniser of our biological clock and it is a powerful antioxidant interacting with the immune system. Melatonin receptors play a role in learning and memory. A natural sleep aid for our circadian cycle: jet lag, working night shifts, up all night partying, and other reasons we disturb our 24-hour sleep–wake cycle, may be helped naturally by taking melatonin together with light therapy. Light therapy upon awakening has been found to help depression and seasonal affective disorder (SAD).

Melatonin regulates lepton. Interestingly, the protein lepton is released by fat cells when we overeat. The hypothalamus normally senses the levels of lepton in the bloodstream and responds by decreasing appetite. Some of us have a mutation in a gene which produces lepton, so our bodies can't tell the hypothalamus we have had enough to eat. However, many overweight people (and obesity is fast becoming a general problem in many societies) do not have this mutation. Could addiction to food have something to do with the somewhat mysterious pineal gland? Indeed, our desire to 'fill the gap within' ties in with the mystical description of this gland as the 'seat of the soul', the 'G-d spot', or the sixth chakra or third eye chakra (in yoga), our inner vision. If Rene Descartes' description is correct, 'food for the soul' takes on new meaning!

Related Areas

Besides those described there are other areas in the structures near to the Limbic System that are intimately connected to it:

The **cingulate gyrus**, providing a pathway from the thalamus to the hippocampus, responsible for focusing attention on emotionally significant events and for associating memories to smells and to pain. Note: 'triggers' can come from all sensory perceptions, including perfume, etc!

The **septum**, which lies in front of the thalamus, has areas that seem to be centres for orgasm.

The **ventral tegmental area** of the brain stem (just below the thalamus) consists of dopamine pathways: the 'Reward Circuit' pathways. The **basal ganglia** lie over and to the sides of the Limbic System, and are tightly connected with the cortex above them. Responsible for repetitive behaviours, reward experiences and focusing attention.

The **prefrontal cortex**, part of the frontal lobe which lies in front of the motor area, involved in thinking about the future, making plans and taking action. It also appears to be involved in the same dopamine pathways as the VTA, and plays a part in pleasure and addiction.

Summary

The Limbic System, the 'home' of our emotions, is affected in every way, shape and form, by the use of mood-altering substances. Our feelings are so tightly bound by chemical distortion (being chemicals themselves), resulting in distorted perceptions and malfunctions of various departments (or areas) in our brain which process all sensory information.

Alterations in our thinking patterns ultimately 'rule' our emotions. Increasingly we prioritise our thoughts towards our D.O.C. Our feelings become ever-more focused on our drinking or using time. Often, the expectation of receiving our 'comfort' preoccupies our mind the majority of the day (which increasingly may become earlier and more often) to 'relax' with our 'reward'. How many hours have you spent thinking about your D.O.C.?

The expectations of fulfilling our need or desire for more drives us in many areas in life. The workaholic will protest it's only to pay the bills, but is there a more basic 'addictive' need for comfort from bigger, better, more? The shopaholic certainly doesn't need more things, and the expectation of pleasure from using the new things often wears off the moment they're placed in the cupboard! Dieting to lose excess weight can become a dangerous obsession (essentially distorted thoughts about our shape and size) and the achievement or expectation of a 'perfect' image manifests itself with surgical enhancement obsession. Expectations of reward can feed our ego and many compulsive behaviours: we receive 'comfort' by gaining or doing more things. Attainment of things and a healthy ego is OK when balanced by the non-physical needs of survival: love and friendship. But when we don't achieve things we can so easily turn to our D.O.C. for comfort, making 'it' the love of our life, and the thought of that false reward keeps us going until we actually receive it. Think about that!

Great Expectations: Where's the reward?

Very often in everyday life we experience the expectation of receiving, taking, gaining 'something', or the expectation of doing things to get something back. If we give and we don't receive back, that can lead us to wanting something more to make us 'happy'.

Or we do things intending to make others happy, but 'miss the boat' because

- if we have the wrong intention or expectation
- if we aren't living in the truth
- if we aren't being mindful of others
- if we're not even aware of what's really going on externally or internally,

how can we ever find a conscious state we call happiness? Being at peace comes from within. And it's a natural state we can achieve if we are self-aware, with no mood-altering drug interfering with our perception of 'reality'.

Obviously this state we get our brain and neuropeptides in is not a natural state of being.

Remember how you could laugh, cry or feel 'just OK' perfectly 'naturally' before you became dependant on a mood-altering substance to do it for you?

Unless there is a biological disorder occurring naturally or created, we humans are behaving perfectly normally if our moods vary slightly! The seasons change, so does the weather, and so do we. And that's real life! We naturally have highs and lows and mellow moments, by doing things which create a feeling, a thought, an emotion. Unfortunately, some of us want to feel different without doing very much, so we take something to do it for us – a quick fix. Just as the Reward Circuit informs us! Incidentally, those of us who like that fix from a psychotropic substance a little too often, and a lot too much, who become dependent upon that substance to make us feel normal, can, in recovery by putting 'something else', something perfectly natural, within ourselves in the gap have the potential to experience a natural fix or high.

Gap 'adapt'

Neurotransmitters, our messengers of sensory information, act like keys, fitting into the receptors on the other side across the gap.

Mood-altering drugs work either by mimicking 'keys' or, with over-use of those drugs, over-stimulating our 'natural' keys, causing a blockage or total shut-down of the receptor site.

Sometimes that site can be so damaged – imagine forcing the wrong key into a lock, it may work but over time damage the mechanism – that our natural ability to produce feel-good chemicals has 'gone'. That's when we may need a little help from psychopharmacology.

But not all of our bodily mis-functions, from the over-use of psychoactive drugs, can be 'fixed' with a pill.

The truth is alcoholism and drug addiction kills, eventually, if we don't stop! Or, can leave us irreversibly damaged – mentally or physically.

The 'Pretenders'

THE 'PRETENDERS'
'False' chemicals mimic, block or prevent reuptake

To conclude the first part of this experience: It is the action potential of our neurotransmitters, the information and the source of that information, which holds the key to release us from the negative emotions of our self-imposed Prison of Addiction.

How we experience or perceive the world and those in it depends upon what we put in the gap.

So now (in Chapter 3), let us take a mood-altering substance and discover what it really does to us physically.

3 The Yo-Yo Effect

'Our greatest glory is not in never falling but in rising every time we fall.'

Confucius

Let's take alcohol. It's the first mood-altering drug known to mankind.

What does alcohol do?

1. It's a depressant of function. It reduces function in the brain and Nervous System. It slows down your reaction time. That's why alcohol-related accidents occur: because reaction time is slowing.
2. It's the first known tranquilliser – it's a euphoric agent. It makes you feel good, it gives you a Party Effect.
3. It's an anaesthetic agent. The first known anaesthetic, it was abandoned as an anaesthetic because it was considered too dangerous to use in humans. It's also a sleep-inducing agent, as we all know.

But we're mainly interested in these two particular characteristics: depressant of function and a pleasure-producing euphoric agent. And the effects occur at the same time as you take the drug: in fact these characteristics occur simultaneously which indicates that different systems in the brain are being involved.

Now, if you depress the function of your leg, by destroying the leg or injuring it or breaking it, what do you think the body tries to do? It tries to get its function back to normal. If you damage or injure your heart, what do you think your heart tries to do? It tries to heal it, get it back to normal. That's known as the **Law of Homeostasis**. And the brain, being the controlling organ of the body, has massive defences and tries to get that function back to normal.

If we take a substance that is depressing in function the body produces biochemicals, or neurohormones that are excitatory and altering in nature, in an attempt to get that function up to par, up to normal.

As these excitatory neurohormones and neurochemicals build up we lose the euphoric, pleasure and Party Effect of the drug. So what do we do?

We take more. What does the body do when its depressed in function? It tries to get its function back to normal. It obeys the Law of Homeostasis, the laws of biology. And it produces more excitatory, more altering neurohormones. As these build up, we begin to lose the euphoric and Party Effect of the drug, so what do we do? We take more. What does the body do when it's depressed? It builds up more excitatory agents to get the function up to normal, up to par, to get the system going. What do we do? We want the effect, so we continue taking the drug. What does the body do when it's depressed?

Now, this will continue without letting up, without cessation, until finally, as we escalate the dosage of the drug, we reach a point called overdose.

This will happen **with every mood-altering drug** we take without exception.

And if we review our lives we will begin to see that there's progression: slowly but surely we have increased tolerance.

Tolerance: Progression of Dis-ease

We make excuses for the side effects, or symptoms of that progression: nausea, eating and sleeping problems, tummy troubles, itching, aches and pains, depression, anxiety, paranoia, panic attacks. We're actually quite proud of our level of tolerance, ignoring our body's cries for help, even if we experience memory loss or a 'blackout', which is actually alcohol affecting our brain stem! One point away from total shut-down and death.

Tolerance disguises from us the fact we are getting closer and closer to overdose: this is **a secret disease**.

Now, at this point we may begin to realise that if we overdose one day we'll die, so we try to limit our intake, 'topping-up' just enough.

That's when we say, '*I don't take my D.O.C. any more to get high, I take it just to feel normal.*' '*I don't drink any more than I need!*' Because to take over and above our 'top-up' amount to get that 'high' we know we're going to have to risk overdose, and self-survival instinct will, more often than not, kick in at this point. We will take enough for our need for relief. But at this point we are in a very, very risky state, close to overdose, close to death.

Now, this doesn't happen as often with alcohol as it does with other drugs. Because at that stage in our tolerance we would have to take an amount way above that which we can consume before we black out, which you know is one point away from death.

At this stage we may find ourselves being forced by 'passing out' or other countless symptoms including gastritis, chest pains, liver and kidney problems, into admitting we need help, or being admitted into a general hospital.

At this point we are unable to eat or drink properly: the only thing we want and can force down is alcohol. *It is the only thing which seems to give us relief.*

It is often at this point that we know, in our heart, we no longer have any control left at all. We are truly powerless over our drinking habit.

This is a frightening prospect. We think we need alcohol for our very survival, but we know it's killing us.

And, like finding out we have any other disease or major health problem which will mean major lifestyle changes, we fight against this prospect with denial – 'I'm not an alcoholic!'

Even though we have to finally admit we are powerless over our need, it may take much more soul-searching before we surrender to the proposition: we can never have another drop again.

This surrendering is a process. And as it is the 'love of our life' we are losing, not dissimilar to any other emotion of grief.

Denial – anger – frustration – fear! Then gradually, resignation, a coming to terms with the possibility that life without our companion can continue.

And finally, full *acceptance and surrender to the truth*.

This does not happen easily for some. It takes time, and patience, and practice.

Note: every time we 'practice' with mood-altering drugs – every time we stop then start again, when our brain goes through that neurochemical and neurohormone conflict and process of adjustment – we 'kill off' or damage, permanently, a number of brain cells.

So, if you decide to start the process of 'recovery' beware of continual relapse and detox. And remember, just like any other process 'things' can happen along the way, which make us feel stuck at any one stage, even sending us back to the beginning of denial.

But, just as summer doesn't immediately turn into winter, we need our 'autumn' of grief, that process to surrender, before we can step into our spring and look forward to a life without our 'support', 'friend' or 'loved one'. To realise, in the loss of a chemical that we haven't really 'lost' anything at all can be made easier if we lose the resentment, change our attitude and make the necessary adjustments to our lifestyle willingly! There may be many grey moments and dark 'winter' nights, but if we take each stage, each step one at a time, we can come through this process. And the gifts that living on a New Pathway bring far surpass being locked in our 'prison'. If only we had known then in the depths of despair that we hold the master key. But, life is a journey, and we can change direction any time we want with the right determination and effort.

'Stop the Yo-Yo, I Want Some Peace!'

So, let's say we want to start that process – we admit, at least to ourselves, that we need to stop and we want to stop. So we stop using whatever mood-altering drug it is we take. What happens now?

Well, when our drug of choice is gone there is a 'lag' effect. And what happens now is that there is an *unmasking*.

The exposing of all those altering and excitatory neurohormones, the biochemicals our body produced to get its function back to normal, now backlash! And cause what is known as the alcohol and *Drug Abstinence Syndrome*.

When we're abstinent from drugs, abstinent from alcohol, we are now **stark raving sober!**

Agitated, aggravated, irritated, tense, jerky, nervous. hyper-reflexive: all of those symptoms have that biological basis of the unmasking of the defences of the neurohormones that are excitatory in nature which were produced when we were under the depressing effect of a drug.

It is that tension, that agitation, excitation and biochemical stress which can lead us back to 'picking up' a drink or drug for relief!

Note: Even if we 'go into treatment' the 'balance' of neurochemicals and neurohormones can only be adjusted. And if we leave that hospital or clinic and return to our usual lifestyle, thinking we are well, because we've detoxed, thinking nothing needs to change except us just not 'picking up', we may remain stark raving sober. Gritting our teeth, hanging on to 'sobriety' for dear life, battling against our need and desire for relief! Not knowing, because we don't understand, why if we've stopped – why do we still feel so bad? Why can't we cope with life? Because it takes time, sometimes a long time, for our body, our whole system to find its own natural rhythm again. And, as we will show you, this disease has *biologically reduced* and *psychologically reduced* our ability to cope with normal tension. Many of us feel a medical 'detox' will 'make us better'. 'A detox' is a myth: how can you 'treat' the abstinence of something? Our bodies 'detox' or get rid of alcohol naturally. It is the abstinence of alcohol we are 'treated' for, an attempt to rebalance all those neurohormones and neurochemicals.

But, if that is done with another chemical, then we are simply replacing one chemical with another. If we continue to replace one drug with another, such as Valium, Methadone, etc., we are still putting something unnatural in the gap. Do you know anyone hooked on a 'replacement'? And, incidentally, if we don't change our lifestyle, all the normal tension remains, reducing our ability to cope as we still crave our drug of choice, which is why those on Methadone will top-up, to get that level of relief. And alcoholics will feel just the same.

Stark Raving Sober

We have biochemically limited our capacity for stress. Because we've sensitised our system in such a way we are super-sensitised to any added tension.

And any added tension means any problems related to our family, our children, our partners, our job, puts us at the *peak point of tension. The point which we cannot biologically surpass.*

At this point we correctly identify with the tension and say to ourselves, and the people around us 'If you don't stop … you're driving me to drink!'; 'I can't take it any longer.'

We storm off, away from the tension, blaming everyone and everything, not realising it is our biological sensitivity that has reduced our ability to cope!

And as we become agitated, aggravated, tense and nervous we immediately think we know what will make us 'feel better'. What do we know will give us instant relief? A mood-altering chemical will relieve the tension!

Now we believe, falsely, that this is the solution. Because when we take any psychotropic drug our tension, obviously, disappears.

We believe we have the solution, and they don't! We're correct, and they're wrong.

And so mentally and psychobiologically the mood-altering drug itself is creating a change in our thinking patterns, into thinking that this is the solution and not the problem!

Well, that is only part of the problem.

Tension: Our Amazing Mind

Our thinking, our process of thought, is, as far as we know, unique to us as humans. We are actually quite simply amazing!

Where do our thoughts come from? Do we have any control over them? How can we alter those we don't want?

Science can supply a limited amount of answers, and perhaps we will never fully understand all the mysteries of our mind, though we do know we only use a small percentage of the capacity of our brain, so the possibilities are endless. For those who embark on a New Pathway, understanding certain aspects of our thought process is essential to alter those thoughts which can *trigger relapse*. Because, as any one of you who has ever tried to stop 'using' a 'substance' to cope with life knows, there are a million and one psychological and tension-producing situations in life we just can't stop or avoid! And it's all very well knowing, now, it's our neurochemical imbalance which started our need for relief, but what is the reason now we're not 'using'? What is it about our thinking which continues to demand relief from a substance, every time we get over-stressed or over-excited, over-happy, over-anything, or even if we're not? Even if we're just sitting quietly, doing nothing! Particularly in the early days along our New Path, our thoughts can trip us up, leaving us confused and vulnerable, sometimes even fearful, which produces stress, something we don't need! It's appropriate to mention here, before we examine our thought process, that just as we can't dismiss our 'problem' as a disease we can do nothing about, so we must not expect others to change because we have a limited tension thermometer, or blame others for 'making' us think or feel something.

The truth is, and we will show you why, *we are 100% responsible for our own thoughts!*

Remember: we can only change ourselves by adjusting the 'heat', by adjusting our thoughts, by self-awareness. And by doing so we may create a change in others; we might make a dish all will want to taste.

Tension Thermometer

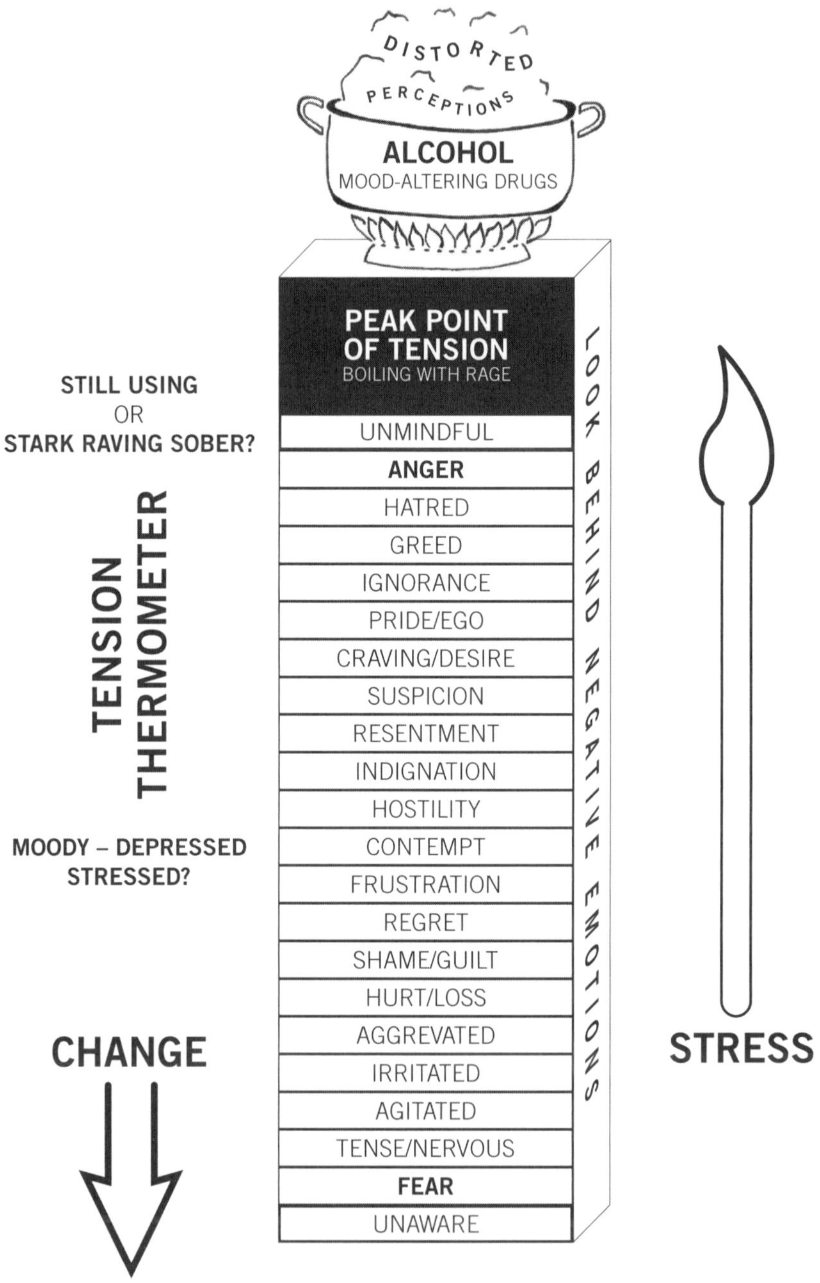

Change

CHANGE

↓

STOP

'BOILING THE SUBSTANCE' – 'GET OUT OF THE KITCHEN'

ALTER YOUR LIFE STYLE
WITH A
NEW WAY OF THINKING!

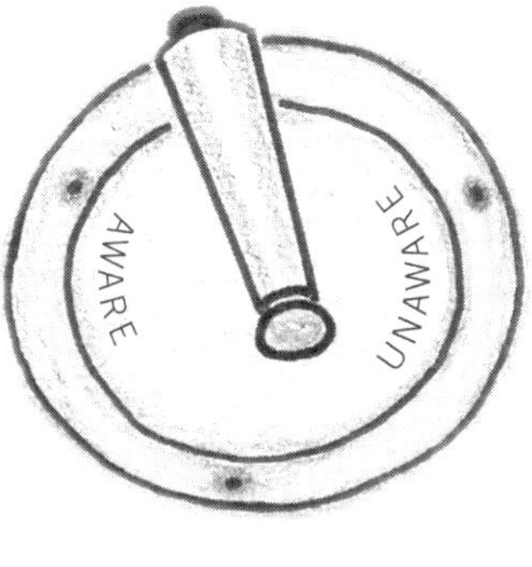

TURN ON THE TENSION TERMINATOR

USE THE 'SPRINKLER SYSTEM' …

The ‘Sprinkler’ System

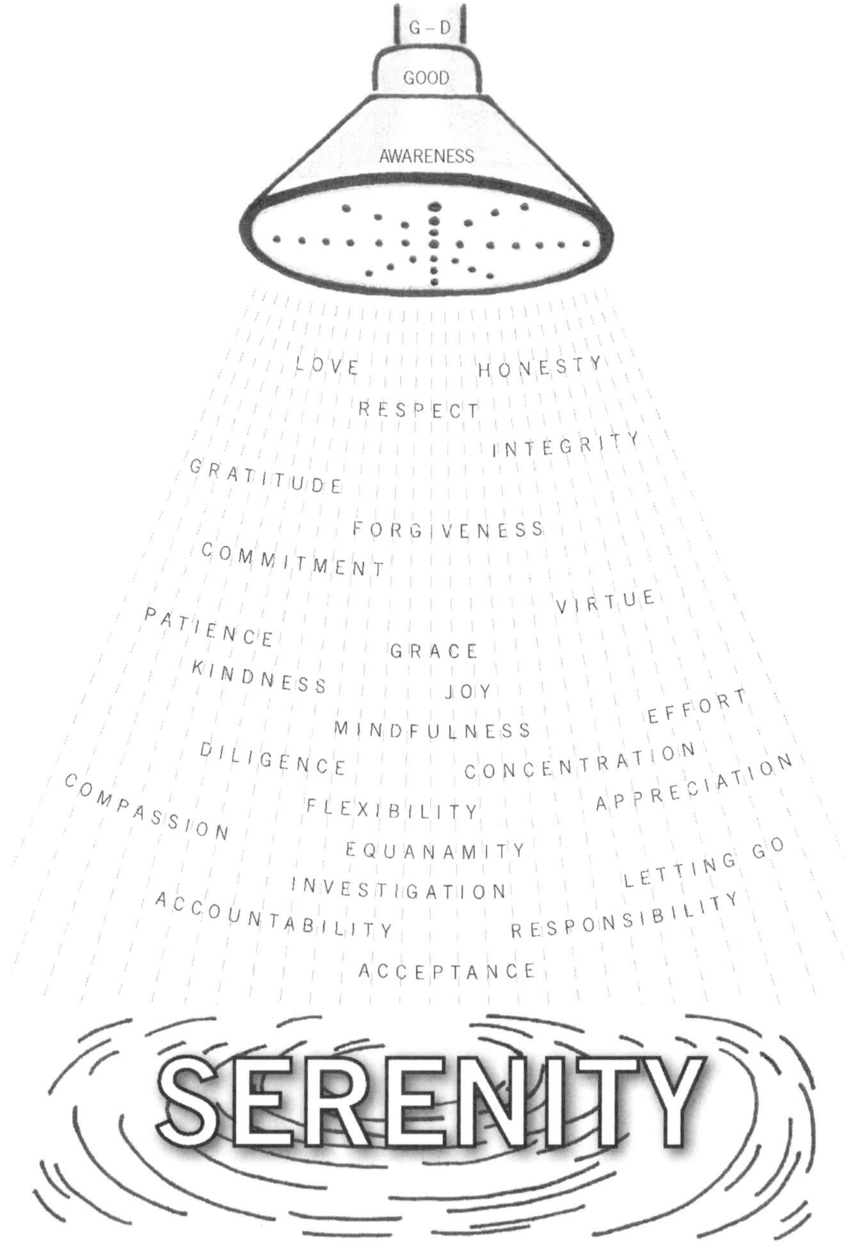

TRUE UNDERSTANDING + EMANCIPATION
LOVE + AWAKENING = ENLIGHTENMENT

4 Pathways: Knowing Neurons

> 'Where there is hope there is life, where there is life there is possibility, and where there is possibility change can occur.'
>
> *Jesse Jackson*

And so, let us move deeper into the human brain, our sensory information processing unit.

Hundreds of thousands of nerve cells collect information and relay 'messages' up and down our spinal cord, in different tracks and patterns. Once these messages are received our brain processes the information to send instructions and process thoughts. Some messages sent to our brain don't require much thought process – we automatically take our hand off something boiling hot, we don't have to think 'Oh, that's hot – I will have to remove my hand'!

Many functions or instructions are subconscious or unconscious. We don't have to think to blink! Or remember to breathe!

This autonomic system is greatly affected by addiction to psychotropic drugs. *We don't have the control that we think we have.*

But why is that? Why do our thoughts seem to be so hard to control?

At some time we've probably all said 'I don't know where that thought came from'; 'The thought of a drink just "popped into" my thoughts, I didn't really need one.' Understanding that our thoughts are quite simply tracks or pathways in our brain is vital if we want to change any pattern of thought, ultimately leading to behaviour patterns, especially if we are altering our lifestyle from addiction.

'It's the thought that counts' is probably one of the truest statements ever made, in more ways than one! And there are countless self-help books to tell us 'you are what you think', 'change your thoughts, change your life'. And you probably know what a positive or a negative thought means.

But to fully understand the power of your thoughts we are going to show you how these pathways of information form into permanent patterns, influencing how we act, which influences how we think, which can seem like a never-ending helicopter going round and round and round inside our head!

Every information processing area in our brain has millions of nerve cells called neurons. From each cell body branches, called dendrites, reach out and connect to other neurons to form a neuronet.

Each place where they connect incubates a thought or a memory. And you know the place where neurons connect, the synapse, or the gap, is where all mood-altering drugs 'work'. In fact science knows alcohol undermines the structural integrity of the membrane surrounding a neuron. No coincidence then that our integrity wears away with the over-use of alcohol! Each thought is linked to another, and another, and so on.

There are approximately 100 billion nerve cells with dendrites linking together in this neuronet or thought system.

Information Highway

Think of this system as a very large road map. Neurotransmitters are the delivery trucks on these 'roads'. Along the way they drop off their messages, units of information, or units of dis-information if we take a mood-altering substance.

Just as we can so easily get lost, take the wrong exit, or get stuck in traffic, so it is with our thoughts. We can get stuck in certain patterns or pathways or thought.

And just as we don't have to think much about where we're going on a well-known road or route, we 'automatically' know the way – so it is with our thoughts; we can respond automatically to certain thoughts.

But we all have an internal 'sat. nav.' or guidance system to help us find the correct route. We will discuss this as part of the prescription later.

For now, let's continue on this journey along the pathways in our brain.

Permanent Pathways: Hard-Wired Thoughts

The brain builds concepts or pathways by the Law of Associative Memory: ideas, thoughts, feelings are all constructed and interconnected in this neuronet.

And all have a possible relationship with one another. So, thoughts just don't come 'out of nowhere' – a vital piece of information if you're trying to change them!

Physiologically nerve cells that fire together wire together.

Meaning, a dendrite will remain in one place, one particular site or 'drop-off' depot, unless the unit of information, the experience, displaces it to another.

The long-term association, or connection between one thought and another, of wired-together nerve cells, creates patterns of thought, which become 'set', or hard-wired, creating permanent pathways.

Science can demonstrate this hard-wiring or learning with what are known as PET scans (Positron Emission Tomography) showing how permanent changes in the structure and function of synapses produce enduring patterns in the brain. Actual structural changes can be seen in PET scans. Specific neuroendocrine cerebral patterns have a defined neurobiological circuitry.

So now we can see how our thoughts, our concepts or ideas are formed, into 'set' patterns.

This acquired neuronal pattern becomes permanent.

But where do feelings fit into this framework or neuronet?

Well, any sensory information we take in from the environment is 'coloured' by the experiences we've had and an emotional response to what that thought brings.

We need our emotions to create an experience in order to 'shift' a dendrite from one depot or 'docking site' to another.

Whatever we think about on a daily basis, whatever we do or experience habitually, becomes a permanent pattern of thought. So a habit can become an obsession, an addiction.

Being hard-wired into a certain way or habit of thinking creates or maps out a permanent route along our thought system. These set thoughts form our behaviour. A set course along that route.

Our internal diagram of that course is coloured by any 'turnings' or 'stop-offs', our emotional response or experience.

This set route of behavioural response is like an internal road map. We may use a map or a plan if we're not sure of the right way, but many of our reactions or thoughts become automatic.

Just as we don't have to follow signs to get somewhere we know, so we automatically respond or react to certain signs and symbols, emotions and thoughts, along our road of life.

Our internal route or plan becomes part of our behaviour.

Note: The use of any psychotropic drug dulls our senses in varying degrees, from mild 'I feel better now' to 'I don't feel anything'. Chemical dependency creates an inability to function on a 'natural' emotional level: the yo-yo effect. We are often frightened by the thought of coping without our drug because of this; we all know we will have to feel, really feel if we stop taking it. Emotions are normally natural chemicals; everyone has them in varying degrees of potency! Basic emotions help us experience sensory information. When we stop taking, we can either be overwhelmed by our emotions, or remain 'stunned' for some time after before our natural body chemistry returns to our normal level. Sometimes we may be in need of a little psychopharmacological help, which, if possible, should not be taken indefinitely as many have their own mood-altering side-effects to dull our senses. Using any prescribed drug should always be under the strict supervision of a doctor.

Our Internal A–Z

This plan or scheme is our automatic navigation system in life. Thank goodness! Imagine if we had to really think all the time of how to respond in any situation!

Daily life would be even more difficult if we had to think 'How do I respond?' and weigh up all the possible alternatives at every turn of thought. So we need a scheme to find our way through life. Unfortunately, this self-navigation system can put us on the wrong path. Sometimes we should think before we speak or act! We shall look at our self-schemas as part of the prescription. Also, how we need to re-wire and re-frame to get back onto the correct path in life.

Each and every one of us has various self-schemas which 'play a part' or become the driver along our road of life. We change 'costumes' to suit every situation in life. We can wear several different 'masks' during one single day (see The Masks we Wear in Chapter 12). One minute we're wearing our job costume, next hour we're in our home suit, later we might take off all our masks and chill, just being our true self. But if we are habitually using a mood-altering substance we may lose our true self and become totally lost.

With each thought somewhere along the 'wire' leading to drink or drugs *we create the psychological change.*

And remember, we have created a *biological change*; our self-schema is driving with dis-information, the messages have been biochemically altered.

So this acquired psychobiological disorder creates a *permanent neuronal pattern in our brain.* This may seem like a never-ending cycle, a negative pathway of thoughts creating a negative pattern of behaviour. Remember, our behaviour is secondary to the disease of addiction.

Unless we find a self-schema within us to create a gap!

And there is a simple solution. By placing a spiritual thought in the gap, which is essentially finding the 'right' information to help us on our journey, we create an emotional experience or thought strong enough to *alter the direction of our thoughts.*

A spiritual thought is essentially a new experience.

Spiritual Thought: A New Experience

(i)

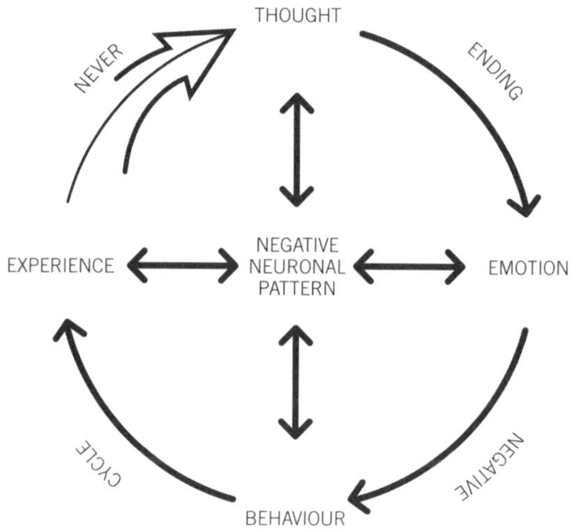

(ii)

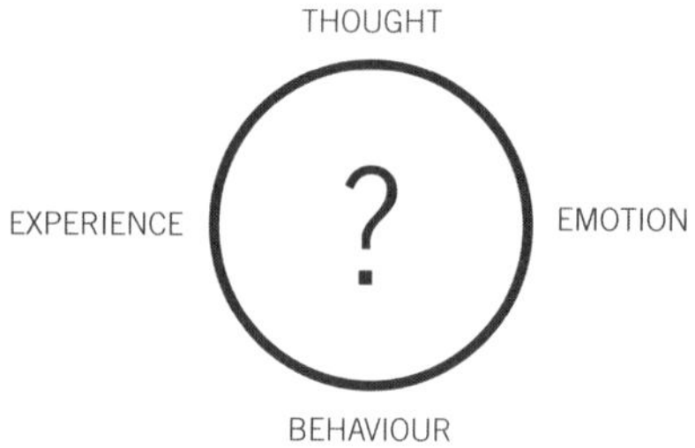

(iii)

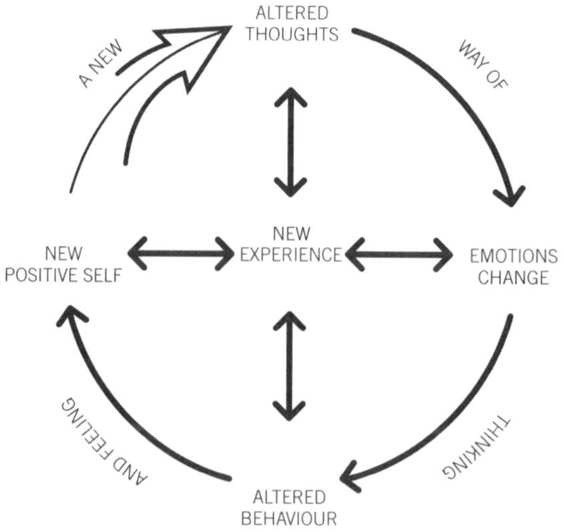

Any new experience, if it comes from the right source, creates a **New Way of Thinking and Feeling** about our self, others and the world around us; finding an awareness of reality, which we can do if we are living in reality, without the dis-information of a mood-altering drug.

When we live in the truth of our own true self we can step out of the self-imposed Prison of Addiction.

Note: The prescription teaches us how to find our true nature of self, so our thoughts are not driven by our addict self-schema. These are simple instructions, units of positive or right information to guide us on the correct pathway.

Highways to Health or Hell

For you to see how these permanent patterns affect our behaviour and way of life, which influences our already limited ability to cope with tension, we have simplified matters by graphically describing negative and positive patterns of thought as two distinct lines:

The Positive Pathway and The Negative Pathway.

See DVD slide (plate 4) to refresh your memory.

Obviously, it's not as simple as that: thoughts grow. By the Law of Associated Memory one thought leads to another, and another, and so on. And every time we even give a reason for thinking or doing something we reinforce that wiring.

The Positive Pathway represents not only a drug-free state, but a way of being which is conducive to our self, others and the world in which we live. This way of life, or tree of life, will be discussed as part of the prescription.

So, we take a mood-altering drug and it passes the blood–brain barrier; there's a barrier there that actually prevents most substances from entering – remember the 'keys'?

And when these substances enter they alter, biochemically, the action potential of neurotransmitters and receptors, which are our messengers and receivers of information with which we form our perceptions of everything we touch, see, smell, taste and hear.

And emotionally respond to.

Diversion: Tree on Road

As we travel on our Path of Life, with its many experiences along the way, we can so easily change our pattern or way of thinking by becoming 'best mates' with our D.O.C. We may consciously or unconsciously prioritise 'its' use (see next chapter). How do we know our pattern of thinking alters? Because patterns of thought are created by repetition; they are 'set' by habitual use of certain pathways created by the Law of Associative Memory.

So, if our perceptions, which form our thoughts, are altered it follows that we have created a psychobiological change. An alteration in our pattern of thought.

Now, how do we know this is a negative pattern, rather than a positive pattern of thought?

Well, if we review our lives honestly, we may admit those altered thoughts have created altered behaviour causing consequences which are negative rather than positive. That as this disease has progressed, with the habitual use of a psychoactive drug, so our thinking and therefore behaviour has deteriorated. The consequences of our mental and physical health cannot be denied. *We are creating a tree of death, the opposite of the tree of life.*

'But,' you might protest, 'there are lots of other factors involved!' And you are right! There are many aspects which influence or determine whether we may become destructively addicted to a substance. There are possibly four main categories:

1. Social, environmental and personal vulnerability.
2. Cultural and religious backgrounds.
3. Causes of an inherent psychiatric or psychological nature.
4. Genetic predisposition. Though there is not one 'single' gene involved, there is current speculation as to whether many genes are an influence.

In each of these instances lie a multitude of possible 'causes', but it is not unreasonable to suggest that the effect of over-use of a mood-altering drug, to help cope with any emotional distress, stress or trauma, makes the initial influence of extenuating factors for our thoughts and behaviour infinitely worse.

	Cause	**Effect**
1.	Social	Extensive social deterioration – job, family, friends, etc.
2.	Cultural and religious	Moral and spiritual deterioration – sex, drugs and rock and roll.
3.	Psychiatric and psychological	Any inherent nature made worse.
4.	Genetic	Biological deterioration.

The implications of cause and effect may influence our use of mood-altering drugs.

Our external environment, the social, cultural and religious aspects of our lives, may have a direct influence on our internal environment, how we think and feel, how we respond and react emotionally to events and experiences.

However, how we prioritise the use of a substance as the 'solution' to our 'problems' creates definitive patterns of thoughts.

The positive or negative pathways; the tree of life or the tree of death.

There is positive proof of this structural change in our brain (see scan slide, plate 7).

The Road to Hell?

Let's now look in detail at the formation of the Negative Pathway, which is an acquired change in our way of thinking.

The choices we make, in our external and internal environment, change with the progression of this disease.

Alcoholism and other drug dependencies are created in two ways:

1. In our body
2. In our mind

That is why we describe this as an adventure, a journey, a trip: To discover the *psychobiology* of destructive addictions.

As we alter, biochemically, neuronal functions in our brain, we alter our lifestyle, by our neuronal patterns, our way of thinking. It is vital to understand this way of thinking will be present: **even if we are sober.**

As you will see, our altered perceptions create a way of thinking which becomes 'set'. Entrenched thought patterns become our dominant attitude or character of our personality. Understanding how we choose our thoughts, which ultimately creates our behaviour, creating a positive attitude or pattern of thought, the tree of life, is vital for recovery on our New Path.

Here we must fully understand the creation of an altered way of thinking by prioritisation in the negative, from over-use of any mood-altering substance. Initially we may take mood-altering drugs, including alcohol, to:

• be part of the group • feel more sociable • increase our confidence	} The Party Effect experience

Many of us will be aware, even in the early days of our 'drinking career', that the experience, the feeling, the reward is something we 'love'. Drinking larger quantities, more often, than others.

As tolerance builds we begin to prioritise: to be with people at places and do things which provide an opportunity to drink or use; being with people who 'like a drink'; only going to places we know we'll 'get something'; organising things in preference of drinking time potential.

As tolerance progresses our time management becomes centred around our 'relaxation' time:

• drinks after work • drinks while making supper • drinks when all the jobs are done	} The Reward Effect

Our set time is not only the reinforcement of a habit, it is becoming a necessity!

We find ourselves really needing a drink to relax. We use a substance for relief, as a reward, not only to feel good but to feel better.

As we experience this need for relief we prioritise and set our thought patterns in the negative: 'I need a drink to relax'; 'I deserve just one'.

But it is never 'just one' is it? As we progress along the path of addiction we need more and yet more to get the relief (tolerance).

At this stage others may question our need to drink or use. Our 'habit' is causing problems with people, in places and causing consequences with things.

How can we view things objectively, in their proper context, if:

1 our thinking is biochemically distorted?
or
2 we are creating negative thought patterns?

How can we view things realistically if we're not experiencing the true reality? We can't.

Because our thoughts and emotions are distorted (this disease affects the very organ, our brain, we use to think and feel), we're often not aware that the consequences of our 'habit' are contributing to the things which are 'going wrong' in our life.

We view our problems with People, Places and Things as the cause, and our need for relief, our use of a substance, as the solution.

As we justify our need we will often bring up the past:

- 'I only drink because . . .'
- 'If People, Places, Things were different I'd change'

} The Comfort Effect

The underlying issues may be perfectly valid, but are not being dealt with realistically when we 'pick up', because distorted thinking renders us incapable of viewing situations in reality. If our emotions are being heightened or depressed how can we think clearly?

Any addiction to people, places, things has an unrealistic aspect to it. When we think logically, using our rational thoughts, we may prioritise, for the good of our self, People, Places, Things so they are conducive to our health.

The very nature of addiction is the Focus of Attention – in our thoughts and actions – on something or someone.

It becomes a destructive addiction when we focus entirely on something or someone, when we prioritise other things around 'it' – no matter what the consequences are.

Destructive addiction from over-use of any mood-altering substance, however, defies logical or rational thought, it defies sanity: our need for relief, biologically and psychologically, is being wired to our very sense of survival. We will keep drinking that first one, each time promising our self and others 'this time it is different', which is totally insane if we remember the Reward Circuit and the creation of a real biological need.

Losing our Way

If our thoughts are negative rather than positive how can we evaluate problems with People, Places, Things? And if we keep referring to the past to justify how we're thinking and feeling, how can we think clearly in the present?

The past can keep us stuck in the present, affecting our future. Until we let go of the past, while we're living in reality, in sobriety, we cannot realistically reconcile events with People, Places, Things.

The very nature of addiction is the focus of attention, in our thoughts and actions, on something or someone. It becomes a destructive addiction when we focus entirely on something or someone, no matter what the consequences are.

How can we deal with the past if we're using a mood-altering substance in the present? How can we possibly sort things out realistically if we're not living in reality? We can't! See Chapter 12: Letting Go for insight into fear, anger, resentment, hate and the alternatives to negative emotions and thoughts.

As problems, past and present, escalate so does our *need for relief*. More problems – more substance – more problems.

As this disease progresses by distorted negative thought patterns so too does negative behaviour: *our behaviour is secondary*, remember? But, because we can't view our problems in a realistic way, the way we deal with them becomes a problem in its own right. And, because people question us and accuse us about our use and behaviour, we lie about our use and justify our behaviour.

This eventually *isolates* us from People, Places, Things. As our 'love affair' with a substance grows our need for other People, Places and Things diminishes.

There is a myth that those with a destructive addiction are weak-willed. In fact, remaining focused above all else on something demands self-will. It is a destructive self-will, we get nothing in return of any real value, yet still we persist, continually, insanely believing we need it for our very survival.

The very nature of this disease is denial. We try to keep it a secret, hiding, planning, plotting our next drink. Just think of all the time we waste! It is a secret disease, for we can't see what it does in our brain. **It is a disease which tells us it isn't a disease!**

What else could make us give up our family, friends, work, sex, play, values, morals, our sense of peace and happiness? It takes an awful lot of will-power (insane though it may seem) to continue anything of a no-win, all-loss, nature!

Many in recovery, on a New Path, refer to their drug of choice as evil or the demon, recognising that it took over who they really are, isolating them in the Prison of Addiction. When we escape in a false reality we drift further away from the truth, and further away from our true self. Believing we are worthless, when it doesn't give us relief any longer, it just makes things worse, yet (we think) we need it.

What we do need is the right information, the truth.

People, Places, Things
our *external* environment
affect our *internal* environment.

Creating either a positive pathway or a negative pathway.

If our habitual thought patterns are those of a spiritual, i.e. of truth and good, nature, the tree of life will flourish. If our thought patterns are continually being distorted by a mood-altering substance, and we prioritise the use of a substance as a way of coping in life; if our primary thoughts are on the attainment of bigger, better, more the Party Effect, the 'I'm only in it for me', self-gain approach, the focus of attention on want and desire, then the tree of death will flourish and will continue to grow, even though we're sober.

Barking up the Wrong Tree!

Every time we think a certain way we maintain that thought pattern. Every time we link, attach or associate a thought to using, the negative pathway becomes more entrenched.

Thoughts are always linked together – the Law of Associative Memory – and can come from all sorts of directions:

- sensory perception (our five senses)
- our 'sixth' sense, our 'other source', 'gut feeling', conscience
- our spiritual or higher self

External influences include:

- media and advertising
- music – vibrations may either calm or excite and lyrics can bring up all sorts of associations!

Internal influences: touch, taste, smell, can all be emotive, bringing up memories of past events, links, attachment and associations to using.

Dis-information and triggers to use are linked to our thought process. The negativity of this may make us lack self-confidence, self-esteem and self-worth. Often we feel inadequate, trying to have it all, because we think we should have the things others have, the things media and advertising tell us we need. Sometimes we forget to just be our true self, we're so busy being part of it all, forgetting the truth: love and peace come from within.

All the good things in life are free! But how many people do you know who say 'I'm happy just being me'?

By using a substance we're not even starting with the right information to make the right choices. We make 'mountains out of molehills' because our thoughts are distorted, often choosing People, Places, Things we wouldn't if living in a substance-free reality!

Our internal environment, our emotions and thoughts, create conflict with our external environment when we use any mood-altering substance.

In recovery, our New Path, situations and events, People, Places and Things won't magically change, but the way we cope and deal with them can, by choosing what we prioritise and choosing what we focus our attention on. Being **100% responsible for our own thoughts and actions!**

On our New Path we find a way to *live in the world, but not of it*, which means by living in reality we are part of everyday life, but by 'watching' our thoughts we are consciously aware to not be part of our old (often chaotic) way of living. More about this in The Prescription.

Before you contemplate on and 'digest' the next 'dose' of information in SECTION TWO, play the *DVD* to familiarise yourself with the graphical representations of the 'Journey' through Destructive Addiction.

Refer to the plates after page 244 whilst reading if you need to refresh your memory.

Section Two

'Live in the world but not of it'

If

If only I felt Peace Within
If only things were different
If only someone knew my pain
If only I felt whole again . . .

Taken from *If* Jane Allen

5 The Journey

'It is never too late to be what you might have been.'
George Eliot

Ask any teenager what they'd like to be when they're in their 20s, 30s or 40s; I doubt the answer would be 'an alcoholic/addict'! Sadly, the invisible line between being addicted and not addicted does not present itself as an ultimatum: 'If you take one more step you'll fall off the edge!' The Journey towards dependence, addiction, or subsequent total reliance to 'feel normal' may take any number of years, depending on the amount of, and how often we use, our D.O.C.

This Journey takes us from 'innocently' looking forward to 'getting-out-of-it' after a hard week's work, making sure we have 'a little for relief' at the end of a day, 'just one' to relieve the tension (or simply enjoy our self) during the day; to needing it to quell the shakes/symptoms of withdrawal, ultimately perhaps as we open our eyes from yet another dreadful night's sleep (nightmares, night terrors, DTs).

Once that invisible line has been crossed Geometric Progression kicks in (for more on this see end of this chapter), with each 'trip' taking us further away from 'reality'. Thereafter, the amount, the frequency, and most importantly – *our Way of Thinking, Our Lifestyle* – dictates to what degree our addiction affects us as a whole.

Our 'level' of prioritisation (how important it is/becomes to us) dictates the speed at which we are affected, ultimately making our lives 'unmanageable' without our D.O.C.

There are millions of 'functioning' alcoholics/addicts, who would be quite appalled if you suggested 'it' was their problem! Many who attribute 'depression' to life's problems/pressures, or earlier emotional life-experiences. Many who seemingly manage to 'cope with' or 'contain' their addiction during the earlier stage of Geometric Progression, by 'cutting-back-a-bit' when times are less stressful but turning to their 'bit-of-relief' during a 'rough patch':

Thereby reinforcing negative thought patterns
(nerve cells that fire together, wire together).

Misconception and stigmatic labelling often prevents us from acknowledging we have a 'problem', at all! The image of a 'park-bench' alcoholic or a 'dark-alley' addict tells us our 'just a habit' isn't a problem ... That when it becomes a problem we'll 'knock it on the head'.

Remember: addiction starts and ends in the brain!

'I only drink/use when I want/need it!'

'Just a "little to help" (again!)'

'I don't do 'it' in the morning: I'm not hooked like an alcoholic/addict!'

The disease itself creates a distorted perception:
A Dis-ease which tells us it isn't one!

All the while it's progressing we don't make the connection: that we're reinforcing our need for relief by the very substance creating a biological and psychological demand for relief!

By prioritising our D.O.C. as a coping mechanism or feel-good Party Effect we reinforce our way of thinking to convince ourselves

'It' is the 'solution', not the 'problem'
But the exact opposite is the truth!

The more we make our D.O.C. our regular companion (socially or alone), the more 'it' invades our privacy. 'It' sneaks into our thoughts, giving us false information, false promises to solve our problems: while our sense of self erodes our broken promises.

Its secret progression continues!

Prioritisation/Time Management

We can easily prioritise in the Negative Pattern. An alcoholic wouldn't think of going to a hotel where there's no alcohol, just as a drug addict wouldn't think of going to a country where there are no drugs.

That's obviously the obvious! But there are far more subtle ways in which drink and drugs become the *Focus of our Attention.*

For the Party Effect or Self-Medication our D.O.C. can become our soul-mate: embedded within our Reward Circuit, inextricably linked to our emotions (the Limbic System), how we consciously or unconsciously prioritise this 'fun' relationship, 'source of comfort' or 'instant energy-fix' by our Process of Thought (with Biological Need) is the *reinforcer* or terminator (with abstinence in recovery) of our addiction.

Often, we are not even consciously aware we are prioritising the use of our D.O.C. over and above People, Places and Things which hold meaning for us, until we are well and truly hooked.

Our distorted way of thinking becomes secondary to the disease itself!

As negative thinking patterns become 'self' we cannot see how our involvement with our D.O.C. is prioritising our *Management of Time.*

Slowly but surely (or with rapid ease depending on 'binges'), as this dis-ease progresses we abandon People, Places and Things which don't fit in with our 'habit' or pattern of thought.

Time Management (Background)

1. We always make time for our D.O.C. Somehow we don't have to fit 'it' in between other commitments – rather, the other way round.
2. Substance mis-use affects cognitive function and memory; so does stress. As this is a dis-ease of stress and we are creating extra biological stress within the very organ (our brain) with which we process and manage stress, we can sometimes forget other things quite easily.
3. Even when we're 'physically' there we're not totally in

'reality' because our perception is altered (remember Cause and Effect earlier).

4. We may become impatient, trying to hurry-things-along so we can get to our D.O.C. at a set time or when we feel stressed. In fact, a prime characteristic of someone with a 'problem' is being **Tense, Nervous, Agitated, Aggravated, Irritated.**
5. When we don't get 'things' done as a consequence of a hangover our frustration causes more tension: a vicious cycle – we 'need' more to relax.
6. If we're using stimulants to keep us going we may either 'crash' physically when we stop or self-balance the Yo-Yo Effect with a depressant such as alcohol (different drug: same biological disease being created).
7. Missed opportunities: anything which interferes with 'using' time gradually gets refused. As we saw in the **Reward Circuit** what was once something 'nice' to do with friends etc, becomes the *sole purpose* of any opportunity to 'get out of it'.

Summary:

- buying/sourcing
- drinking/using
- hangover/consequences

Count the Cost of Time
Time = Your life

As we re-emphasise and reinforce the negative, we set the pattern. How can we learn coping skills in reality, if we're not there, not living in reality? We can't!

As the disease of addiction progresses we

Link, Attach and Associate People, Places, Things
to this negative thought pattern.

Take a look at the 'Positive Proof' scan (Plate 7) for proof of these neuronal changes. (More on the structural and functional change in Chapter 7.)

The split

Every time we take any mood-altering substance it distorts reality. We have simplified matters by visually explaining this change or switch in our perception of reality as The Split.

Information coming from the reality of our *external environment* via our five senses is *altered* by alcohol or other mood-altering drugs.

Our 'habit' links our *internal environment* (our thoughts and feelings) to our *external actions* i.e. *behaviour.*

habitual use – habitual thoughts = habit reinforced

The 'split' in our personality as we alter our mood is being created by the mood-altering substance: **biologically.**

As we progress along the route of addiction we are *altering our thinking and changing our behaviour.* We even start *hiding* our D.O.C.

We hide the amount we really drink/use: verbally minimising – 'I've only had one (or two)'; physically hiding our 'stash'; keeping a 'spare' for our self. And panic sets in when we run out!

We lie, cheat and sometimes steal as we prioritise our D.O.C. above all else.

Like a drug dealer smuggling 'gear' through customs, we can all be devious and extremely ingenious when it comes to hiding our supply: sheds, drawers, laundry baskets, car boots, in between other bits of junk we'll hide our 'junk'. Anywhere there's a space, just in case we *need relief.*

Entrenchment

As time goes by this negative pattern becomes more entrenched, more set, by use of a mood-altering substance and other forms of dis-information (a negative lifestyle) creating their own negative patterns.

As these negative patterns of thought become more set, which can occur **even if we're sober**, the positive pattern of thought fades.

As the negative is being fed, with negative thoughts, from distorted perceptions, it grows and develops, becoming our predominant 'personality' or pattern of thought (see the Prescription for the self-scheming patterns of thought). As with anything else undernourished, abandoned, starved of thought, care and attention, the positive pattern of thought withers and dies when we prioritise in a negative lifestyle.

Think of the growth of our neuronets as a tree. Habitual thought patterns are its roots (entrenchment). As time passes, prioritisation helps dictate whether its branches (dendrites) either grow in health, able to withstand the stress of a storm (Emotional Muscle) or, become susceptible to breakage (from the blockage by a substance) to snap or simply die. (Emotional Muscle is created by participation in reality life, not a quick-fix attitude. It's the 'doing' that which is 'right' and 'good' which takes us through the tough times: '*When the going gets tough, the tough get going* . . .')

Patterns of thought can be likened to the **Tree of Life** or the **Tree of Death**. A Positive Pattern of Thought or a Negative Pattern of Thought.

As the tree of death grows, the tree of life fades. We will see how the effect of taking any mood-altering drug directly affects our lifestyle outcomes, the quality of our life, as a direct *mirror image*, opposites and contraries in every way, later in this book (Endless Possibilities).

Invisible Line/Panic/Relief

This abnormally created and acquired pattern (explained in detail in Chapter 7) will **biologically** divide for ever the addicted from the non-addicted.

From this point, crossing an *invisible line* there is no cure. There is no cure because **biologically** speaking there cannot be: we can't cut out bits of our brain, taking out all our negative thought patterns!

But we can **re-wire** and change our thought patterns **if we are sober**, taking no mood-altering drugs.

Creating Tension

At various points along Progression we may become aware of our tolerance, concerned about our health (Yo-Yo Effect), and be responsible enough to admit the consequences of our 'habit' are taking their toll on us and others.

We decide to *stop* our *D.O.C.* (at least for a while), not knowing we have a serious **neuroendocrine disorder of the brain,** which is linked to our Sympathetic Nervous System (which means we don't have the control we think we have), and not understanding this is an **acquired dis-ease** and a real **biological need** has been set up within the brain with consistent *false information* from **A dis-ease which tells us it's not a disease.** What happens when we stop drinking or using our D.O.C.?

The blockage goes away, of course. The drugs caused the blockage so we return to the normal reality pattern.

But, horror of horrors, the negative remains!

When we revert to the normal reality pattern all the *tension* shows up: the reflex, the rebound tension of all those excitatory chemicals that were built up to get rid of the depressing effect of the drug (in the case of alcohol).

Tension is now *exposed* and *unmasked* in the reality pattern, when our thinking is 'normal'.

All the biochemical tension is exposed. Our internal tension (thoughts and feelings) is unmasked. External *triggers* are exposed with nothing to mask them in *reality*

when we are sober

(Now we are Stark Raving Sober and we need relief!)

Need for Relief

When we stop our D.O.C. we may look to another drug to reduce the tension. As we are *tense, nervous, agitated, aggravated* and easily *irritated* – because this disease creates dis-ease and biologically reduces our ability to cope with 'normal' tension – we may ask our physician (G.P.) for something to relieve the anxiety.

'Doctor, if you don't give me something ... I can't sleep ... etc.'

Or, we may simply start using or drinking again, unable to reduce cravings (i.e. the need for relief): we *relapse* simply because of *internal and external tension.* Often because we haven't had the right information, the truth of the matter; we pick up because we don't understand.

We have this Disease

When we are Sober!

So, unless we learn how to manage this dis-ease in sobriety while we are living in reality, we may continue taking 'substitutes' or even 'top-up' with our drug of choice.

Anxiety – Panic!

Our need for relief is created by the biochemical stress, the tension and anxiety of reality, and the panic of coping in reality.

There is nothing more terrifying than the sheer panic of having to cope with People, Places and Things without our drug of choice to help. The non-addicted simply do not understand that need, the overwhelming, all-consuming need: a need linked to all our thoughts, to our very sense of survival; a need, so much more than a craving, which defies all rational, realistic, sane thought!

Biologically the addicted need the amount of the tolerance level. That is, if we're tolerant of x amount when we stop we have to take x amount + more to get our relief, should we start again – there are no exceptions.

And, should we start again, because it gives us relief, a false relief, we think it is the solution! We cannot see the progression of this disease, in our brain. We do not understand. Every time we pick up our negative thought patterns grow. *When the tension seems to go away tension is being built up.*

That is the secret of this disease!

Placing good in the gap – relief!

However, all is not as it seems, a hopeless situation: there is a way out, for every negative has a positive. So let's go back into our brain and remember where all the tension starts. *Our need for relief is in the gap.* The secret of lasting recovery, on our New Path, is to place something good in the gap. When we replace negative, destructive thoughts – the tree of death – with positive good thoughts – the tree of life – we can grow, in every way possible, in a manner which is conducive to our True Self, doing no harm to our self, others or the world around us.

The collective word for this re-wiring, replacement of negative thoughts, connection to good, is spirituality. This does not mean religion. Spirituality is the essence of life – spirit. Whether we choose to be accountable to a particular higher power is a highly personal, emotive issue. Being accountable to our true self, accepting right from wrong, is simply playing a responsible part in our human existence on earth, being part of the universe as beings of light and life, as spirit and love, something everyone can connect with!

Spirituality Counteracts the Dis-ease of Addiction

When we fill the gap with true spirit we find relief and that is the *right solution*. The Prescription gives a more detailed account of the right way of thinking.

Cycle of Addiction

Before we continue our experience, our journey on a New Path, let's go over the cycle of addiction:

a. Tension
    i. shows up when we live in reality taking no mood-altering substances
    ii. is created by the 'lag' effect of excitatory chemicals
    iii. negative pattern of thought remains causing stress
b. Need for relief
    i. Why? Because of the tension
    ii. Where? In the gap
    iii. What is created? Craving and anxiety
c. Solution
    i. False belief, tells you substance is solution (remember this is a secret of the disease)
    ii. Why? Because the tension seems to go away
    iii. What can happen? We pick up to relieve tension
d. Substance/relapse
    We relapse for relief not knowing we simply increase the tension!

And so the cycle goes on, and on . . .

Flashbacks/H.A.L.T.

If we analyse what has happened, in our pattern of thought, knowing the Law of Associated Memory dictates how one thought leads to another, we can see how easy it is to flash back into an old negative pattern of thought, *even if we're sober*.

At any time we are able to **tune in** to that pattern.

The flashbacks will remain, in sobriety, for as long as we allow them to be fed by conscious thought. The Dry Drunk Syndrome is of someone who has stopped drinking, but has not replaced old thoughts with new. If our attitude and our basic lifestyle does not change nothing new is being created, so our thought patterns (negative) will remain the same. We will continue a negative way of being, the only difference being we don't drink or use our D.O.C.

To go through the remainder of life, just holding on to our sobriety for dear life, is something AA calls 'white-knuckling' – a sorry state to try to enjoy all the possibilities life does have to offer. And dangerous, for each time we flash back, each time a memory flashes through our thoughts there is a potential trigger for relapse.

As we can flash back any time we want, by the way we choose to think, even when we are sober: the disease of addiction can continue to grow in our thinking, in sobriety.

True sobriety means we have tuned out of negative patterns – our thinking has changed.

Watch your Thoughts!

We lose our 'sobriety' long before we pick up. We lose our sobriety when our thinking changes and we tune in to that negative pattern. Just take one simple scenario, then think of all your own triggers and flashbacks: It's just gone 5 o'clock. Every night for the past few years you've gone to the pub after work. Noting the time can make you think of drink or your D.O.C.

Or: It's just gone 5 o'clock. Kids will do their homework, get off to bed, then I can get a drink. It's just gone 5 o'clock, all my mates will just be getting in from partying. I miss that. It's just gone 5 o'clock, I'm on 'early', I need a boost. I've been on 'lates', I need a sleep. I need a drink, my D.O.C. There are a million and one times every single day in every possible way when we flash back, at any time, into a negative pattern of thought!

There is always the danger, in flashbacks, of being drawn back to our substance use. People, Places, Things don't always change, we do! But, only if our thinking changes. If we remain stuck in a negative attitude it is very easy to tune in to the destructive pattern of thought. The Dry Drunk will not drink, not because he's enjoying living, but because he doesn't want to die.

If we are at war with the world our anger can cause all sorts of negative emotions. In fact, anger is a huge cause for relapse. So is being lonely, tired or hungry. All are basic human emotions. Things we need for our well-being: companionship/love/rest/food. If ever you find yourself needing relief

H.A.L.T.

Ask yourself 'Am I **Hungry**, **Angry**, **Lonely** or **Tired**?'

Sometimes we can be all four! By changing our attitude, making the effort to do the right thing, we can find the alternative, the opposite, of each negative thought and emotion we experience.

Reward Circuit Flashbacks

But how about positive thoughts and happy emotions?

Another horror of horrors!

When we think we're well we can still tune in to the negative.

In fact, being happy, thinking we're well is another huge potential for relapse. Doing something good is also a trigger, linked to our Reward Circuit: our pattern of thought may flash back. Here are a few examples:

'I've finished all my jobs, I deserve a drink.'

'It's a party, I can have one to celebrate.'

'I've not had a drink for months, I can have just one.'

We have a name for this feeling good, feeling well: The Pink Cloud.

The Pink Cloud – Endless Possibilities

The Pink Cloud can be a major stumbling block or trigger for relapse. Sometimes everyone around us can see we've slipped back into our old way of thinking, old patterns of behaviour, even if we're sober, but because of the Pink Cloud we will deny there's anything wrong! The biggest danger, when we feel well, and we look better too, is that we abandon the Prescription. If a diabetic, because he felt better, abandoned his prescription, what would happen? He'd relapse. And that's the same reason we relapse.

When we tune in to the negative because we abandon the Prescription we feel well. The tension escalates because we're not thinking of our recovery and we forget our New Path. Everywhere around us are units of dis-information. Media, advertising, People, Places, Things, signs and symbols, lots of triggers. If we don't watch our thoughts which can bring us to boiling point we will reach the biological point when we need relief!

Rising Tension: A Choice

Take a simple example. The start of a new day. You get up, have breakfast – because you're doing the right thing. You have a quick conversation with whoever's around. They have issues they want to discuss. 'We'll talk later,' you say – because you're doing the right thing. *Anticipation of tension.* Off you set on your day. As you go along the mobile goes – problems to sort out. *Tension starts to build.* You breathe deeply, keeping positive thinking in a positive way – because you're doing the right thing. There's traffic, road works. Now you're going to be late! *Tension increases.* You begin to panic and at that moment you see a sign or symbol of comfort: an advert for a drink, a place you used to 'pick up' and *without realising it, you tune in to negative thoughts*! Subconsciously this may have started as the tension began in the morning.

As you're late you hurry along. *Tension increases.* You meet an old friend who invites you to have 'just one' because you seem so stressed. You resist – because you're doing the right thing. Then you hear some music. An old, emotive song, the flashbacks occur. *You tune in even more.*

Now, there are a million and one other triggers, in our thoughts, from external and internal sources, which can occur during one day, one hour, one minute! We have to watch our thoughts 24/7 until we tune out enough that those old thoughts fade. Don't ever be surprised by a thought: the negatives always come from somewhere. It's a case of tracing them back and learning to re-direct them!

So, you're tense, nervous, full of anxiety.
You've tuned in to signs, symbols, people, places, things.
You've got the 'flashbacks'.

But you continue to do the right thing. Instead of old behaviour, seeking out relief from a substance, you finish your working day without picking up and go home. And you don't take home anything for relief! *Tension drops slightly.* Phew! Made it! (*The Pink Cloud creeps in.*)

There, however, you're confronted with all the household problems. And because others think you're well, and you look well, no one holds back any of their own emotional issues. 'This needs to be done; that needs paying [and often our finances are depleted from addiction]; we need to sort things out!' You might reply, 'Let's discuss things later,' knowing your anxiety and tension levels are rising. You're still trying to do the right thing.

But the other person may feel or perceive this as a lack of your ability to listen to them, or confront issues, as old behaviour sending them into a panic. As a direct result of our anxiety *they* may become tense. *At this point honesty is needed! And an ability to listen.*

However, what can so often happen is the boiling-over point is reached on both sides: 'You're driving me to drink!'; 'I can't talk to you when you're drunk!'; 'I can't talk to you when you're sober!'

All sorts of issues emerge when we're on our New Path. The past may keep popping up: things we've both done or said. Remember, others need their own New Path. Even in the present we can be so disconnected from each other, wrapped up in our own problems and issues, we forget to really listen.

The art of communication is listening.

When we listen, not just hear, if we look beyond the anger or accusations we realise that fear, insecurity and a whole range of human emotions which are attached to memories create everyone's thoughts. When we look for the similarities rather than differences, in feelings and emotions, then we have a chance of reconciliation. If we are honest, and sometimes the truth hurts, with our self, it is never one-sided. It takes two to have an argument, even in silence.

Between every line of conflict lies the truth, the real reason (if it's need for control the conflict will continue). Ideally, however, when you have one honest statement on one side and another honest statement on the other, there will be a gap in the middle, a space for compromise. Many people are not used to or good at compromise, finding common ground, or accepting a solution of mutual understanding. When we are used to taking a substance to help us cope with difficult emotions, getting a quick fix and sense of relief, learning how to communicate our feelings can be scary and cause tension in its own right. Our stock of Emotional Muscle, situations and events we've learnt from, together with our natural emotional make-up and all previous experiences from life as other people manage their emotions, dictates how easy or hard we find communications and compromise.

We can learn to be better at expressing our feelings: if we remember where the thoughts originate from, when we remove past reactions to those thoughts, if we accept now is all we really ever have, when we live in reality and listen.

Note: It is vitally important we are heard. This is not always possible, or appropriate, if it concerns those we have caused upset or emotional harm to. Our point of view may come across as justification. Finding someone we can off-load to, who is impartial and detached from the emotional content and impact, someone who will not be judgemental, someone who will just listen, is a true blessing. If we're not used to talking about feelings it is important to find someone we feel safe with, and can trust not to break our confidence.

Just as we have to forgive the past, so do others. As we can only change our self: *we may have to accept others may not change*. The Ripple Effect of destructive addiction is far and wide. Some things may never be healed completely. We have to accept the consequences of our addiction. And so, at the end of the day, *we have a choice*. We either allow the tension to boil over creating immense need for relief and pick up, or we watch and take notice of our thoughts along our New Path, aware where each of them is taking us, and put something else in the gap! Unless we are *responsible for our thoughts and actions*, aware of the signs and symbols, tension will create relapse.

Sometimes we don't want to listen to our thoughts, because they are too painful, or we feel we can't cope with the truth of reality. Some things are better simply accepted for *we can never change the past*.

And often, when we change the things we can, the emotional content and strength of negative experiences fades. Learning to re-wire our thinking is worth the effort. If we truly want to change we can! We must need and want to desire change with all our heart, as much, if not more, than we needed our substance. If we put in all the determination and time we spent using into our New Path of transformation, we can grow into our true self. This means going to *any lengths* to create harmony and balance *to maintain sobriety*: doing no harm to our self, others or the world in which we live. Matching our spiritual (good) thoughts with the needs of our human form!

Note: If we don't really want recovery, a new life, we won't achieve it. Sometimes we'd rather stay stuck in the past, because it's a known feeling. There are lots of people who remain in awful situations because acknowledging we may have to change to facilitate change is too scary a prospect to even consider. We may choose to remain where we are if the fear of change, the unknown outcome of changing our self, how others will respond and react to us, is likely to turn our world upside down. Even chaotic circumstances have a hidden agenda, a pay-off. It may suit us to feel the under-dog, the victim of circumstances, the person who can't do anything to help themselves. If we're honest, we may choose to stay stuck because it's weirdly comforting: 'things' may be bad, but feeling bad may be a known experience. At least we know what we're dealing with. We may have experienced unhappiness all our lives, neither expecting nor thinking we either deserve or are able to change things, learning to accept feeling good is scary, when we simply don't' know any other way to feel. So we accept second best for and of our self. But if we want change, we won't: we'll make more out of life. And we'll risk changing everything to achieve that!

When we embrace real life, *living on life's terms*, with all the human emotional experiences that come with being alive, *accepting those things we cannot change, having the courage to change the things we can, and learning the difference*, when we are *honest, open and wiling* to change, *life opens its doors with endless possibilities.*

'Endless Possibilities': the Good, the Bad and the Downright Ugly

Any possiblity of positive change is hard to imagine if you're stuck in a destructive addiction. Even the encouragement that millions of us find a New Path, not only those of us in addiction, but millions of people make positive life changes, can be depressing. 'Why should things work out for me?' Well, why not? What makes you so different? There are countless others, with all sorts of diseases and illnesses and dreadful circumstances, that through sheer determination, belief and effort manage to either turn their life around or cope as best they can, maintaining a positive outlook on life.

There is no cure for this disease. We either manage it, or we don't. Eventually, directly or indirectly, it may kill us if we don't. The choice is ours.

Consider The Paradoxical Law in Addiction.

Realise the meaning of these words. In your heart look at every opposite thought and possibility to those you may have, or had in the past, and consider what can be now, or in the future.

Mirror Image

Life	Death
Love	Hate
Good	Evil
Peace	Conflict
Truth	Lies
Hope	Fear
Reality	False Perceptions
Growth/Creation	Destruction/Despair
Choice/Freedom	Monotonous Prison of Addiction
Joy	Grief

Remember: substance mis-use is the problem not the solution: everything's the opposite!

Either you, or someone who cares for you, which is a real blessing, bought this book for one reason – to gain information. When we're not well we need answers to such questions as 'What is wrong with me?'; 'How do I get better?' So we search to find a way to 'get our head together'. This information, this truth, tells you and explains to you what lies behind every other 'thing' you may have known about addiction from other sources of information.

The Good

You have learnt about the brain: the science of addiction. How it affects our body (brain) and our mind (thoughts). *You now know about the psychobiology of addiction.* When we integrate knowledge with action we cause growth. As we cause growth, we create: we create life, rather than death. These are mirror images of each other. **Everything in this disease is the opposite**.

The Bad

We take drugs to calm our self down, and they create more tension. We take tranquillisers to tranquillise, and they create more tension. We drink in the winter to warm up and we drink in the summer to cool down! (We come off heroin and get hooked on methadone. We stop drinking and take other mood-altering drugs!)

These are *mirror images*. Instead of causing creation we cause destruction. Instead of finding love we nurture hate. Instead of a life full of possibilities we face the prospect of death.

The Downright Ugly

And as we continue to disintegrate and deteriorate the tension escalates, and that tells us we ought to take only more.

Don't think that as we progress we will want it less – we will want it, need it, more. Even when we get to the point when we can no longer hold down food, when everyone is fed up with us and abandons us, when we have nothing left but our substance, we still want it!

Geometric Progression/Pressure to Stop

The disease of addiction is progressive. It is progressing, not in an arithmetic way – 1, 2, 3, 4, 5 – but geometrically – 2, 4, 8 16, 32, 64.

And once we have crossed that *invisible line* of addiction *it does not ever go back to the beginning*. It does not matter how long we stop for, *we will always return to the level of tolerance at which we left off!* And if we switch or change one drug for another we progress without any interruption, our brain does not differentiate one mood-altering substance from another. (Alcohol, cocaine, meth etc., though different in their effects, have the same outcome regarding progression.)

Which is why those of us in recovery, on our New Path, must 'always check the label' of anything we take, including non-prescription medicines. Codeine is an example. Anything which alters our mood, chemically, should be avoided unless supervised by a doctor.

Note: There are many natural alternatives, supplements or foods. In fact, vitamins and minerals are depleted when we're using false chemicals, especially vitamin B. There are many brain food supplements and foods we can eat which can help our body and brain return to optimum functioning. Always consult an expert such as a registered nutritionist.

Summary:

Now we understand the psychobiology of addiction, the progression of the disease. But will you take it in, understand the information and decide to stop? Giving up, giving in, to the truth – that we are powerless over alcohol and other mood-altering drugs – is the most fearful thought! When we are in the grips of a destructive addiction, surrendering to the fact we can never drink or use again is like asking us to cut off our arms and legs! In fact, death itself may not be a deterrent; sometimes it may seem preferable. That's why there are many suicides, intentional and unintentional. Because this is **a secret disease, a disease which tells you it isn't one**: until we are fully in the grips of addiction, we won't see its progression *until it's too late*!

Initially the tension goes away, you have a party! The girls get sweeter, the lights get brighter, the music gets mellower, so *your life appears to be getting better*. And of course, *the tension when you're sober* tells you you ought to take more to relieve it! And if you switch drugs, it makes no difference. Tranquillisers don't tranquillise, they create more tension. Sleeping pills don't cause you to sleep, they give you insomnia. Progression will continue, until something happens to make you want to stop.

Pressure to Stop

The first and foremost reason we address addiction is the pressure to stop. Pressure put on us by our partners, our friends, our children, our relatives, those in authority – the courts, the 'boss' of our job. When the *pressure to stop overcomes the pressure to take* we admit, at least to our self, 'I need to do something'.

When the *fear of losing* our partners, our friends, our children, etc. *overcomes the need to continue* we are forced into trying to stop.

All of us can stop when that pressure is great enough.

However, because we do not know the truth that the disease is within us, that we now have a limited amount of tension we can take before this disease demands relief, very often we will only 'stop drinking'. We most probably won't make lifestyle changes! And so the 'problems' remain.

'All my problems cause me to drink!' *Everything's the opposite: we can't see our problems are linked to drinking and drinking is not their solution.*

'All my family told me that I had a problem. That I had to stop, so I stopped.' Who can't stop when that pressure becomes so much greater than the pressure to take? *Because self-will through fear kicks in, we put down the drink*. This may relieve the pressure to stop, from others, and makes us think '*That proves to me, and them, that I can stop at any time I want.*'

But if we do not make lifestyle changes, the pressure to take will continue. And we will have 'just one' for relief – 'I'm still drinking, but I'm not an alcoholic!'

Now, remember, **the need to take is biological, we have a set level of tolerance.** We will always return to that level of consumption, where we left off. Always, if it takes one day, one week, one month, one year. **The addicted can never have 'just one'.**

Perhaps we feel the need for relief, but are determined, through the fear of the consequences, not to drink. We may go to our doctor and say: 'Doctor, doctor, I'm tense, nervous, depressed, anxious, emotional, agitated, aggravated. I can't sleep. My head's confused, I can't think properly. I need something to help me relax, help cope with this tension!'

When we stop our D.O.C. all those chemicals in our body, which are excitatory and depressive in nature, are screaming for relief! And every time we need relief we think drink is the solution!

The doctor may give us a replacement to help. If we have not been entirely honest, told the whole truth, they may prescribe another drug which is mood-altering, to counteract the symptoms of this disease.

Never forget, all who jump in the water get wet!

This is another phenomenon of this disease: cross addiction/cross tolerance.

Cross Susceptibility: Geographical Cure

If you're addicted to one, you're addicted to all.

If you're tolerant of one, you're tolerant of all.

If you're susceptible to one, you're susceptible to all.

And you can't move from one to the other and expect that not to happen. Many can become dependant too on the replacement. Just as we cannot replace one drug for another, we also cannot substitute one place for another. This is called the Geographical Cure. When we think that by moving out of certain places, being away from certain people and not doing certain things that we will not have the same old thoughts of using. All we are doing, in truth, is either moving away from those who would stop us drinking, or often running away from our problems.

We cannot run away from our self! The need to take is within us.

6 A New Way of Thinking

'Wisdom begins in wonder ... Know thy self.'
Socrates

Basically it's the thought that counts, which is often why we take any mood-altering substance in the first place: to change or alter the way we're thinking, our mood.

When we have a need for relief, that need has been created by our thoughts.

Tension has built up by our response and reactions to People, Places, Things. We have allowed our *external environment* to affect our *internal environment*. Our thoughts tell us drink solves the problem and our set tolerance level demands we drink enough to relieve the *biological peak point* of tension.

It's a simple truth, with a simple solution: stop drinking and **replace old negative thoughts** with a **New Way of Thinking.**

What with? How can we stop thinking the way we've thought for years?

By replacing past thought with positive present thinking!

1. Be consciously aware of the content: where are our negative thoughts originating from? Where are they leading other thoughts?
2. Watch our thoughts: be mindful of everything we say and do. Are our words and actions conducive to a healthy attitude, doing no harm to our self, others or the world in which we live?

3. Be fully present in the present, with balance and harmony in all things. Don't respond and react on automatic pilot - this is explained in greater detail in The Prescription.
4. Don't allow People, Places, Things to activate old patterns of thought, and if they do, simply re-direct those thoughts. Don't allow negative thoughts to continue.

If a negative thought sneaks in H.A.L.T. – are you Hungry, Angry, Lonely, Tired?

Literally tell a negative thought to go away.

Remember, it's what we put in the gap.

New Way of Thinking

a. Tension builds to point we need
b. Relief
c. Old patterns of thought tell us to use a false solution
d. To place a mood-altering substance in the gap
e. If we stop: stop using and stop old patterns of thought when the tension comes, everything has the possibility to become the opposite
f. With a New Way of Thinking
g. We find the truthful solution
h. Which gives us relief
i. The cycle is interrupted

Sometimes it is hard to even imagine, now, how our life in the present and future can be a mirror image of how it has been in the past.

Nothing happens unless first a dream, a thought. Everything was once a thought, an idea, a conception. A table, chair, landscaped garden, dress, car, book, light bulb – all things are the product of someone's, or more than one person's, imagination. Even the conception of who we are and our ideas of how others perceive us are all products of our own thoughts. How we communicate our feelings to others, how we respond and react to People, Places, Things, can be a highly difficult, time-consuming and tiring experience. To re-direct our thoughts, born out of a lifetime's experience, requires patience and practice. Just like any other habit, we can prioritise our thoughts to the positive, rather than the negative.

We are 100% responsible for our own thoughts and actions!

Everyone has the ability to turn, however humble or vast, their thoughts into action and achievement. Bringing the thought from our internal reality into external reality requires determination and effort, and sometimes flexibility, diversity and compromise. Compromise does not mean we relinquish our values, morals, the truth, it does not mean we condone that which we inherently feel and know to be wrong in order to achieve our aims or goals, doing any 'thing' it takes no matter how the consequences harm the good of our self, others or the world in which we live. Finding compromise, being diverse and flexible, simply requires looking at things as a mirror image of each thought, replacing a bad thought with a good one. Looking for the good in people and places in everything we do, when we replace a wrong-doing thought with a doing-right thought, we enter into spirituality. Good will always, eventually, overcome evil as many traditions affirm: *the truth shall set us free.*

Expressions of Thought

An essentially human characteristic or quality is our ability to think. To make a choice between one thing or another. But what do we do with our gift of thought? Our ability to think? Do we choose thoughts conducive to our health, or our detriment? Thinking is often tinged with the past or fearful of the future. We feel in the Present, in the Now. The gift of language gives us an ability to think, choose, then articulate our feelings. Words give us this ability. Words are our verbal or written thoughts, our main form of communication with one another. The evolution of the human brain enables us to share our thoughts and express our feelings.

We are not unique in using our vocal skills to communicate. Many less 'intelligent' animals use sound. The power of vibrations, though, should never be underestimated. Music can touch that precious place within, which some call our soul. *Sound, vibrations, can evoke meaningful experiences, far beyond the meaning of words*. Take note! Be aware of the sounds, the music, you listen to, including the TV, etc. The volume and content of sound can quickly change our thought patterns or mood. Altering our lifestyle to create less tension will often include what we listen to.

Especially in the early days along our New Pathway of thinking. (See also notes in Chapter 8.)

Many living creatures communicate through body language. What is unsaid in the gap is instinctive awareness. Human beings attach meaning to feelings with words, and have the power of thought to express instinct, but we should never underestimate body language as another form of communication.

Indeed, our internal body language, how we are feeling inside, is often portrayed unconsciously, externally ('a look can say a thousand words'). And **learning to listen to our internal feelings, connecting our heart to our head**, is extremely necessary and will be discussed in The Prescription. Music and body language are just two other ways by which we communicate our thoughts. But, *we are more than our thoughts.* Some emotions go beyond words or expressions of thought. Sometimes a 'feeling' has no explanation. It is 'just a feeling'. Sometimes there is no rational, logical or explicable reason for a thought. These are most likely to be of positive content. Negative thoughts most usually pertain to the past or projection of fear for the future.

Some things we just know, we feel it. Words to express that feeling may include trust, faith, hope. Something else, separate, yet part of our mind and body, 'it' is our spirit. And the most important aspect of recovery is spirituality! *The most successful way to change our thoughts is to mirror a 'spiritual' thought against a 'negative' thought.* Although old patterns of thought must be altered, and that requires intensive thinking, **addiction is not something we can actually 'think' our way out of.**

Because our emotions are so tightly bound to the creation of this disease (remember the Limbic System and Reward Circuit), and the fact that an alteration of thought requires an 'emotional' shift, something to move one 'arm' (dendrite) of the thought pattern (neuronet) to another. **We have to feel our way out of addiction.**

A New Way of Thinking gives a new way of feeling and vice versa.

This renewal or transformation of our self can begin when we stop using any mood-altering substance.

A New Path: Putting Good in the Gap

A journey of a thousand miles begins with one step.

True feelings may be hard to manage, that's often why we drink, and it may be some time before our hormones, etc. (remember the Yo-Yo Effect) return to our natural balance. But when we reach that true state of being, and appreciate being able *to feel for real,* we literally *wake up* from our unnatural, false, chemically-induced dis-information, distorted and often desperately depressing state of existence, to being alive in the true sense of the word. To feel, touch, taste, see, hear, smell, to communicate our thoughts, to share, to be, accepting our self and others, to love and love life, is the simplest form of spiritual awakening.

An awakening of our true spirit is essential in recovery, our New Path.

This new way of feeling about our self, others and the world in which we live isn't difficult. It is not like having to learn something totally new or alien to our very essence of being. We have all felt good about our self at one point in our life and it's never too late to start if we haven't. We all want and need to feel good about ourselves. *Acknowledging our spirit within is simply waking up the good within.*

Our personality, our character traits, born out of our way of thinking and our life experiences, may be negative, causing us to do harm, but *our true spirit, the way we were meant to be, is pure, embracing the positive human qualities in life.*

Negative character traits most certainly have to be seriously addressed if we are to achieve and maintain sobriety. We have to be perfectly *honest* with ourselves and take a 'fearless' look at our self in the mirror. Only the truth will set us free from the Prison of Addiction. When we examine our self, truthfully, admitting who we are and who we have become, through the process of this disease, we can honestly admit our lack of certain 'good' thoughts and behaviour: not only when we are in active addiction (the character 'defects' AA speaks of), but, most importantly, when we are sober.

If we do not change our thinking and our lifestyle we will remain sick, when we are sober.

If we put down our substance, **abandon the addiction**, and **concentrate on the created disease**, in our thinking, to change our thoughts and alter our lifestyle, we will naturally make the 'amendments' needed for a 'good' sober life.

There are so many reasons why so many of us have difficulty, particularly in the early days of our New Way of Thinking, before we actually experience any of the astounding changes which occur, from the inside out, when we alter and transform our self, getting our head round the very words spirit or spirituality. An intensely personal subject, one which fills many volumes, written from many different perspectives, *spirituality is, in essence, a feeling*. The importance of finding our own meaning is not just for 'recovery' from a destructive addiction, but *for meaning in life itself*.

Endless possibilities, free will, choice, motivation, life!

Whichever way we 'find' our true self, our spirit, always comes from doing what is inherently good. Good for our self, others and the whole world in which we live.

The English Dictionary defines the word spirit as life-force. *If we use our life-force for good we are being spiritual, simple.*

There's no mystery in spirituality, the only 'thing' we have to get is being 'good': defined as better, complete, positive qualities, virtuous, beneficial, generous or genuine, honourable, satisfying, pleasurable and favourable, just to mention a few! It's no wonder good is a euphemism for G–d, for at the heart of what is good, its essence, is G–d. But that is a personal perspective. Spirituality does not have to include either religious or 'New Age' conceptions. Neither do we have to adhere to a particular 'organised' set of ideas or practices to believe in G–d Himself. Whatever we may conceive Him to be, or whichever higher power or connection to spirit, even the simplicity of knowing that ultimately everything is connected, that we choose the feeling of connection, to something greater than our self or others (who, let's face it, lack perfect goodness), gives us an *inner support system*. We no longer have to feel alone. G–d or 'Goodness' is on hand 24/7. We simply have to look and ask for guidance and strength of spirit. His light is pure. Above the confines of this imperfect, often chaotic world, shining to illuminate even our darkest times. Darkness is only the absence of light. When we fill our life with 'good' we shine.

Take a look at the following. Ask yourself, honestly, which qualities:

- You possess
- You'd like to possess
- You need to possess

No one is expected to be a saint, but the simple fact remains this disease leaves us with a limited amount of tension we can take when we are sober. If we learn to nurture a good spirit, to live in a more peaceful way, which includes all positive qualities, the direct opposite of how our lives have usually been, we will have a successful, peaceful, New Path on which to enjoy our life.

Foster 'good' positive thoughts. Abandon the substance of negativity!

Human Qualities

Positive		*Negative*	
Morals		Unprincipled	
Values	Integrity	Unscrupulous	Sinful
Ethics		Dishonest	
Compassionate		Indifference	
Responsible	Self-aware	Unreliable	Thoughtless
Accountable		Oblivious	
Modest, decent		Promiscuous, dissatisfied	
Tolerant, restrained	Virtue	Prejudiced, controlling	Unrighteous
Faith, hope charity		Doubt, despair, selfish	
(theological values)			
Self-esteem		Conceitful	
Self-worth	Respect	Egotistical	Irreverence
Humility		Arrogant	
Dignity, integrity		Shame, Disorderly	
Conscientious	Principles	Guilty	Unaware
Honest		Disgrace	
Balanced	Governed by	Unstable	Disorder
Inspired	Good/G–d	Chaotic	(disease)
Animation of life/spirit		Decay	
Affinity		Hostility	

Feel what each word means to you. Connect your heart to your head and 'watch' what each thought brings to mind.

A Wisdom Way of Knowing

Most people are conscious of 'good'. Most of us have an inner voice or conscience which tells us the right from wrong in People, Places, Things.

This knowledge may come from others telling us, or we may discover right/wrong from our own life experiences. This cause/effect of thought, behaviour, consequences, is something we all understand. We can see and feel certain consequences and qualities in life.

But how about the things we cannot see? Such as our spirit in its pure form? Or the concept of G–d, who is within yet outside of people, places, things? Many people struggle with belief. For most of us our ideas and concepts are gathered from others. From an early age we are influenced by others' opinions. Past thoughts and experiences may either endear us to the 'unseen' or vehemently propel us against anything of that nature. Some exclude themselves even from nature itself. Sometimes life experiences can make us question what we know or what we believe in. Faith is the ultimate acceptance of the 'unseen' feeling. But faiths can make us question our belief. We can lose faith even though we still believe, and vice versa. If past concepts of religion and experiences in life are based upon retribution of everlasting consequences, or questioning why certain things happen, we may either reject or live in fear of G–d, or we may struggle with the concept of being accountable to the 'unseen'.

Or we may forget the true nature of G–d being 'good', using teachings or faiths to justify those thoughts and actions which conclude in negativity, wars and conflicts over religious beliefs (as seen throughout history), or watching others do so may turn us away from every concept of G–d. Spiritual belief and faith in G–d is, to many, a different concept altogether, or part of, but not pertaining to, any particular set of rules or conditions other than each thought or action being inherently 'good'.

Spirituality is, perhaps, a 'wisdom way of knowing', a spiritual intelligence.

Each and every one of us has intelligence. We are all different, unique in our own way, as to what type and quality and quantity of each individual intelligence or gifts we have. Some of us have a natural ability to learn certain things intellectually. Some of us instinctively know things, and nurture our creative gifts. For some of us, inner wisdom comes with age, and life experiences.

Whether *intellectual, creative or emotional intelligence* is learnt from scratch or nurtured by experience and determination, there is one 'intelligence' which rises above them all: *spiritual intelligence.*

The human being is a *mixtus orbis*, a mixed realm of mind/body/spirit.

We need our intellectual skills. We build our *Emotional Muscles* to help us cope in life. It is vitally important we question and ask why. Knowledge and action precipitate wisdom, and wisdom brings peace. But to answer the question of meaning, the 'matter' behind the 'matter', the purpose of being, beyond the material aspects of our existence, we surely must include all aspects of this human form: mind, body and spirit. If we pay attention only to the needs of the first two we disregard our life-force and run the risk of becoming closed, confined, stuck in one particular way of being. *Including our spiritual needs opens our mind and heart to all the possibilities life has to offer*, to attain all we can be while on earth.

If we exclude all 'things unseen' just because we cannot use our five senses to experience or rationalise or justify, we run the risk of disbelief simply because we cannot imagine or have no proof! A bit like someone from the first century being unable to accept the earth is round! In each and every age of mankind new discoveries, new concepts push the boundaries of belief and acceptance. Perhaps our journey of earthly experiences is simply to discover new things.

Everything Changes

The astounding miracle of life is change. Things will always change. Views, ideas, concepts, proof that certain things exist – *everything changes.* Our perceptions when we use any mood-altering drug; our life when we stop using any mood-altering drug!

Who are any of us in this transient mortal existence to question what lies above and beyond our limited perception of reality – especially when science itself knows we don't use all our brain's capacity – simply because we don't have the knowledge to prove or disprove facts?

One fact remains the truth: we cannot separate our self from our life-force or spirit. Endless searching for proof must be, by its nature, inconclusive.

Everything's the opposite
Everything changes
Mirror image
(states of being)

Positive		*Negative*	
Serenity Vitality Prosperity (To thrive in all aspects of life)	Unlimited	Anxiety Apathy Depression	Turmoil
Whole Transformed Fulfilled	Ideal	Empty Wretched Failure	Incomplete

Endless possibilities by clear thinking/confined or blocked perceptions.

Placing the spiritual dimension opposite negative thoughts and actions as a mirror image of human qualities is essential in recovery on our New Path. By creating 'good' we create good growth. By surrender we do not lose, we gain. By admitting we are powerless over alcohol or other mood-altering drugs we regain our power of spirit, our life-force. We become authentic not false. Acceptance is the beginning of waking up our true state of being. **Self-awareness is the beginning of spiritual awakening.**

When we place the spiritual part of being opposite everyday thoughts and actions, actively looking for the 'good' in life, we engage the Law of Attraction: Good begets good. Out of the disease of disorder comes order and peace. From the weakness of pressure comes strength and wisdom. Acceptance of People, Places, Things, of G–d, brings proof and victory of 'Good' *v* 'Evil'. Restlessness and agitation are replaced with serenity. Fear and impulse give way and pave the way for the courage to change. Change just is – part of every state of being.

Ask yourself, who do you want to be? Do you want to transform yourself? Do you need the miracle of change? Do you desire a different way of being? Simply start with what you already have – your spirit. Wake it up! With determination, effort, imagination and belief!

Be the architect of your existence, create a 'good' reality.

Note: Those of us who are naturally creative may believe, falsely, our inspiration is enhanced by drinking or taking mood-altering drugs, like those who think a drink helps with intellectual 'pressure' of thought. Or we may think we feel a more intense experience while observing creativity. Whether we make music or listen to it, is one example. As with all other false beliefs, while in the Prison of Addiction this stems from disinformation, the disease within us and the way we think.

Everything's the Opposite

Inspiration comes from within, not from 'false' chemicals. Everything's the opposite! The source of creativity lies in our spirit. As any 'recovering' person, including highly acclaimed actors, musicians, artists prove: passion, excitement, imagination, talent, that exquisite feeling of creating or appreciating things, does not disappear. In fact many will tell how excess 'use' destroys our capacity and capability to bring any vision, dream or feeling to life!

You know now, *mood-altering drugs don't give us anything*. They don't make us do anything better than we are already capable of doing. 'I play better, I write/draw/paint better. My ideas come and flow better.' This illusion is simply not the truth. 'I think better'; '"It" solves things' is an absurd statement. 'I feel better.' Well, maybe we did, for many moments, long before we became dependant, addicted, ultimately destroying all the good in our lives. **Happy hours/sad years**.

But the truth is our lives become unmanageable. Including the unmanageability of emotions, thoughts, feelings and expressions of creativity! No, if we are honest, the only thing drink gives our self, others, and the world in which we live, if we over-use, over-rely on and over-indulge in 'it' is grief! We must never forget the Pink Cloud: what chaos over-use of a substance creates. So, when we feel well, feel creative, feel positive, are doing good things and achieving our 'dreams', beware! Watch your thoughts! Remember the Reward Circuit. 'I'll just have one to celebrate this marvellous piece of creativity, this miraculous change, I'm feeling and looking so good. Things have changed, I'm in charge now, I'll just have one!'

Hah! It's got you!
This disease exists in sobriety!
In our brain and in our thinking
The only way to manage is to
Change our thinking
Alter our lifestyle
And place G–D in the gap!
And never, never, *ever* pick up a drink for relief.
There are no substitutes, no alternatives to this truth.

Look at the graphical representation for Chapter 6 on the DVD:

When we feel our **Tension** Thermometer rising
with a **New Way of Thinking**
we find the **Solution**
to our **Need for Relief**
without 'picking up'
thereby **interrupting the cycle** of addiction.

Just as the addiction cycle can go round and round one destructive way after another, so – if we Re-Wire our Thoughts to *Create Change* – we can 'reverse' our direction of destruction:

Everything's the Opposite!

Successful recovery demands a New Path in all aspects:

1 Stopping our use of all mood-altering drugs.
2 Altering our life-style – people, places, things.
3 Most importantly, changing our thinking, our thoughts!

We must change our internal as well as our external environment.

This requires a **New Way of Thinking:** the secret of keeping sober and emotionally well.

This may seem an absolute impossibility, if you are in the grips of a destructive addiction, but *everything's the opposite*. Once we have found the correct, the right replacement, *our lives can have endless possibilities*.

7 An Acquired Dis-ease

'Life should not only be lived. It should be celebrated.'
Osho

Addiction to any mood-altering substance ultimately creates a dis-ease within our very being, which is compounded and maintained by 'stress'.

The neuroanatomical (structural) and physiological (functional) aspects which biologically create this disease, causing psychological symptoms result in a *maladaption between us and our environment.*

Drug dependency is an acquired disease, affecting our 'whole' being.

Misuse of any psychotropic (mind-altering) substance interferes with the processing of all sensory information, *i.e. everything we see, hear, smell, taste, touch*, altering how we think and feel which alters how we act, i.e. our behaviour.

Scientific fact:

Alcohol and other mood-altering drugs affect our brain. They can be 'destructive'. Over-use causes a change of function and structure (anatomical) within the network (neurons) of the human brain.

Therefore *addiction to destructive drugs is a neuroanatomical disease.*

Definition of disease:

The physiological function of an organism, especially a pathological change caused by stress, producing characteristic symptoms. (English Dictionary)

The physiological and neuroanatomical aspects of the disease of addiction to destructive psychotropic chemicals are fact. The truth. Reality.

Our perception of reality, as you now know, is altered or changed by alcohol and other mood-altering drugs. Our brain perceives actual sensory information, existing and occurring in the physical world, no differently to imaginary or theoretical information, i.e. stored thoughts (memories), ideas (content of conscious mind), beliefs (what we accept as true) and learnt thoughts (often the content of our unconscious mind).

'Learnt' behaviour, our automatic response to People, Places, Things, forms certain 'habits' and 'addictive' ways of thinking. If we are forming our behaviour from a distorted way of thinking by distorting our perceptions with psychotropic chemicals, which creates this disease, then once we have crossed the invisible line from habit to addiction our 'need' for those chemicals is biological, not only a pattern or 'habit' of thought.

Then our behaviour becomes secondary to the Disease of Destructive Addiction.

If we understand the neurobiology of behaviour, wherein feelings and mood are reflections of specific biological changes and shifting neurocellular patterns – that the brain, the centre of our consciousness and communication, is the primary centre of this disease and physical centre of consciousness and communication and physical centre of the recovery process as well – we begin to understand the psychobiology of addiction.

Medical Dictionary Definition:

1. A disease is a morbus, an illness, a sickness that causes an interruption, cessation, or disorder of bodily functions, systems or organs.
2. A disease is an entity characterised by at least two of these criteria:
   (i) a reorganised etiologic agent (or agents)
   (ii) an identifiable group of signs and symptoms or
   (iii) consistent anatomical alterations of known body systems.

(Stedman's Medical Dictionary)

Alcoholism is a disease. This position is shared by many prestigious organisations including:

- The World Health Organization (WHO)
- The American Medical Association (AMA)
- The American Psychiatric Association (APA)

The Congress of the United States of America formally acknowledged that alcoholism was a disease with the passage of the Hughes Act in 1970.

'Addiction, like heart disease, cancers, and type II diabetes, is a real and complex disease.' National Institute on Drug Abuse (NIDA)

The Director of NIDA, Nora D. Volkow, M.D., pioneered the use of brain imaging to investigate the toxic effects of drugs and their addictive properties. Her work has been instrumental in demonstrating that **drug addiction is a disease of the human brain.**

Consciousness – Human Behaviour

The physiological aspect of consciousness – thought process – gives us an understanding of the psychobiological aspect of human behaviour (in relation to addictive disorders).

Consciousness is part of our physiological system. Human experience is a complex amalgam of processed structural units of sensory information.

'The Mind' is not separate from 'The Body', which dispels the myth of the psychiatric + psychological models for 'treating' addictive disorders.

All information we receive – internal or external – affects the 'whole' person to give an 'experience'.

If you affect human experience you affect behaviour Once a true conversion – biologically – has occurred the true reality is blocked out both physically and psychologically.

Therefore drinking and drugging are not the disease,
merely the symptoms.
The addictive disease exists primarily in sobriety.

Choice of our sociological and psychological environments, where we are and what we think, determines real expressions of physical manifestations as biological effects on the Neuroendocrine System causing permanent disease.

Remember: The destructively addicted search out and crave for much more than psychological relief. *There is a real biological need created by the disease.*

The psychological and neuroanatomical (functional and structural) aspects of the disease of addiction are fact. The 'need' for drugs and alcohol created by misuse changes our ability to observe and recognise 'true' reality. But what is 'true' reality?

The perspective of attachments between the self and a transitory reality – material objects/sensations, People, Places, Things – form our perception of new and stored information creating our thoughts in our mind: consciousness is mere electrical activity in our brain.

However, consciousness as an external soul, part of the spiritual dimension, transcendent higher sphere of being and the mysteries of the quantum nature of matter, suggests a different kind of awareness.

True conception of 'self' and 'consciousness' includes 'spirit' or 'soul'.
Psychobiology = spiritbiology

The human organism functions within the external limiting framework of a larger 'life unit' culture of the universe. External style and spirit impacts on the internal environment to either reinforce positive creative lifestyles or induce personal stress and establish destructive patterns, i.e. disease states. The soul of the universe is limitless. By tapping into our higher power we create endless possibilities for transformation.

Psychobiology as spiritbiology – our 'whole' being.

There is no practical cure for the organic disease of drug dependency or alcoholism. Addictive disorders are truly chronic, but can be arrested with the right prescription for management of dis-ease.

Spirituality counteracts the disease of addiction.

Recovery is dependent on the external constructive confrontation of information, i.e. changing behaviour including People, Places,

Things. Behaviour changes require rejection of sensory information at the level of the internal environment, i.e. changing perception and patterns of thought (level of consciousness, mindfulness, being alert) by a *New Way of Thinking and Being.*

Destructive Addiction affects our Whole Being

The Autonomic (Sympathetic) Nervous System relates to the base level on which all addicts tend to live: the emotional, pleasure or mood division, of an animal instinct or sexual nature. This system can either control or be controlled by the primary Conscious Nervous System, i.e. Endocrine System. Therefore we can define the physical aspect of this biological disease problem which has psychological, spiritual and social aspects as a primary, chronic, neuroendocrine disorder of the brain and Autonomic, mainly Sympathetic, Nervous System that has adverse behavioural consequences.

Why 'One' is Never Enough

This disease is acquired by over-use of psychotropic chemicals.

Once we have crossed that invisible line we can never:

1. 'cut out' neuronal pathways of thought, only change their direction to facilitate New Pathways;
2. return our neuroanatomical structure within the brain to its pre-addicted form. Structure or functional changes are permanent. That's why there is no cure for the Disease of Destructive Addiction.

To understand the exact 'workings' of psychotropic drugs in the gap is not necessary here. Should you wish, on your New Path, to discover more, there are numerous sources to keep you fascinated and enthralled at just how absolutely amazingly intricate, spectacular, clever and quite simply miraculous we are!

Here is a simple explanation. Information we need to understand why there is no cure and why, no matter how long ago we had our 'last', if we pick up just 'one' we will very quickly need to return to the level of consumption at which we left off.

Fig. 1 shows the normal transmission of chemical information from

Tolerant Terminals Trap

FIG 1. **NORMAL TRANSMISSION**

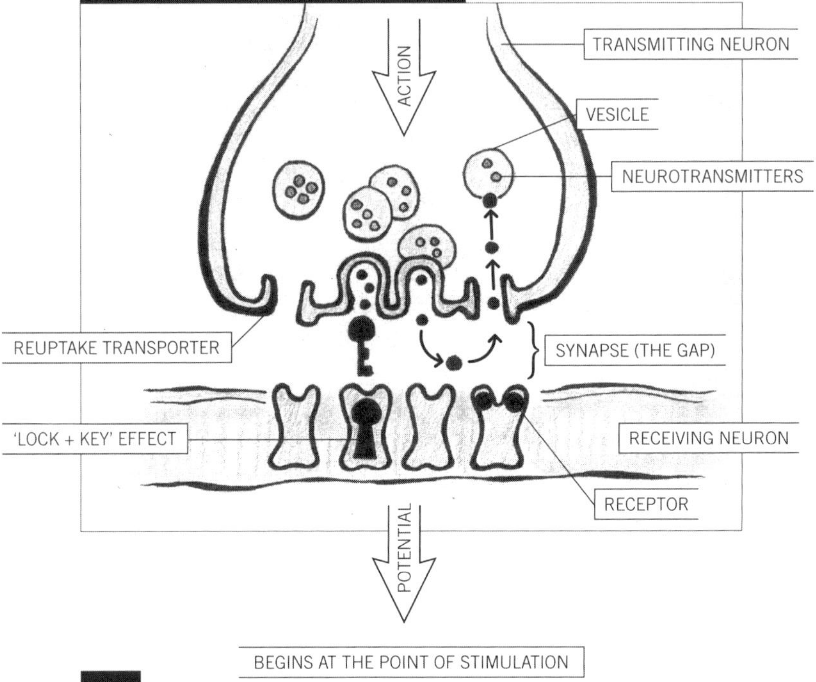

FIG 2.

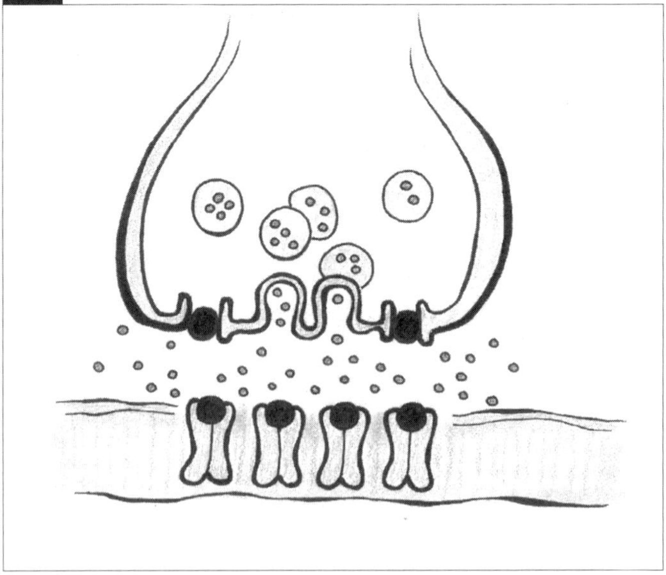

Psychotropic chemicals mimic, block or inhibit reuptake, flooding Synapse (e.g. with Dopamine, see Reward Circuit).

'False' messengers of sensory information distort reality.

Tolerant Terminals Trap

FIG 3A.

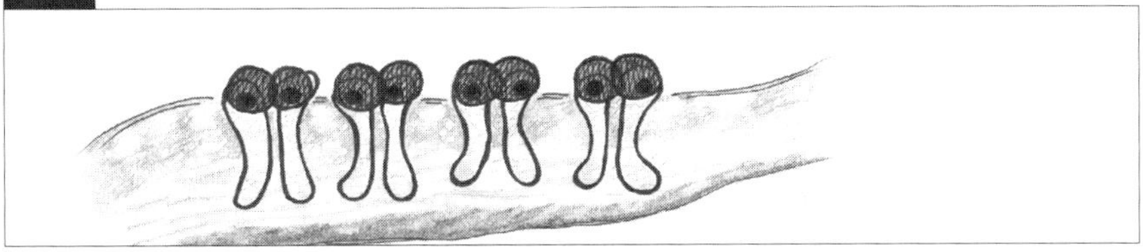

Use of mood-altering substances 'blocks' receptors / reuptake transporters.

FIG 3B.

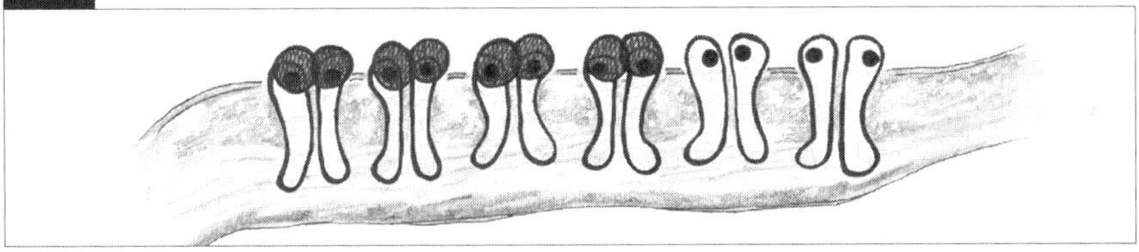

With overuse of mood-altering substances, our brain attempts to restore homeosatis by 'opening' more receptors.

FIG 3C.

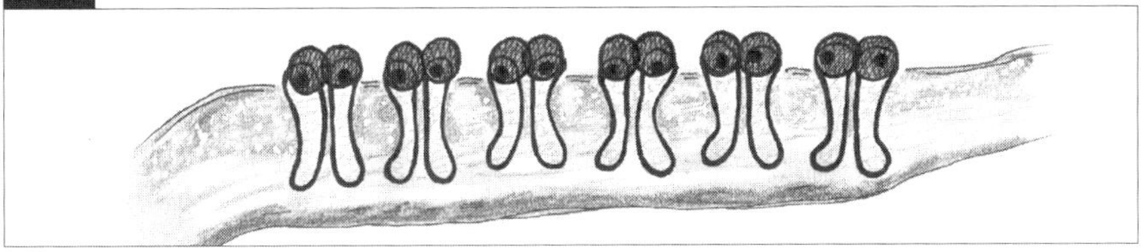

These 'new' receptors are permanent. This leads to tolerance. Overdose happens when receptors are blocked quicker than the brain can 'open' new ones.

FIG 3D.

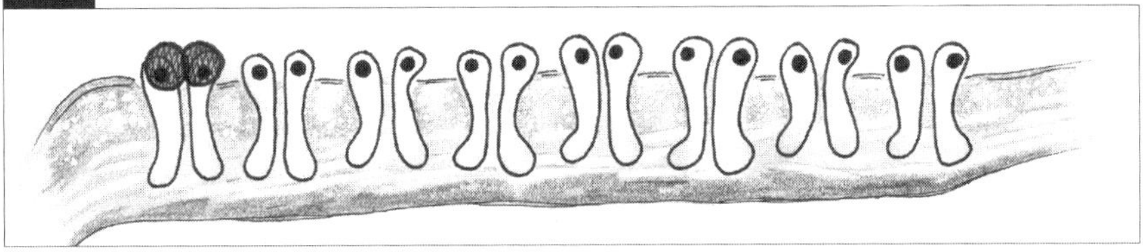

'One' will never be enough!

one side of the synapse (the gap) to the other. When there is no interference neurotransmitters will 'naturally' regulate the flow of chemical messages to and from (reuptake) one neuron to another.

Regulation of receptor density is affected by many different aspects. In pharmacology an agonist is a substance that binds to a specific receptor and triggers a response in the cell. It mimics the action of an endogenous ligands (such as a hormone or neurotransmitter) that binds to the same receptor.

A receptor antagonist is a drug that does not provoke a biological response itself upon binding to a receptor, but blocks or attenuates agonist-mediated responses. In pharmacology an antagonist is a binding partner (ligands) of a receptor by disrupting the interaction and inhibiting the function of an agonist or inverse agonist at their receptors.

In simple terms, drugs can either mimic, block or inhibit reuptake of 'normal' neurotransmitters. They are 'false' messengers of information. See Fig. 2.

Any 'false' messengers from psychotropic chemicals interfere with the transmission of sensory information, either external or internal. Our body, being the amazing organism it is, tries to regulate itself to return to normal homeostasis.

It will do this in one of two ways:

1. Downregulation – if there are too many neurotransmitters, i.e. over-stimulation (which is what many drugs do) our body will shut down receptor sites. This is what makes us tolerant to drugs and stimulants and is why we crave more to get the effect they once gave.

   Downregulation – more neurotransmitters, fewer receptors. Desensitisation is a decreased response to a neurotransmitter or agonist drug, i.e. tolerance.

2. Upregulation – possibly the defining (invisible) moment of 'addiction'. If sites are blocked or shut down the function of our 'normal' feel-good neurotransmitters becomes depressed or depleted. Our body produces excitatory chemicals to get that function back to normal.

   To help this process of chemical rebalance our body opens up or 'builds' more receptor sites, making us more sensitive to our own natural neurotransmitters.

   Upregulation – fewer neurotransmitters, more receptors.

The more we 'push the drug', the more 'blockages' and the more receptor sites our body opens up to return our body to normal homeostasis. This is the Yo-Yo Effect.

Upregulation and supersensitivity:

Upregulation – an increase in the number or density of receptor binding sites. Supersensitivity – an increased response to a neurotransmitter, e.g. stress hormones

Consequences of receptor downregulation and upregulation: the more blocked sites there are the more we feel the effects of withdrawal when we stop 'pushing the drug' until our body adjusts itself chemically. So, what happens with all those 'opened' sites when we stop? They remain, permanently. Which is why we can never have 'just one'. Those receptor sites remain forever: a structural and functional change has been acquired which is the definition of the disease. Fig. 3.

Remember:

'One is too many'

ABANDON THE SUBSTANCE

focus on the disease

Physiology of the High

Both sensitisation and desensitisation can develop within a few minutes.

Tolerance (desensitisation) may in fact occur after only a single exposure to a drug.

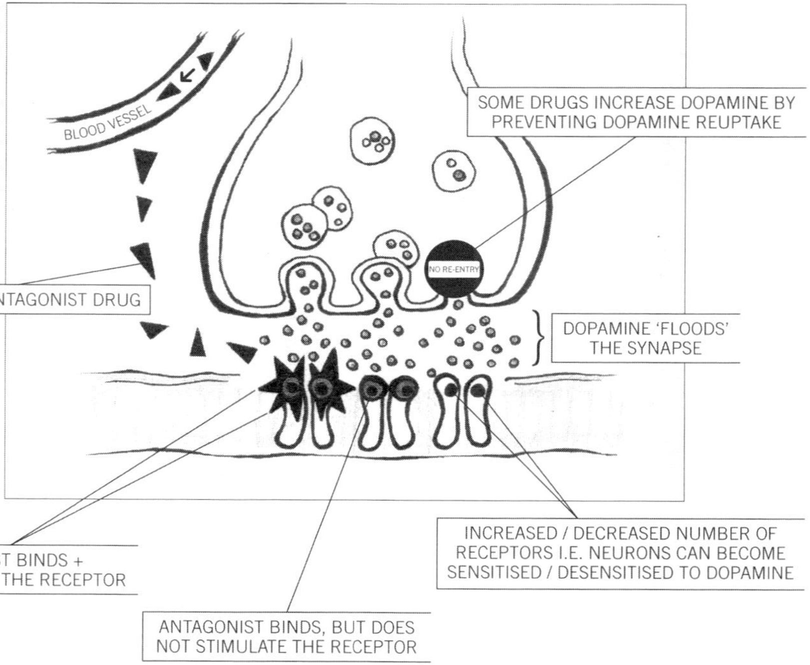

Physiology of the High

For those 'technically minded' the following is a brief indication of how certain drugs influence amine synapse functions either presynaptically, or postsynaptically:

Presynaptic effects may include interference with

1. transmitter synthesis by inhibiting the synthesising enzyme tyrosine hydroxylase;
2. transmitter storage in vesicles;
3. transmitter release from vesicles;
4. reuptake of transmitter after release.

Postsynaptic actions include

1. stimulation or blockage of receptor binding by the transmitter;
2. inhibition of the deactivating enzyme.

All mood-altering drugs over-stimulate the neuron cell in some way. Here are a few examples:

Amphetamine (an 'upper' drug) increases release of dopamine (our natural feel-good chemical) and blocks transmitter reuptake, so leaving dopamine 'bouncing-up-and-down' in the Gap!

Cocaine, like amphetamine, causes nerve cells to release lots of dopamine but blocks dopamine transporters, so dopamine is excessively released but cannot go back up i.e. cocaine prevents reuptake.

Methamphetamine mimics dopamine. Meth enters dopamine vesicles and forces dopamine out, so there is excess dopamine in the synapse.

Heroin mimics natural opiates and binds to opiate receptors, therefore flooding the synapse with dopamine.

The active chemical (THC) in **Marijuana** mimics the natural neurotransmitter anandamide, which binds to receptors releasing excess dopamine.

Ecstasy mimics serotonin and confuses serotonin reuptake transporters. These transporters are responsible for removing serotonin molecules from the Gap after they have done their job as mood-regulating chemicals. By mimicking serotonin Ecstasy is taken up (more readily than serotonin itself). The transporter becomes confused and does its job in reverse by 'spitting out' serotonin in the Gap. Excess serotonin becomes trapped and binds again and again to receptors.

LSD acts almost exclusively on serotonin neurons. It chemically resembles serotonin and binds to serotonin receptors. Sometimes it 'inhibits', sometimes it 'excites', therefore LSD has complex sensory effects.

Alcohol serves a 'double sedative punch'. It interacts with our natural GABA transmitter which controls neural activity along many brain pathways. When GABA binds to its receptor the cell is less likely to fire. Alcohol interacts with GABA receptors to make them even more inhibitory. As a 'double whammy' alcohol also binds to glutamate (the general purpose excitatory neurotransmitter), preventing the glutamate from exciting the cell. This is when our body tries to return to natural homeostasis (the Yo-Yo Effect), just as it does when our natural balance or equilibrium is thrown into turmoil by any mood-altering substance.

Release of opiod peptides (endorphins, enkephalin) are also implicated in addiction and drug tolerance. These reduce pain and increase feelings of pleasure and well-being i.e. further reinforcing the Reward Circuit Pathways.

As we can see from Figs 1, 2 and 3 changes can occur to modify properties of the synaptic membranes (receptors, enzymes): changes to existing synapses and formation of new ones, as well as in intracellular synaptic compartments (presynaptic and postsynaptic). The functional abilities of a synapse – **synaptic facilitation** – has a direct influence on learning i.e. memory.

Changes can increase synaptic facilitation so that the stimulus in a presynaptic neuron could result in a different (more or less intense) response in the postsynaptic neuron. New synapses can form in response to new experience – **synaptic growth** – as the diagram of a meth addict's neuronal structure showed, earlier.

Sensitisation and habituation occur as a result of changes in the function of presynaptic sensory terminals. Instantaneous learning is followed by short-term memory and terminates in long-term permanent physiochemical changes in the brain i.e. modified or new synapses.

Rapid learning may involve **reverberating circuits** i.e., even when the initial stimulus ceases the activity 'carries on' as recurrent positive feedback connections, e.g. sensory neurons, activate parallel excitatory interneurons.

Reverberating circuits can explain instantaneous memories = 'That felt good, I need to do that again!'

Memory consolidation occurs in the hippocampus and amygdala of the Limbic System, which you know is the 'home' of our emotions, inextricably linked to the formation of learning (memory and behaviour), which in turn is influenced by what goes on in the Gap!

Neural Mechanisms	*Learning/memory (Behaviour)*
Reverberation	Instantaneous
↓	and
Facilitation	Short-term memory
↓	
Protein synthesis	Consolidation (Limbic System)
↓	
Synaptic growth	Long-term (permanent synaptic changes)

Faulty Wiring/Faulty Connections

In conclusion:

When we interfere with our natural chemical balance by taking any mood-altering substance we 'give our gaps' false information. We put our brain (neuronal networks) and inter-related systems – our internal environment – into confusion and disharmony, often creating confusion and disharmony in our external environment.

We are no-longer 'connected' to 'reality'.

This disorder or disregulated system we acquire by mis-use of any psychotropic chemical creates a real biological need.

Our 'need' regulates our 'disordered' thoughts and behaviour which 'disconnects' us from our own True Self.

We become unable to pay proper attention to what our body can experience from sensory perception: instead, we form our ideas and concepts on distorted information, falsely believing the experience is real, resulting in a whole system of instability and inaccuracies of thought.

creating MALADAPTION between
our self and our environment
particularly
WHEN WE ARE SOBER

When, however, we become mindful in recovery, we can reverse this dis-ease. By paying attention to our thoughts we re-establish connectedness with our True Self: restoring balance and harmony. There are endless possibilities when we are free from the Prison of Addiction to create new synaptic growth by a New Way of Thinking.

Maladaption

Our maladaption to our external and internal environment most usually manifests itself in one well-known word – stress. Stress is the foremost trigger for relapse. Stress is an all-encompassing descriptive word for many types of emotional response to many different events, each of which has a wide range of psychological and physiological effects on our well-being. Each 'stress' has a personal meaning and intensity depending on our pervious life experiences and our personal ability to cope. What is stressful to one person is not to another.

But, all of us in destructive addiction **have biologically reduced our ability to cope with stress.** Each of us has falsely believed 'it' helps us cope. To help you understand 'stress', how you can 'adapt' to life and cope with stress without your substance, read the Stress chapter (Chapter 8) and The Prescription.

Some of us say we're 'stressed' when the underlying emotion is:

- Anger
- Resentment/disgust
- Disappointment/hurt
- Guilt/denial
- Fear/panic

Fear and love are possibly the most powerful emotions we experience, and opposites! For if we use the goodness of love, for our self, others and the world in which we live, we enter into spiritual goodness, which can dissipate the flow of fear, its intensity and power. The power of love will eventually outweigh negative emotions of hate. Everything's the opposite! If we are honest about our feelings, where they are 'coming from' and where they are leading, are our thoughts positive or negative, for good or evil? We become truthful.

In the truth there lies the spiritual. The divine. Above evil. For goodness, truth and love personify G–d. We 'enter into' spirituality the moment we start being honest.

If we are truthful we may find the two most powerful (and destructive) emotions underlying feeling 'stressed' are either anger or fear. Love counteracts both, particularly anger. Something 'outside the box' of our limited conception or negative perceptions, i.e. greater than our mortal, vulnerable, self, can subdue that most debilitating core emotion/feeling of fear which lies so often at the heart of much 'dis-stress' or 'dis-ease'.

We often feel the maladjustment to life without our coping mechanism of substance misuse in the form of fear and panic. Dizzy spells, tightness in our throat or chest, shortness of breath, racing heart with 'tingle' sensations, obsessive worries and unwanted thoughts, overwhelming fear that something awful is about to occur. The anticipation of a 'panic attack', the fear of not being 'in control' starts the cycle of anxiety, that 'stress' feeling. Sometimes the foundation of panic is laid hours before and the slightest added tension will launch a 'panic attack' into full motion unless we are aware of rising stress levels, leading to the need for relief. Break the cycle: fear–panic–anxiety–stress–panic, by interrupting the thought of having a 'panic attack'.

Each 'variation' of stress can give us a Helicopter Head, when we feel we can't think properly (read about concentration and memory in Chapter 8). Some say they feel 'trapped within their head', craving internal peace. **To find peace, inner contentment, requires us to live in the world but not of it**, sometimes! Meaning: we must find ways to 'adjust' or 'adapt' to our environment without picking up!

At times of 'maladaption' it helps enormously to literally take a step back. Close your eyes for a second and breathe deeply, in and out. Focus, be aware. Create a moment of peace internally. Open your mind for a second . . . .

Open it W – I – D – E – R and put G–d in the gap.

Create a different response – a New Way of Thinking. When we 'get through' the moment, and our head stops pounding and our ears stop buzzing and we stop feeling like we're going to throw up or faint, we realise we haven't died from anxiety and panic, in fact we've just built some Emotional Muscle.

Anything we have to 'get through' is one moment, one step at a time.

One day at a time

The mind generally hates change. Whether we're trapped in addiction or not. To combat our mind-set being resistant we must be ever-more persistent; focused; aware; determined; positively creating a New Way of Thinking.

Some of us just want to be 'like everyone else', plodding on, with the same old patterns of thought, because the effort to change either seems too much, we don't seem to be feeling any better, or we simply can't be bothered. Or, we're so used to that permanent state of agitation or depression, that 'sick to our soul' feeling inside, that we simply can't imagine ever feeling any different.

The pressure to stop gives us an opportunity, life gives us opportunities. Yours is now. Take this knowledge and act to create change to 'adapt' in whatever way you possibly can your lifestyle for positive thoughts and behaviour to take you into 'recovery'.

Even if we are overwhelmed, emotionally, in the early days or months, as our homeostasis returns, if we watch our thoughts and pay attention to our stress levels, we can gain all the gifts of transformation.

Often this renewal of our mind needs only the spark of a new thought to set alight the light, the gift of hope.

Finding a different perspective, hope, thinking and 'seeing' the good, i.e. spiritual, in things, immediately changes the way we feel. The glass can be half full or half empty, or have nothing in it at all, in which case it becomes a vessel ready and waiting to be filled. Anything empty can be filled! Including our self!

When we change our lifestyle, when we let go and let G-d in, the part of us which makes us whole, which fills us up, our spirit, returns to feed our soul, to 'content' our whole being. Hope is enough to enable us to 'fake it to make it'. Say to yourself, 'This is not all I am'. When 'maladaption' to your environment makes you feel like giving in: '*I am going to change my mind's scrapbook' with good thoughts and positive action*!

The Serenity Prayer (p. 228) does not mean accepting the negative, giving us the permission to sit back and say 'That's just the way things are'. Sometimes we need to grow up, become emotionally responsible for our own thoughts and actions, take control of our 'destiny' and be accountable. Neither does simply handing our 'will' over to G–d give us the wisdom we require for a healthy, stable new way of living. We have to play our part! G–d will give us the recipe but we have to bake the cake!

Millions of us have changed a miserable 'maladaptive' existence by acknowledging their own true spiritual self and asking a Higher Power for help and guidance. Why should you not? Lose the attitude and have a little faith, hope and trust. Take one step at a time, retaining humility, grace and gratitude in the acceptance of His love.

8 Stress

'In the middle of difficulty lies opportunity.'
Albert Einstein

Stress. This is such a relatively small word for such a big meaning! To help understand the 'workings' of stress, how it affects us in so many ways and why it is so inextricably linked to destructive addiction, a cause and effect of internal and external disharmony, there are three main sections to this chapter, covering a wide spectrum of necessary information and knowledge to help 'maintenance' of the recovering process from what is ultimately a disease maintained by stress:

1. Introduction:
2. Background: What stress means on an emotional level
   Why not all stress is bad
   The stress of noise (or the Startle Reflex)
   Behavioural implications of stress
3. Attack of the Adrenals – review of flight/fight response.

Introduction

Very few people have not experienced stress. What is vitally important to remember throughout the recovering process (i.e. the rest of our life), particularly in the early days: we have biologically reduced our ability to cope with tension and stress by over-use of alcohol and other mood-altering drugs.

When we are sober!!

Stress begets stress, i.e. tension and need for relief.

Tension feeds anxiety.

Anxiety breeds fear.

Fear causes more stress.

S.T.A.R.

All of which can lead us to picking up for relief.

There are two simple ways we can reduce stress:

1. Change our lifestyle to reduce pressure–tension thermometer
2. Learn coping mechanisms for times we cannot avoid stress – put G–d in the gap: Good is our 'sprinkler' system

See Chapter 3 for diagrams.

Above all else, whatever is going on around you remember:

We are 100% responsible for our own thoughts and actions!
We can live as part of the world, but not of it.

We can do this if we:

- remain self-aware;
- focus and be mindful of the moment, now;
- place a spiritual thought in the gap.

It is often extremely hard to think objectively when faced with a stressful situation, particularly in the early days of recovery when our 'instinct' tells us the solution to any problem or stress is a drink! It helps to look at the building blocks of stress. For stress or being stressed-out, unlike the real physiological instinct it's meant for, is not usually an immediate threat of life/death, but rather a building of tension, anxiety and fear.

Stress, ultimately, is built-up tension. The level of stress depends on the frequency, intensity and duration of tension which, as we know, can come from may external influences. How they affect us internally is our responsibility.

We can only change our self, not the world!

From a medical perspective, our sensitised Autonomic Nervous System produces chronic anxiety at extremely high levels. Science knows even simple forms of anxiety produce profound structural as well as functional changes in the Nervous System. Sustained anxiety results in altering the functional expression of various Nervous System circuits and connections within the brain.

Anxiety is a truly biological event.

We may not be able to stop the physiological, biological reaction to stress, but we can alter our response by changing the pattern of our thoughts when confronted with anxiety, if we bring our conscious awareness to exactly what is happening and how we are feeling.

The pace of living and changes in social, political and religious aspects of twenty-first-century life have created a great deal of global and personal insecurity as the 'fabric' of society disintegrates, with less emphasis placed on the spiritual aspects of living, concentrating rather on the bigger, better, more of 'affluence', i.e. what we want and desire, rather than what we actually need for the true purpose of being.

When we relentlessly focus our attention on our pursuit of things, stress becomes part of everyday life, to the detriment of everyone's health. For stress is also quite contagious, as is 'affluensa'. Ever noticed how your own tension level goes up when around stressed-out others? We respond to others' facial expression and body language as well as their words and actions.

Distorted thinking sustains depression and anxiety. Many surgeries and counselling rooms are full of patients with symptoms related to stress, but which may actually be symptoms of over-use of alcohol or other mood-altering drugs which we take to relieve our stress. Perhaps we could be taught simple coping mechanisms at school? For everyone, at some time in their life, gets stressed. No one has a perfect existence. Many medical conditions and behavioural traits can be as a direct or indirect result of stress. We need to learn how to cope without simply picking up something else for a quick fix.

The world of literature, media and TV is now full of practical everyday resources for relaxation. The learning of a new form of natural relaxation is therapeutic in itself. For it is in the doing of something positive that we gain our reward of natural 'feel good' chemicals. Yoga, meditation, sport, cooking, DIY, etc. With programmes, DVDs, books and tapes, the mind/body/spirit 'industry' has something for everyone – there is no excuse! We have a wealth of suggestions to help us de-stress and become self-aware, self-successful, etc. and they don't all cost money to learn – try libraries! Discovering ways to relax, naturally, as a complement to our health is important for everyone. Time out may seem like a luxury, but lifestyle change with People, Places, Things is not a luxury for those with the disease of addiction (or indeed, any other life-threatening illness), it's an absolute must!

There is physical stress and emotional stress. We can often cope with one or the other separately, but if we have the two together our health can suffer greatly. There's an old saying: 'Hard work never actually killed anyone.' We can work extremely hard if we look after our emotional, i.e. spiritual, well-being and recover from a hard day's work naturally. It is when we put our body and mind under more stress, from using false chemicals, that we really suffer.

We need to learn to relax, naturally, from both kinds of stress, to keep our mind/body healthy.

The missing component to a healthy whole being is in our spirit.

The action potential of spirit
Thinking good thoughts
Putting G-d in the gap
Can
Freeze-frame
The moment
In the theatre of our mind
Stopping
Negative thought process
Releasing
Tension

Background

The feeling of being stressed-out is actually based on a primitive survival mechanism, to supply us with adrenaline for *flight or fight*. This may have been an absolute physiological necessity at the beginning of evolution, i.e. man *v* wild beasts, but the 'lion' of stress, in the shape of People, Places, Things is not actually going to eat us! *It is the emotional response we attach to the perception of fear which causes 'stress' and the need for relief.*

Note: We are not talking here about Post-Traumatic Stress Disorder, or similar highly emotional life-threatening situations and events. Such psychologically disturbing experiences require trained therapists and counsellors; medical professionals to help us 'work through' emotions in a safe, supportive and systematic 'healing' process. Trauma has been shown to have correlations with the Freeze Response (see end of book for recommended help with this 'inbetween' flight / fight brain state).

Rather, it is everyday situations and events: standing in a queue, waiting for a bus/train/plane/someone. Someone arguing with us, or not willing to engage in discussion. Being questioned, told off, accused. Stuck in a traffic jam, at home with the kids, in the office. Cross at the burnt toast, your best friend, your parents, your partner. Frustrated at unfairness, at life itself sometimes. Angry with the 'system', the telephone sale calls, the shoes from the sale that don't fit. The inefficient car/hoover/drill/bank manager. Fearful of the future, 'amendments', finishing homework/dinner, letting others down, not being 'good enough'.

You name it!

One thing every stress emotion has in common is that flight/fight instinct in it, somewhere!

And where do we 'fly' to? The pub/club/bar/off-licence!

How do we 'fight' stress? Armed with a bottle/unit of substance!

Whether we're one or a hundred and one we all feel some type of physiological, biological (including pollutants) and emotional stress. It's those of us who add spiritual stress, from the over-use of any mood-altering chemical substance, that add extra physiological stress to our very being. Growing up itself is a stressful time, and adolescence is the age when most of us are introduced to alcohol, etc., when we are particularly vulnerable (we shall look at this in more detail in the Pathophysiological Chart, at the end of Stress). What was intended, for our survival, has, particularly in *modern-day bigger, better, more* society, backfired on us; turned round, not to save us being bitten, but to bite us at our core of being. Fed by a multitude of spiritually depleting ways of being, e.g.:

1. The pursuit of things. Possession is not a 'bad' thing. Neither is having an ego. They simply require balance and harmony with other aspects of our self and being, to be healthy.
2. Isolation. TV, video games, internet addiction (just replace alcohol and drugs with the word technology in the Reward Circuit), non-participation with fellow human beings (take texting), and there is no bigger cause of isolation than Destructive Addiction.
3. Lack of prioritisation for natural relaxation. It is not only healthy and perfectly natural to relax, but a physiological necessity. Why do so many of us feel guilty or have an inability to just sit still and do nothing other than contemplate? Finding time to ask yourself questions and discover various answers is the very essence of being human! Even those who don't experience the continual internal agitation and perpetual restlessness created by the Yo-Yo Effect of mood-altering chemicals and bodily reactions, often find it hard to make time to still the mind as well as rest the body.

Making time (and we've discussed Time Management in respect of addiction) for reflection on People, Places, Things is important Quality Time. Introspection, the ability to look objectively and constructively at others, things and, most importantly, our self, is within us all. *The creative process of transforming thought into reality starts with the gathering of information.* Right from birth we have our own natural ability for creative thought, to process all information we receive and create our own views, concepts and ideas. All information, external and internal, creates our thoughts which creates our reality.

As babies we spend all our time absorbing sensory information. As small children we usually have time to question and learn. In the vast arrangement of information hopefully we learn how to analyse, accept or reject. The impact of imagery through the media however, seems to place little emphasis on gaining knowledge in things of true worth. As 'little people' our imaginations soar – who hasn't 'pretended' or spent time 'day-dreaming' at some time in childhood? *We need to encourage that versatility and diversity of thought through introspection, not merely the storage in our mind of facts and figures, in our places of learning*, especially in adolescence, when we 'separate' our views from those of others, to find our 'place' in the Great Scheme of Things. Perhaps we could foster emphasis on who we are, rather than what we've got! Teenagers are bombarded with twenty-first-century 'needs'. But do we equip our future minds with ways to relax in this ever-increasing stressful world? We often ask 'What's wrong with them?'. Perhaps it's us feeding them the wrong information. Youngsters don't have a problem asking – maybe we need to change our answers!

The intrinsic human quality, the ability to ask why, what, how? Our thirst and appetite for information, our desire to know, experience and feel more; to ask what makes us 'tick', including others and the world in which we live, has kept mankind busy in thought since time began!

Problems themselves are a source of information. They offer an opportunity to ask our self questions, to look at areas in our thoughts and behaviour which need more self-awareness and re-framing. At the beginning of this book it was suggested you use your imagination, if necessary to make it up, to visualise how you would like to see yourself: out of the Prison of Addiction, free to live as a whole being. Your New Pathway of thoughts started with a request for information. You have spent quality time for your own true self reading this, to ask and learn:

'Why am I like this?'
'Why can't I stop?'
'What makes me pick up?'
'How can I get better?'

Without doing anything yet but read, you have started to create a shift in your thought patterns.

The pressure to stop precipitated this process of transformation in thought and feelings. This opportunity, to take time out, to break the cycle of addiction, is happening right now! *Digest the information up to now. This gives a clear insight to why and what. The how comes by asking more questions about our self and only we can give our self the honest answers.* Finding out how to turn the tables on tension requires us to find the time to be still.

Be Still
Be still.
In calmness of self lies
Peace,
Intentions are seeded in tranquillity,
Given time and space they flourish,
Watered from above with love
Each inspiration grows strong, from our soul.

Therefore be still.
Allow the spirit to be whole.

Making time for true spiritual thoughts and reflection on our reactions to People, Places, Things – time to discover who we are, making time to discover more information from within, *by connecting our heart to our head*, is essential.

Remember: **information is the key to everything**. If you distort information at its very core, at the beginning of its process, distorting perception of external and internal stimuli, by taking alcohol or any other mood-altering drug, *how can you discover the truth of the matter*?

Our Rational Intelligence – what we think, is affected.

Our Emotional Intelligence – what we feel, is affected.

Our Spiritual Intelligence – what we are, is distorted.

Our true spirit and the truth, which will set us free to discover all the wonders of being in this amazing universe, never dies. Like spirituality, there is no mystery about relaxing, just a simple requirement of connecting approximately twelve inches of our being together: our heart to our head! Contemplation, mindfulness, relaxation, being still is a natural state of being. When mankind first evolved we didn't have so many outside pressures to attain, achieve, to survive, other than keeping alive, or external pollutants to 'stress' our physical well-being. Now our lives often seem to be 'living to work' not 'working to live', leaving us stressed out with seemingly no time for mental and physical relaxation.

But just as we find time to work at things of no spiritual value, we can make time for being still. Even if it's just a minute: *Hectic in your head? Go JAMMING in your soul! Just a minute! Mindfully imagine now is good* (with G–d in the gap!).

If we make and take the time to look at our self, the matter behind the matter, and ask big questions: 'Why am I like this?' we can *act for positive change* on the answers we get. If we ask 'What is the true meaning of life?' we may *discover the meaning of acceptance.* That all things are part of the great scheme, that each and every one of us has a purpose, that nothing lasts for eternity except the spirit, the essence of light, the 'matter behind the matter'. Fifteen billion years ago 'there was light' and 'all will come to pass'. As Shakespeare wrote in *The Tempest*, 'What's past is prologue'. *Now is the time for change. The scene is set for your true spirit to emerge!*

Asking big questions puts us in touch with something larger than our self. It allows us to aspire to higher motivations. This can be viewed as our *soul's intelligence.* We search for the truth by asking why. As human beings the bulk of our existence is primarily made up of our instinct to survive. Destructive addiction affects our primitive survival mechanisms, leaving our very being in turmoil.

As human beings we strive for information, knowledge, answers and the fact remains: even those totally against anything to do with G–d often find themselves putting Him in the frame, asking: Why? What? How? 'Oh G–d!' is just a figure of speech you might say. Possibly, yet there are more things on earth and out there we have yet to find answers for. That's the beauty of life. The journey, the discovery, the experience of People, Places, Things to which we are all connected.

If we re-frame our 'Why? What? How?' by putting good or G–d in the gap, rather than distorting the truth with false chemicals, our time on earth, our perceptions and perspectives, our questions and answers become things which are truly important.

We need information to help us manage the disease of addiction. We may struggle to remain sober until we understand: **stress helps to create and maintain this disease or disorder, in sobriety**. How can we help our self cope unless we understand our self? What makes us tick? What do we like/what makes us happy inside? Not just a quick 'fix'.

Unless we make time, just as we did for our drinking or using, for quality time, getting to know our self creating order in our life, prioritising the spiritual (good or G–d), we flounder like a ship on the waves with no rudder, just going with the flow of life with nothing to steer us. We are like a 'fish out of water' when our spirit is disconnected from our whole being through an addiction. An empty vessel makes the most noise of discontent! We need to return to a natural state of being, look behind the desires of our earthly form, to our true nature, and replace confusion with contentment.

The tides of life are giving you this opportunity, this chance, now! Take it! Grasp the information and knowledge and do something with it!

Do the opposite of what you've done in the past.

Knowledge + action = success.

Walk the walk, not talk the talk.

Contrary to what most of us think we need for contentment, that rush of our feel-good chemicals, dopamine and serotonin come not from something we take, but from within our self, and they're free! Even the simplest act or thought can give us a 'good feeling'. A smile, 'please' and 'thank you' show gratitude and respect, spiritual qualities, and if we don't succumb to the 'I want it now!' syndrome, appreciation, patience and acceptance qualities come along too!

Provoke the presence of G–d by an attitude of gratitude. Freedom of spirit is nurtured by generosity of spirit.

The only thing we really need to make happen is our new way of spiritual being, which we can do now, in the moment, by a New Way of Thinking. Adrenaline is derived from the 'feel good' neurotransmitter dopamine. Excess adrenaline release, i.e. stress, leads to dopamine deficiency, which can lead to physical exhaustion and mental exhaustion, e.g. depression: but remember – everything's the opposite!

If we naturally increase our dopamine and serotonin levels by doing and thinking 'things' spiritually, i.e. in a good way, we learn to manage our 'stress' response in an appropriate manner which is conducive to our survival and our health. *Our physical, emotional equilibrium is affected by our spiritual well-being.*

Not all Stress is Bad – Noise

One of the principal excitatory neurotransmitters, norepinephrine, is needed to create new memories. It also improves mood. If we look upon problems more as challenges to stimulate motivation, effort and creative thinking, norepinephrine helps grow new connections within our brain itself!

Stress management is the lock, spirituality is the key!

One of the most successful techniques to activate our relaxation response is meditation. Simply taking time to be mindful of our recovery. Some kinds of stress are even beneficial. For example, Ohio State University researchers found that stress from engaging in a memory task activated the immune system, whereas stress from passively watching a violent video weakened immunity. We all often suspect we're susceptible to colds, etc., when we're stressed and we're right to think that.

Their results suggest that challenges, deadlines to make for completing something – work, college, getting the kids off to school, making supper, finishing a project, DIY, etc. – in fact anything creative, and active, rather than passive, even if annoying for a short time, could be instrumental in strengthening the body's defences, as well as improving our self-esteem and self-worth.

Very Important Note: Eustress

Many stressors emerge from happy situations: parties, meeting new people, new relationships, organising events, moving house, new jobs, holidays, etc. The thrill of achievement can be stressing in itself! Feeling like a 'pick-me-up' or reward for doing something good is part of our old way of thinking: 'Oh, thank goodness I've finished that! Well done me! Phew, that took ages!'.

Particularly in the early days on our New Path of doing good the thought of a drink can pop along on old patterns of thought so easily! A drink to celebrate! (Especially if we don't seem to be appreciated by others, which can tinge our good deed with 'I'll congratulate myself!' Or add a biological need for relief from tension as our frustration or anger rises within us.)

Pleasure from 'eustress' or 'good stress', butterflies in our stomach, that feeling of anticipation, keeps the basic flight/fight Nervous System response in 'working order'. Pleasurable feelings keep stress manageable. The natural feeling of expectation or excitement, in anticipation of that good feeling neurotransmitter, dopamine which can be released naturally by doing something good, makes a job-well-done a reward itself.

Unfortunately, for those on a New Path a simple act of happily doing good can trigger our Reward Circuit, especially early on! This can seem very confusing and contradictory. Why do good? Why pick up a pile of newspapers instead of leaving them on the floor as you'd usually do, if half an hour later you have a notion for a drink? Because **our New Way of Thinking is a process**, a re-framing, a re-training of our mind to how we respond and what response and reward we obtain for 'changing our old ways'.

The greatest acknowledgement of doing good comes from within. Knowing in our heart we've done the 'right' thing is reward enough. Pleasurable stress can catch us 'off guard'. Remember the **Pink Cloud!** Others may warn us, 'Don't go to that party, there will be lots of drink,' to which we'll honestly reply, 'It doesn't bother me!' But beware: we may abandon our substance of choice but stress in sobriety can be an enormous trigger.

That's when lifestyle changes mean exactly that, changes to make our life and the style of life we've led different, to make a difference to our level of stress. We cannot expect things to change if we don't make changes! Simple cause and effect. And we can only change our self, not People, Places, Things.

It is our responsibility to remain self-aware, mindful of our thoughts in whatever stressful situation we find our self: H.A.L.T. automatic reactions. Ask yourself 'is this situation putting my recovery at risk?' Choose a different way of thinking, diffuse the smoke from the fire by using The Sprinkler System!

The Startle Response: Noise

Even before birth we are designed to react to sound. Known as the Startle Response, this instinctual, often unconscious trigger is crucial to survival. A baby in the womb will move more in an externally noisy environment, and infants focus on every word they hear, so they can learn to speak. The Startle Response enables us to go from a deep sleep to a quick sprint in a mater of seconds, or to do 'battle' with surprising strength. This response is most probably why, if someone shouts at us, our immediate reaction is to shout back. But, caught 'off guard', getting lost, making wrong assumptions, feeling anger or fear when we don't expect something, an unexpected outcome can easily upset our internal equilibrium. Frustration and disappointment may follow, bringing more internal stress.

Noise stress, which abounds in twenty-first-century life, can impair cognitive function though its influence on dopamine, which is a key neurotransmitter involved in many psychiatric disorders including ADHD and Parkinson's Disease.

Incidentally, many of us, particularly in early 'recovery' are sensitive to noise levels. Simply walking down a crowded street may disrupt our internal Tension Thermometer! Often we choose a quieter way of being on our New Path, wisely avoiding People, Places, Things, which our old chaotic self would have revelled in: personal lifestyle changes to perpetuate peace means acknowledging the effect external environmental noise has on our internal equilibrium. Don't become a recluse, just live in the world but not part of its noisy business: make time for 'quietening the mind'.

Behavioural implications of stress

Too numerous to explore fully here, these are possibly the ones which stand out the most:

1. Reasonable or unreasonable reactions to People, Places, Things

2 Sleep disturbances: inability or too much
3 Eating problems: too little or too much
4 Motivation, i.e. concentration and memory
5 Sexual activity and relationships

All of which are also affected by destructive addiction.

1. Behavioural traits

Some behavioural traits are already present before over-use of a substance. There are those whose conduct towards People, Places, Things has always been 'undesirable' to put it mildly! Individuals who, for whatever reason, have an inability to perceive 'right' from 'wrong'. Whose attitudes and actions towards themselves, others and the world in which we live are not only 'misguided' by external stressful influences, but who inwardly decide and make the choice to deliberately confront life head-on. 'Stinking thinking' as it is known! In an age where it can be politically incorrect not to look behind someone's behaviour for a reason there lies the danger of making excuses. Sometimes 'what you see is what you get'. Certain personalities with 'unhealthy' attitudes or egos, certain characters or ways of being, are just plain rotten, insubordinate, unfavourable, damaging and dangerous. While it can be protested all behaviour is linked to our thoughts and perceptions from our environment, there lies the possible trap of the modern-day get-out: 'It's not my fault!' (Though I personally maintain there is 'good' in everyone: the spirit without ego is pure.)

Just as we have to take responsibility for this disease, it is not an excuse for continuing to drink, etc. Accountability exists whatever circumstances of stress are happening now. Those whose behaviour 'stinks' even before over-use of a substance may have to work doubly hard on their thought patterns, but nothing is impossible if we are willing to change. If we nurture our true spirit even the most 'evil' personality can find peace in repentance and changing old destructive patterns of thought.

2. Sleeping patterns

Disturbed sleeping patterns are often the first sign of stress and a direct outcome of over-use of any mood-altering substance. We may use 'sleep-time' to 'escape' from the world. Those with 'depression' or depletion of feel-good chemicals, from stressor substance over-use, may either sleep as if they were hibernating, continually nod off, or being unable to sleep through stress, use a substance to achieve false relaxation (when we pass out more than nod off!). The opposite is also true. We may take drugs to keep us awake (caffeine etc. included) depleting all our natural energy and feel-good chemicals, leaving us exhausted and 'depressed'.

Incidentally, one of the greatest gifts of sobriety is to wake up feeling good, refreshed, grateful we slept, with no night-terrors, sweats, cramps, etc. The joy of feeling alive and looking alive (no red eyes, puffy skin and pale pallor), feeling proud and grateful we didn't drink the night before!

Our natural sleeping rhythm does return. If we live in a busy, noisy household, evenings can be our most stressful time. Or, if we live alone, our most lonely. Night-time is one of the most vulnerable times for old patterns of thought and behaviour. If ever you feel like picking up – H.A.L.T. Review your day: what's happened in it to create stress in your thoughts? Say the Serenity Prayer (p. 228) over and over and over again. Put G–d in the gap.

3. Eating

This is another vast subject, tied up with emotions and physiological reactions. Stress can have an effect on the third branch of our Sympathetic Nervous System, the enteric (see also Attack of the Adrenals), making us feel queasy or sick to the stomach. Some people will eat more, particularly sugary foods, for the feel-good chemicals, when they're stressed or depressed (note: with the depletion of chemicals, bad foods deplete us more). Some people don't feel like eating when they're upset. Some, who perhaps feel unable to 'control' their external environment or circumstances, may falsely believe they can regain their 'power' by taking 'control' of their eating, either not eating or eating too much. As with many habits or self-medication, eating disorders can take on their own addictive and destructive patterns of thought and behaviour.

At the risk of simplifying matters, for our eating habits are so inextricably linked to our thoughts and our thoughts are 'governed' by the Law of Associative Memory, whether we 'mentally' lean to one end of the scale (not eating) or the other (too much), it may be said our eating habits have been constructed over time by our feelings connected to food and feelings about our self.

Many of us with eating problems have self-worth issues which can stem from the past. Some of us need to let go of past issues and patterns of thought concerning our long-term relationship with food, the memories of mealtimes, etc., how others' attitudes influenced us. If we eat to fill a gap inside, or get used to feeling 'empty inside' we cannot simply abstain from food as sobriety demands from mood-altering drugs. It is a suggestion to use the *Letting Go Ritual* (p. 235), replacing the 'drug' with 'food issues', to allow a space or gap to move into a healthy relationship with food.

Mindful of eating, being aware of how certain foods (chemicals therein) have a direct influence on our mood has never been easier to discover. There are many books on this subject and plenty of other resources to use for information.

Finding the good within our self to replace that feeling of emptiness, the desire to look after our self, our body, is part of 'recovering' from the destructive addictions cycle. *Any cycle can be broken.*

Note: We don't feel like eating when we drink too much, particularly because our Reward Circuit is telling us we don't need to; our survival instinct to eat is replaced with the need to take a false chemical messenger.

Nutrition, when we are on our New Path, is extremely important. There are certain minerals and vitamins we lack: drink and drugs deplete and interfere with the absorption of nutrients, which contribute to the symptoms of physical damage from substance over-use. Specific supplements for regeneration to achieve optimum cognitive functioning can be recommended by your doctor, homeopath or professional nutritionist. Non-addictive 'brain food' will help relieve anxiety, mood swings, depression, sleep disorders as well as malnutrition. (See also Gene Therapy at the end of the book.)

A healthy body/mind/spirit = a healthy self = a contented, satisfied whole!

It is important to mention that some of us cross-addictive personalities may 'use' food in an equally destructive manner as any mood-altering drug. Paying attention to our eating habits, healing our Nervous System by giving our self nourishment of 'good' foodstuffs, not false empty calories of alcohol or 'junk' food, is a vital part of valuing who we are.

4. Motivation

But, you may protest, 'I start out with good intentions, but lose my motivation, particularly when any stress comes along!' *Change requires discipline, something we lose when we over-use a substance.* Once we are addicted we need a certain amount to top up our level of tolerance, to feel 'normal', and more to achieve a 'higher' feeling, biologically reducing our capacity to cope with stress.

Add to this the effect of stress on concentration and memory: sustained stress can affect the hippocampus, the part of the Limbic System (the 'home' of our emotions), which is central to learning and memory. Using the analogy of the telephone exchange (when we discussed neurotransmitters and mechanical messengers at the beginning), 'the lines go down' when we are in certain stressful situations. Hormones are secreted from the adrenal glands. During a perceived threat these glands release adrenaline. If the threat persists then they release cortisol, which remains in the brain much longer than adrenaline, continuing to affect brain cells.

Cortisol affects memory, formation of new and retrieval of existing thoughts, and learning. Normally the hypothalamus secretes a hormone that causes the pituitary gland to secrete another hormone that causes the adrenals to secrete cortisol.

Interestingly, the hippocampus (specifically the limbic region) is where the 'wanting' response is observed. 'Wanting' a substance is more directly connected to relapse. Dopamine, the feel-good neurotransmitter, is connected to the 'liking' region of the brain.

Adrenaline is derived from dopamine. So when our stress levels go up excess adrenaline demands lead to dopamine deficiency which leads to chemical and emotional 'depression' or depletion. Substance over-use also depletes dopamine, the Yo-Yo Effect.

GABA controls the release of dopamine. It is the 'chilled'

neurotransmitter which 'calms us down'. Alcohol and Valium (to name just two) mimic GABA's effect in the brain. It is interesting to note every cell in our body has GABA receptor sites and spiritual yogis and those who attain 'peaceful' states of consciousness are often found to have very high levels of GABA – another reason to practice meditation.

Warning: barbiturates, e.g. sleeping pills and alcohol, bind to a subset of GABA receptors, which can be a fatal combination, slowing our systems down to the point of death.

5. Sexual Activity

From a pure survival perspective, we have to procreate. From a love and feelings aspect it is fairly safe to say there is no more a complicated human emotion than love! Indeed, we can become 'addicted' to others (co-dependency, etc.) and 'addicted' to sex. Both of these 'problems' should be addressed with as much seriousness and professional help as any other addiction. Part of our very essence of being, sex and love can either fill us with the joys of being alive, or take us to the depths of despair. Rational intelligence can pale in the sight of love. It is truly a force to 'move mountains'.

A vast and never-ending exploration of the meaning of love has been and possibly always will be the inspiration of writers, painters, poets, sculptors, and every human being has a personal interpretation of their own. From a destructive mood-altering substance-using point of view we simply end up replacing any other love with our love for a drug.

Any love we feel for others ultimately gets pushed aside as we prioritise our need for more – the 'love' of our life, our substance or our substitute, falsely fills our senses. 'It' is always ready to make us feel good. Always willing to listen. Always there for us (as long as we can afford 'it'). But, as we know, our 'best friend' turns out to be our 'worst enemy' destroying any other love or anything good in our life. 'It' is truly evil. 'It' eats away at our very core of being. 'It' will do anything in its power to destroy our true spirit. 'It' will leave us with nothing but an empty heart, mind and soul. 'It' will take our life and create devastating consequences in the 'ripple effect' of our demise. The sheer stress, physical, mental and emotional, for all those in or around destructive addiction is a true scourge of society.

As we isolate our self with the progression of this disease, others turn away. We lose love. However much someone cares, eventually their own self-survival instinct may kick in and they walk away to protect their own life. This can be the pressure to stop that we need to address our 'problem'. There are a few who hang on in there for personal reasons, but mostly *love is simply exhausted by our addiction* and consequent behaviour.

There is nothing more un-loving than drunken sexual behaviour. There is often lack of self-respect, forgotten principles of loyalty, commitment, virtue and decency from distorted perceptions by over-use of alcohol and other mood-altering drugs.

Sometimes taken to get us in the mood, large quantities can have the opposite effect. How many times has 'it' loosened your tongue and you've woken up regretting, or worse not knowing, what you've said to someone?

Consider this cycle:

Pressure and Damage

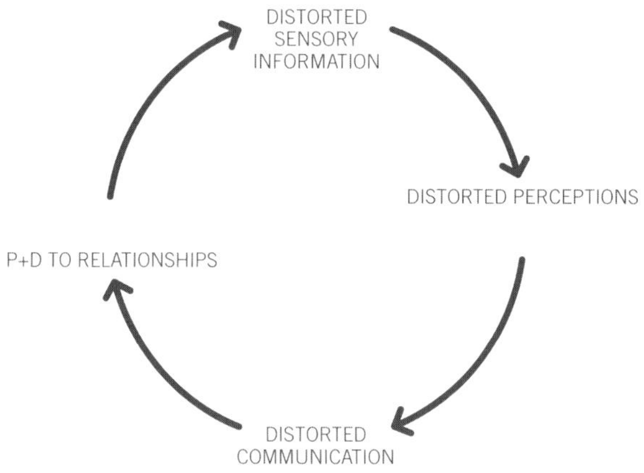

Fact: over-use of alcohol can easily ruin or distort relationships.

Fact: stressful relationships can easily foster substance misuse.

Some relationships may never 'work' for the good of both: as individuals our perceptions of the same situation can be vastly different. But, if we're not receiving the truth of the matter from our external and internal environment, if we are altering our feelings with a false chemical messenger, how will we know the 'reality' or 'suitability' of a relationship?

Distorted perceptions create numerous sexual and relationship problems. From casual sex, unwanted pregnancies, unsafe sex, thrill-seeking practices, prostitution, to hot-headed arguments, jealousy, uncontrollable anger, domestic violence and rape. Watch any 'chat show' where relationships have broken down and note how many of those somewhere along the line involve or are influenced, directly or indirectly, by the misuse of alcohol or other mood-altering drugs. Be honest, how many times has 'it' ruined a relationship for you?

On our New Path we must be fearless in our moral inventory. Our self-love depends on virtuous, the opposite of promiscuous or immoral, sexual and relationship behaviour. Self-respect and self-love, go hand-in-hand with self-esteem and self-worth. If we don't have those for our self how can we possibly love another? We can't give something we haven't got!

The best relationships are founded on and grow with spiritual qualities of trust, respect, acceptance, appreciation, affection, warmth and regard. These are essentials for lasting commitment and a tenderness of love which lasts long after the initial passion of sexual desire. Delighting in each other and the ardour of pleasurable union can be just as intense an emotional experience after many years together. Maybe just not as often!

Infatuation or lust, attachment or co-dependency sell love short of its true meaning. *Stress can add pressure to a relationship, but the over-use of alcohol can destroy love totally.*

Sexual intimacy can be scary in sobriety. What do we do? How do we really feel? Even if we've been with our partner for some time. In fact, many of us meet our partner while starting or mid-way on our progression: false perceptions of each other at the beginning! While in active addiction we may reject any intimacy, our Reward Circuit 'tells' us we don't need sex, we have all we need in our 'love' of our substance, or our drunken urges repel our partner. In both cases we lose the 'naturalness' of love-making. Sometimes we don't really know our self. So how can we share our self or know another?

It takes time, honesty and commitment to our New Way of Thinking to re-frame and build strong foundations for any relationship, new or old, sexual or friendship. *Repairing damaged relationships is a process*. New relationships can bring stress, good and bad. Try to get to know yourself before you search for another.

Taking time to nurture our recovery builds our confidence in all areas of relationships. When we understand our self we can love on a different level. True intimacy can be a wonderful journey for two separate 'wholes' to come together. An opportunity to discover 'as one' new heights of pleasure. True love-making with all senses alive can satisfy body, mind and spirit!

Making time to discover new ways to please each other, without the use of a false chemical, may require a little more effort, but it's definitely worth it, and no better way to relieve stress! Sexual 'sacredness', the union of two beings, two spirits, can bring all our GABA receptors to a state of bliss.

There is one love we can always count on. The source of love itself. One whose love will never fail. Unconditional. The spirit of Good resides in All, and His love gives us hope and strength in the face of adversity. He helps us make true 'amendments' – change, alterations for the good of our self, others and the world in which we live, clarifying the truth, satisfying, rectifying, enhancing, restoring our spirit through His love. All we have to do is show and seek faith and trust Him.

So, let's put this part together: we feel, perceiving threat, stress. We want a cigarette, cup of coffee, chocolate or sticky bun. We desire instant relief from alcohol, drugs, sleeping tablets, etc. Progression of the disease changes the 'liking' or 'desire' to need for relief!

So, does substance misuse work? No! It just produces more biological, more psychological and physical stress. A vicious cycle.

Attack of the Adrenals

The 'mechanism' of stress:

Body goes on alert with perceived threat – flight/fight. Pituitary gland hurls us into a physiological and psychological condition known as hyper-arousal – brain signals to adrenal glands and produces about forty hormones including adrenaline, cortisol and DHEA. We have more oxygen and sugar available, pushing more blood to the brain and instantly become more alert. (Some get 'addicted' to this 'rush'. We get the same physiological high from dopamine and the endorphin-enhancing effects of adrenaline that we do from a stimulant; and the same come-down, leaving us

A Vicious Cycle

Susceptibility to Depletion of Motivation at each turn…

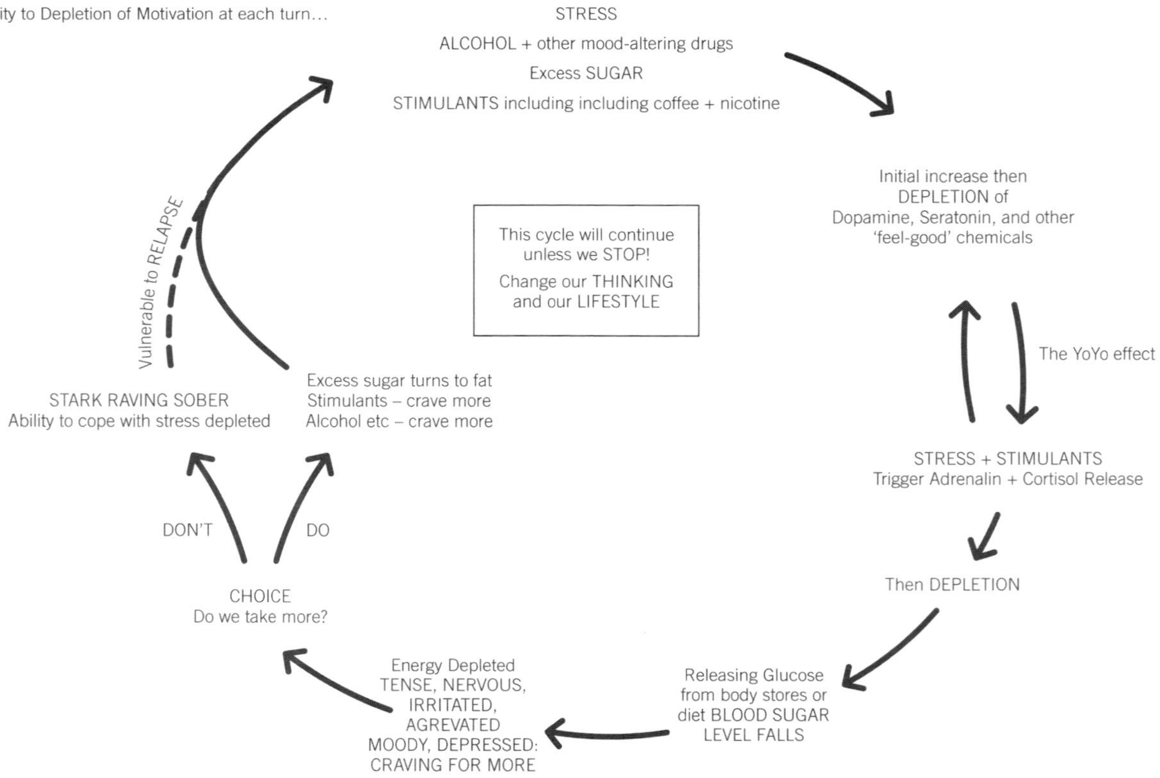

feeling exhausted, 'burnt out' and often depressed.) Initial 'threat' over, our body attempts to return to homeostasis, a state of chemical balance, just as it tries to do when we take a mood-altering substance. Either choice, of flight/fight exhausts our body, allowing our heart to stop pounding, our blood pressure to calm down and our muscles to recuperate.

However, this return to normal homeostasis may not be so easy, and becomes even more difficult with age. Although the hyper-activating system jumps into action immediately, it is very slow to shut down. Once our stress response has been activated the system keeps us in a state of readiness.

Internal imbalance, hyper-arousal, can continue if we do nothing positive to diminish a sense of loss of power or loss of control, leaving us feeling a heightened sense of vulnerability.

We can exhaust ourselves with worry and anxiety, never actually doing anything positive to relieve either the physical or emotional state of tension and stress. This too can be a negative cycle with the perceived threat creating a stress response.

P.T.A. (Power to the Adrenals)

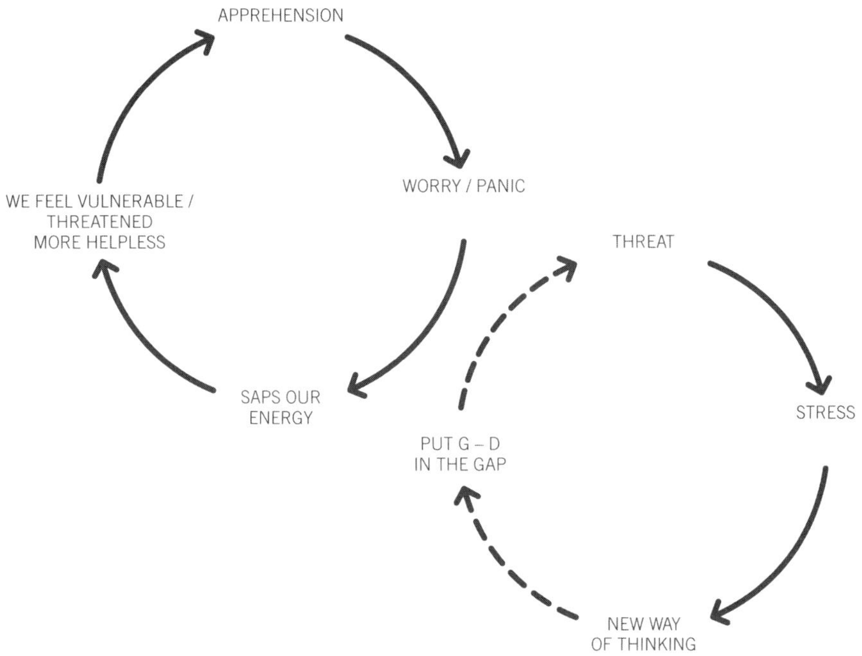

This is when we need to do something positive to counteract our physiological response by a new reaction – a New Way of Thinking.

We can do this! The three Ps:

- Stay Present in the now – don't procrastinate or project.
- Prioritise your recovery – is a situation worth a negative reaction and consequent trigger thinking?
- Perform your intention, i.e. New Way of Thinking – stop to think, don't automatically respond.

The stress response is managed by our Autonomic Nervous System, which is controlled by the hypothalamus which regulates the body's involuntary functions.

The hypothalamus can't distinguish between a real threat and an imagined threat. It bases its conscious response on the perception of threat and danger.

We all know mood-altering substances alter our perceptions, that through the distortion of perception we have altered our way of thinking, changing our thoughts from positive to negative.

This negative pattern of thought, by the Law of Associated Memory, can also be 'unconscious', i.e. automatic. Therefore, an unconscious thought for a drink, while we are in the stress process, becomes a trigger, i.e. need for relief.

We may not reach for a drink while in a state of stress, but the thought, *the 'seed of need' has been planted.*

It may only come into our conscious thought later, when something else happens to push us over the edge, or as a reward for coping earlier.

We may be unaware of rising stress levels for days, or weeks, or even months, unless we are mindful of our day-to-day thoughts and actions.

'I don't know what made me pick up!' – it's up to us to work back through our thoughts and behaviour with People, Places, Things to discover what 'stress' or process of thought contributed to that final action – to our decision to say 'Blow it, this is not working, I need a drink'.

Note: Even if we have 'it' in our hand, it's never too late to call a spiritual thought in, to prevent us actually allowing the rest of our thoughts to run riot! Or, we simply reach for our instant 'fix' saying to our self 'just one, just this once'.

Remember:

1. The stress process is managed by our Autonomic Nervous System (ANS).
2. Once we have 'one' the disease of addiction biologically demands we top up to our level of tolerance (where we left off) to achieve the 'relief' we need.

The Autonomic Nervous System consists of two main parts:

1. the Sympathetic Nervous System (SNS) which turns on our flight/fight response;
2. the Parasympathetic Nervous System (PNS) which promotes the relaxation response.

Like two 'tug-of-war' teams the SNS and PNS maintain metabolic equilibrium

Push – pull   PNS – SNS

The instigators of this hormonal 'tug-of-war' are our chemical messengers produced by the endocrine glands, which travel through the blood system, to and from the brain, through which alcohol is also transported.

Stress weakens the blood–brain barrier, making it easier for the false chemical messengers to affect our Endocrine System. Now add the biological neurohormone stress of our neurotransmitter's confusion, the distorted chemical messengers of the sensory information, then add distorted negative thought patterns. *It's easy to conclude stress and alcohol don't mix!* It is certainly not an answer! The solution to the problem of stress does not lie in the quick false fix.

There is another, lesser-known part of the ANS: The Enteric Nervous System. This is a complex of nerves that regulates the activity of the stomach, e.g. when we get sick to our stomach or 'feel butterflies in our tummy'; when we get nervous; this is our body's way of telling us something isn't right either externally or internally. *If we are mindful and self-aware we can notice 'warning signs' of disturbed equilibrium and change our thought pattern.* Prevention is always easier than cure: if we're 'in tune' with our self we can minimise, if not stop completely, those negative trigger thoughts from ruling our Helicopter Head.

The Enteric Nervous System

Our 'gut brain', the *Enteric Nervous System*, is the third branch of the ANS. In normal operation this system directs the muscles surrounding the small intestine to contract in an organised way, moving food down to our stomach, allowing the mixing motion with digestive chemicals, and decomposing, sorting out useful bits for energy, etc. begins.

Unwanted bits are excreted. The reason why we're sick or have diarrhoea or 'tummy troubles' when we drink too much, take too many drugs, or eat the wrong foods, is because they seem toxic to our body: our systems perceive them as a direct internal threat for our survival.

This simple expulsion mechanism is also a basic protection for our body from external threats. Emptying the digestive system prepares the body for flight or fight, both of which are easier on an empty stomach.

The Enteric System is far more subtle though than this, through evolution. A danger signal from the brain causes the immune system to kick into gear and help protect the body from modern hazards like fights, arguments and confrontation of many kinds; one explanation to why we can feel sick when we're nervous, or hear or see something which makes us fearful for our own safety!

The ancestral function of our Enteric Nervous System was to protect, to prepare us for flight or fight against danger, i.e. anything which could kill us or infect us, if it bit us! This ancient anti-inflammatory response can cause no end of problems, like irritable colon or ulcerative colitis. This autonomic system also explains why we cannot, or don't feel like, eating when we are tense, irritable, aggravated or depressed. Problems that are sometimes considered to be psychological in origin, like difficulty swallowing, ulcers and chronic abdominal pain, may be linked to this primal gut-reaction to stress.

While we are on the subject of not eating and our 'gut', it is worth mentioning several points which affect those of us with a destructive addiction:

1. 'Tummy troubles' are often one of the first outward and internal signs of over-use. Definitely a problem at some time, particularly in the latter stages of this disease.

2 Often we prioritise drink over food. Have you ever gone out for a night's drinking not wanting to eat beforehand because you instinctively know that (a) the drink will fill you up; (b) you'll feel the effects of drink more if you don't eat? Or, do you start a meal while hungry, with a drink, and leave the food after a few mouthfuls?
3 Many of us will push food away in favour of our substance. That comes first. Snacks, usually a sugar or junk food 'high', are of secondary importance.
4 In the later stages of progression we simply don't want or perceive a need for food because that survival instinct is being met by our substance of choice in our Reward Circuit.
5 Stimulation such as caffeine, nicotine, amphetamines and cocaine block the re-uptake of dopamine (and noradrenaline). This Reward Circuit not only facilitates the pleasure, Party Effect, but also suppresses appetite. Stimulants will falsely keep us going, so we burn off any stored fat (sugar) – the 'emaciated' look. Sedatives, e.g. alcohol, induce inactivity and storage of high sugar levels (fat), – the 'bloated' look.
6 Opiates, such as morphine, codeine, heroin and methadone depress nerve transmissions that signal pain. They also inhibit brain centres controlling coughing (beware cough medicines with codeine), breathing and intestinal mobility, with the same effect on the Reward Circuit, making us think and feel we don't want or need food.
7 One other drug to mention here is marijuana. This may both improve appetite or, in some cases, suppress appetite. We may get 'the munchies' but not really want any proper food because our survival instincts are being met already by the drug.

Our appearance, i.e. body weight, is not the only aspect to be affected. Stress and over-use of alcohol and other mood-altering drugs quite simply interferes with all our body's systems; even the inter-related biological systems supporting the skin. The cause and effect of stress on our physical appearance – accelerated ageing, tiny red bumps (spots), broken blood vessels particularly around our nose, easily bruising, etc., are all part and parcel of the dysfunction of our Endocrine System. The chemical messengers that repair, regulate and are responsible for our body's health are seriously affected by stress, alcohol and other drugs, which is why those of us trapped in destructive addiction look like death-warmed-up as well as feeling like we're being destroyed from the inside out!

Sobriety: Stress

Let's conclude the mechanism of stress to expand this insight and knowledge of the disease of addiction. The more information we gain, the more understanding, the greater our capability to 'move into' and 'maintain' recovery. No more 'secrets', no more 'I don't know why!'

Massive myths have simple solutions if we recognise the truth.

This is a disease that we don't think we have. A disease which tells us it's not a disease. A disease which changes our very perception which alters our ability for recognition of the truth. A disease which changes the structural and function ability for rational and emotional thoughts which is conducive to our health. A disease which affects the very organ we need to gain 'insight' with, our brain.

When we are sober!! Until we are abstinent in stable recovery to change our way of thinking!

Summary:

1. We know all mood-altering drugs act in our brain.
2. Our brain is made up of different parts, which have evolved over a time as part of evolution.
3. The hindbrain evolved hundreds of millions of years ago. In charge of our primal instincts and most basic functions, made up of the spinal cord, medula oblangata, the pons and the cerebellum, all of which are affected by alcohol and other mood-altering drugs.
4. The Limbic System, sometimes called the 'emotional' brain, evolved about 150 million years ago. First to be affected by alcohol and other emotion-altering drugs.
5. The neocortex, last and most advanced brain to evolve (to date). Our 'rational' brain. Divided into two hemispheres, right and left. Located in the neocortex are several different 'lobes', all of which are affected by alcohol and other drugs.

> The frontal lobe is primarily responsible for planning, organising and controlling. It is the last to develop when we are young adults. So, when we drink too much in adolescence we really are damaging our brain at the most important time of cognitive function 'learning'.

Consistent findings from imaging studies of over-use of alcohol, etc., show 'abnormalities' in the pre-frontal cortex. This exerts 'disruption' over the amygdala (part of our Limbic System).

The Limbic System is the primary area of the brain that deals with stress, and the primary area that is affected by alcohol, and other mood-altering drugs. It is the 'home' of our Reward Circuit.

Therefore, it can be reasonably concluded: stress affects our capacity to 'manage' destructive addictions and vice versa. This disease reduces our ability to cope with stress: biologically, physically and emotionally.

This 'secret' disease affects our body/mind/spirit, but now you know the truth of how 'it' works, you can do something about 'it'. Now you can change your lifestyle to reduce stress and your way of thinking about People, Places, Things to reduce tension. Now you know the why and what of the disease of addiction. The how is the miracle of transformation when we step onto our New Path of self-discovery, when we 'shift' our thoughts from our earthly 'needs' and invite the spiritual into our lives, to be our own true spiritual self!

When 'One" IS Enough!

One thought, one minute, one hour, one day at a time.

And how do we create perceptional change?

How do we re-wire and reframe our reality?

first and foremost by

ENTERING INTO THE TRUTH

and *really wanting* recovery

Then:

1. By sticking to The Prescription – daily, 24/7.
2. Learning and awareness of self, others and the world around us. Learning means a change in the direction of messages that occur in the Central Nervous System.
3. Reorganise your life and change your priorities with the specific goal of decreasing personal tension and stress.
4. Remember at all times: addictive disorder exists primarily in sobriety.
5. Being conscious or mindful of the self-schema will arrest the primary symptoms.

Reinforcement and repetition of The Prescription
Spiritual integrity
Order
Regain personal power
True reality and essence of things
Creation: nurture and growth of positive mindfulness
Expansion of consciousness and potential
Revitalised, transformed personality
Prescription = transformation = freedom and peace

9 Pathophysiological Chart

‘You must be the change you wish to see in the world.’

Gandhi

Pathophysiological Chart

This shows the progression and development of the Disease of Destructive Addiction (Plate 7).

There are several defining points of reference on the chart. As each stage is reached internal tension is increasing while our ability to cope with external tension directly decreases.

Adolescence

A period of change from childhood dependence to adult responsibility that indicates stress. Change always indicates stress. Internal biological changes, external pressures from family, school, friends, etc. At a time when we are vulnerable to influences of People, Places, Things we are often exposed to the ‘culture’ of alcohol and drugs. Socially acceptable in many societies, alcohol in particular is often readily available, with plenty of opportunities for us to experience the Party Effect and discover the pleasurable change of mood it creates. *Alcohol is toxic. Our bodies vehemently try to get rid of it.* We are often sick with stomach problems. As the body produces massive amounts of excitatory chemicals to metabolise the drug out of our body, it prioritises the function of our brain, the control centre of all other systems.

The Hangover

Tension in our intestinal system, tension headaches. Our hangover should be a massive warning sign: the body doesn't want alcohol in it! Does the hangover or 'passing out' in a heap of sick put us off? Sometimes. Other times cultural 'conditioning', far from expressing deep concern on a general basis of 'moral decline' of the consistent over-use of alcohol, often accepts being 'drunk and disorderly' as part of growing up for some! 'What a party!' 'What a hangover!' In psychology, the more rewards we have following an act the more it reinforces the act. The introduction to the drug- and alcohol-orientated 'club' is almost 'initiated' with the obligatory hangover. Having 'one too many' can be a lesson to remain self-aware of our alcohol intake limit. If we learn not to push that limit we can enjoy alcohol as an accompaniment to other things. It is when the sole purpose of an evening out (or in) is to 'get hammered' or 'get out of it' that external and internal disorder are created. Distorted thinking is part of and the consequence of the disease. Irresponsible, aggressive, disruptive behaviour; lost days off work; poor concentration; lack of motivation; the quick fix attitude; discontent and the bigger, better more fixation on things; the Party Effect we don't want to end and when it does we feel the tension in everyday life. We can't wait until our next 'binge' to escape the reality of our thoughts or have a 'great time'. A 'simple' hangover or an increasing 'way of feeling' after a night out? The more we push a drug, the closer we reach the point of no return – addiction. *The more we accept a hangover as part of a 'good night out', the more our thoughts are already changing*: altered thought patterns are part of this disease. A 'simple' hangover or the indication from our body to 'take note'? Other 'club' members sympathise. We all have a remedy! (Which usually doesn't mean not drinking too much again.) *The consequences of alcohol over-use can easily become 'part of life' on a regular basis*, with an excuse for each episode. A 'simple' hangover or a subtle warning something is 'missing' from our life? We drink or take mood-altering drugs for the effect. To alter or change our mood, our thoughts, the way we are feeling at that time just isn't 'good enough' for us. The 'reward' of increasing tolerance – 'Man, can you hold your drink!' is one of many biological outcomes of alcohol misuse. The false 'rewards' may also include the party persona: 'You're so funny when you've had a few!'; the confidence booster: 'I'm the lad/ladette!'; the Dutch courage or agitated aggression activator: 'I'll show them!'/'Let's fight!' A 'simple' hangover or part of the 'I don't care!' culture? A precursor to distorted thinking and the consequences of the disease of addiction. As we continue along our path of life, drinking, hangovers, consequences, we are totally unaware of the potential damage 'it' is creating in our brain, biologically and in our way of thinking. **This is the 'secret' of this disease.**

The 'Hair of the Dog'

How many times have you looked forward to 'feeling normal' after that first one of the day? That moment your homeostasis, your chemical balance is relieved by a top-up? A drink early evening, lunchtime, morning. *Tolerance goes hand-in-hand with progression.* We don't start off needing a drink as soon as we open our eyes when we wake, we don't do lots of things – yet! Geometric progression of this disease! We can find our self crossing every personal boundary, promise or limit in our need for relief. We know in our heart the difference between 'I'd like', 'I want', 'I need' a drink or any other mood-altering drug.

Addiction – first point

The first point of 'no return'. **That invisible line.** The moment our body opens up more receptors? The hard-wiring of negative thought patterns? One thing is certain, *geometric progression will not stop until we stop.*

Progression may be slightly put on hold throughout our life. We may 'binge' when we're in our teens, early twenties, but with maturity and added responsibility we may either slow down or contain our drinking. At times of stress it may escalate but in general we may remain aware of our level of intake. During our thirties and early forties we may either push the drug or simply be 'too busy' to have too many hangovers! **Keeping our 'top-up' level 'manageable' does not mean the disease is not 'secretly' progressing!** Depending upon what age we started and the amount we've 'pushed', middle age can be the time addiction truly rears its ugly head, manifesting itself to the point we lose 'control'. Middle age is a time of change for most of us. Biological, psychological, physical and emotional stress. Changes within our family and social systems, teenagers at home, children leaving home, business at its busiest or collapsing financial status, care of elderly parents, job changes, losses, house moves, slowing down pre-retirement with more time on our hands, or 'if I don't make it now, I'll never make it'. So many social pressures. Biological changes, particularly for women (menopause) and mid-life crisis. As we grow older health problems in general occur, as our previous lifestyle catches up with us. Death of others, relationship problems, the list is endless! The more we have used alcohol and other mood-altering substances to solve our problems over the years, the more likely we are to turn to it; the very nature of this disease reduces our ability to cope with stress. The amount we could deal with when we're young is far more than in middle age – look at the chart. If the 'seed of addiction' was sown in our twenties, geometric progression throughout the years of this 'secret' disease comes to fruition mid-forties, for many, when either our need escalates or the effects of over-use simply catch up with us.

However, the earlier we start excessive or regular use of alcohol (or any other drug of choice), the earlier we reach that biological 'need' or 'addiction'. Many youngsters not only look upon alcohol as 'part of life' but drink spirits as if they were fizzy drinks (many alcoholic drinks are deliberately made sweet and 'attractive' by an industry whose marketing campaigns unfortunately don't carry a Government Health Warning and beers in general have a higher alcohol content than, say, ten years ago). Not only does our 'immature' brain feel the effects greatly, but we have less 'reality' (time without distorted information) to fall back on if we choose to stop. Add to this peer pressure, and the general 'drinking culture'. Then the insecurities, trials and tribulations of maturing, a desire to 'fit in' and 'have a good time'. Plus an ambition to be fulfilled . . .

It's easy to see why, not only are many in their twenties (having been partaking of the Party Effect since 14 or 15 years old) suffering chronic addiction symptoms; but moving onto a New Path is fraught with the complications of youth itself.

Without proper understanding of *all aspects*: psychological, biological, physical, social and spiritual, a New Path can be filled with 'pot-holes' (literally!). If we could but realise, that desire to 'feel good', that craving to be part of 'something', is actually an internal desire for peace, contentment. Happiness within is achievable at any age. With information and education, I personally find most 'youngsters' able to grasp much more than we adults give them credit for. We live in a technically sophisticated age: why can't we imbue certain 'simplicities of life' – like goodness, truth, honesty, love, acceptance, respect, gratitude – to nurture the strength of our spiritual bank balance rather than portraying temptation (of many kinds) as the ultimate goal, then complaining when they partake, 'They're out of control!'

Treatment

The pressure to stop can propel us into 'treatment'. 'Detox' is a mere starting point on our New Path.

If we can afford the luxury (time and money) of residential treatment it can provide a safe, secure, drug-free environment. If we have the opportunity to listen to others and share our own story, gaining knowledge and having time out from daily stresses can be an excellent starting point. But our 'problems' don't exist when we're 'in' somewhere. Our problems are waiting outside! If we leave, no matter how long we've been in, thinking we're well and go straight back to our old way of thinking and usual lifestyle, the chances of relapse are extremely high. *Learning to cope with reality while living in reality is an ongoing process.* Any 'tools' we pick up from anywhere can only help us on our journey. Maintaining recovery is an inside job of our self. Getting the right information and acting on it is what ultimately counts. We don't **'treat' the addiction, i.e. the symptoms**, we **abandon it and focus on the disease**, i.e. the truth of the matter, the solution.

A New Way of Thinking with major lifestyle changes is required for true recovery. Encompassing the spiritual aspect of our being, in whichever way we can, contributes in unimaginable ways to our healing from the inside out, our 'weapon' and our 'strength' for 'maintenance' of recovery from this devastating, chronic, relapsing disorder and disease.

Terminal – Second Point

The second point of 'no return'. **This disease exists in sobriety.** Stress or dis-ease can trigger relapse time and time again, to the point of directly or indirectly causing our death unless we understand:

1. This disease is a primary condition, i.e. it causes symptoms, with chronic, i.e. geometric progression, and will not stop until we stop, for good. It is a neuroendocrine disorder of the brain, which has serious implications on our entire physical, psychological and spiritual well-being, affecting our Sympathetic Nervous System over which we have little control. It is a disease which changes the structure and function of our brain, creating a real biological need for our substance of choice.
2. Physical dependency, craving and tolerance are symptoms and major characteristics of addiction. 'Withdrawal' is the symptom of chemical imbalance, when we stop taking our D.O.C.
3. When the tension in our body gets to the peak point that we need relief from alcohol or any other mood-altering drugs, that's the beginning of this disease and there is no cure.
4. When tension in our body rises, remembering we've got a limit to the tension we can take, biologically, our ability to cope with tension outside goes down, i.e. maladaption to our external environment. More tension, less ability to cope.

We will struggle in sobriety unless we focus on the disease, first!

Once we surrender to the acceptance of this disease, abandon our substance and focus on reducing the tension, reorganise our life, change our priorities, include the spiritual in daily life, we find the correct solution.

As the tension goes down, what's driving us to seek relief is being reduced. As we follow this Prescription, doing and thinking about People, Places, Things in a spiritual manner, i.e. 'good' for our self, others and the world in which we live, we change our perceptions naturally, the reward of sobriety pushes our self-esteem, self-worth, self-acceptance up!

As long as we continue to make the right choices and do the right things for our new lifestyle, being careful not to forget we have a disease that exists in sobriety, watching for any Pink Cloud or old negative thought patterns, maintaining our recovery becomes an amazing journey of self-discovery, of new People, Places, Things of **a New Way of Being – a miracle of transformation!**

Remember: When we **Need Relief**
Alcohol and Drugs are
Not the Solution!

Before we conclude this experience with

Section Three: The Prescription

Take 'time-out' to consider a question asked at the start: What is it *you want* ...

CHANGE?

If you: *desire* a New Way of Thinking
need an Alteration of Behaviour
admit your Solution for Relief is making your life unmanageable

accept you are Powerless over 'just one' D.O.C.

Abandon The Tree of Death
Break out of the Prison of Addiction
Plant a seed of Hope and nurture
The Tree of Life

ENTER INTO RECOVERY!

Section Three

‘If you could get rid
of yourself just once,
The secret of secrets
would open to you,
The face of the unknown,
Hidden beyond the
universe
Would appear on the
Mirror of your perception.’

Rumi

The Prescription

'All that we are is the result of what we have thought'
Buddha

Introduction

As human beings we like rewards, a 'good time' and most of us – if we're honest! – prefer to have those as soon as possible! We also need to feel loved, appreciated, have a sense of purpose and of 'fitting in'. One of the purposes of feelings or emotions is to have physiological states that motivate action; each 'gives' us a direction or 'energy' to solve 'problems'. If we have never really learnt to deal with our emotions in a mature way, weighing up right from wrong to form an opinion based on Reality Information; or if we have learnt not to trust or respect our feelings, based on others' opinions, we may be emotionally 'stuck'. There is a definite connection between emotional maturity and sobriety. Learning how to accept and use our feelings constructively and appropriately is part of 'growing up' and part of the Prescription.

Our New Path is similar to that experienced when maturing in age: we don't learn to run before we learn how to walk! In fact, while in early 'recovery' our Thoughts and Actions can often be likened to 'maturing', that self-discovery of what we can (and cannot) do ... we're a little insecure, we're unsure of or have difficulty expressing our true feelings, we get frustrated at not getting our own way, instant gratification seems more appealing than long-term satisfaction! Learning to cope with 'difficult' emotions is hard. Life is hard, sometimes. We just have to work hard at and walk through certain 'lessons' to achieve emotional maturity and self-sufficiency. To build self-esteem we must do 'esteemable' things.

Maturity helps sobriety and vice versa. Being emotionally responsible means direct participation with People, Places, Things. Without artificially changing the way we think or feel to help us cope. New coping skills to relax from the stresses of life bring acceptance of our self and others, which encourages healthy relationships and the sheer joy of having 'good clean fun'. The prospect of ever 'having fun' in the future seems remote when we're used to getting an 'instant fix' and we have to surrender to the fact we just can't ever do 'it' again! But we know that 'instant fix' led us to addiction and destructive behaviour. So, like a maturing adult we must learn boundaries along our New Path. If we've never had any guidelines given to us, or any self-imposed codes of conduct, the process to the acceptance of boundaries will take lots of practice. Like any 'habit', checking our self to put our self back on track within our limits of acceptability, will eventually work. Mistakes – reframing - off track – rerouting! That's the process of our New Way of Thinking.

An important point to remember: Destructive Addiction, particularly in our Way of Thinking, doesn't happen overnight. Neither will our New Way of Thinking and Being. But with the right determination and effort we will change. So will our life. For the better of our self and others.

When we 'grow up' and 'grow into our self' life itself opens its doors! When we live in the Truth, of the 'good' we find in spirituality, within our own True Self endless possibilities lie just around the corner . . .

The Miracle of Transformation may happen so slowly as to be unperceivable to ourselves at first. As we change our Way of Thinking, ever aware of People, Places, Things which can disrupt our internal harmony (i.e. stress us out and create triggers), our demeanour changes to the external world in which we live. Though sceptical and wary – trust takes time – others will notice the change in us! 'You're so different! You look great! Alive! Happy! Content! I didn't recognise you!' We may feel a whole lot better – instantly, sometimes – from just stopping our substance. But when we work on our Whole Being, from the inside out, it simply shows!

Unfortunately, old habits 'die hard'. On a metaphysical level the 'evil' of this disease won't let go of its grip on us without a 'real good fight'. 'It' will fling every possible Thing 'it' can at us to 'win us back'. The 'devil in disguise' triggers have many faces and will pile one on top of the other to test our Emotional Muscle. Always remember: this is a disease which tells us it's not a disease. A distorted way of thinking – which we can reroute or reframe.

Like nature itself recovery g-r-o-w-s. If we feed our spirit with the right information we will blossom and flourish. Just as the earth moves in orbit round the sun, if we orbit round 'good' our time to shine from within will come with moon 'shadows' being a natural part of life's twists and turns, darkness and light!

Our natural circadian rhythm (sleep/wake cycle) dictates we wake up when it's light . . . when we wake up spiritually our New Path truly begins. This awakening takes time.

There is no magic formula and no pill we can take (substituting one chemical for another should only be done if absolutely necessary), for the Real Experience. Bear in mind God's time is not Man's time. The Law of Attraction etc., will work. So will prayer, meditation etc., but not always when we want it, in the way that we want it – now!

That's the New Journey . . . that's what makes the experience along our New Path so exciting! Even the depressing times can remind us it's just so great to truly feel alive. The first time you cry – really cry – real emotion, right from your gut, like your heart is going to split in two – you may feel a sense of humility, then acceptance and a strange sense of relief. For it's at times when we feel totally helpless and surrender to the frailty of life, the fragility of human emotion and ask for help outside this often helpless world that we touch that part within us, feeling so empty inside, which is just waiting to be filled!

The D.O.C. (our drug of choice) can't fill that space in reality. Our true spirit can! The Prescription is really nothing more than that – finding our self on our New Path on our Great New Experience of life!

When we break free of the isolation of addiction we rejoin humanity. We experience life by participation – aware the world is imperfect, but learning to cope by doing and feeling things using nothing more than our complete self. Complete awareness of the True Nature of Things is impossible – we are human – but if we are mindful of the matter behind the matter, by examining our attitudes and beliefs, looking within for answers and solutions, we can find our True Self and become who we were meant to be.

The aim of 'recovery' for most is to find Peace Within (Internal). This involves making peace with People, Places, Things (External). Not an easy task!

But by 'plugging our self in' to the spiritual – meaning the good in everyday life, to which we are all connected – we can experience that feeling we searched for and found temporarily, in our drink or drug of choice.

Honesty, Anger and Optimism. H.O.W.

One major contributing factor to successful 'recovery' is honesty. As you know, this breaks down the cycle of denial and that perpetual state of anguish: 'Shall I, shan't I, admit?' On our New Path 'honesty' is a permanent key. If we are honest with our thoughts and feelings while remaining aware of emotional maturity and responsibility towards other i.e. we don't go around 'blurting out our truth', we remain self-aware and mindful with compassion, acceptance and understanding we are all human. We can live in our own truth without having to always be 'right'.

Anger, fear and its opposite, love, are our three most basic underlying emotions. They can trigger old patterns of thought in an instant. When we deny them, repress them, don't 'own' them or 'stuff them down' they don't go away – they just bubble and boil in the Tension Thermometer! We may talk but not truly feel our feelings.

We may analyse things to the smallest detail but avoid feeling, really feeling. We are often afraid of our True Self, our deepest feelings, especially in early recovery because we're not used to Real Emotions, let alone expressing them in a way others have half a chance of understanding. When we learn to be honest and mindful of our anger we can learn ways to 'release' the experience of such a 'true' emotion.

Core emotions:

Joy, Sadness, Anger, Acceptance, Anticipation, Fear, Surprise and Disgust can be overwhelming at times. Note how one is often the mirror image of another!

We often feel fear at expressing our honest emotions. Will we appear vulnerable or weak? Will others laugh? Will we be misunderstood?

How do we cope if we can not suppress such strong hormonal, biological, chemical messages by using false chemical information?

By being honest and realising we are not only our thoughts. Our mind is cosmic. Truth, dignity, integrity, faith, hope and love are the main ingredients of spirituality, which need to be lived – actively!

As mentioned several times, imagining, i.e. visualisation, is a fantastic 'tool' for helping us to deal with our emotions. Now *science has proved that optimism is related to physical and mental health and a pessimistic view is correlated with depression symptoms.*

Researchers, using functional magnetic resonance imaging, examined brain function while volunteers thought of future possible events such as winning the lottery or ending a love affair. Positive future event thought enhanced activation in the amygdala (Reward Circuit). Results suggest that while the past is constrained, the future is open to interpretation, which allows us to distance our self from possible negative events and move closer toward Positive Thought and Positive Outcome.

When we consciously choose not to think about negative things our ability to recall that memory gradually weakens – call it *motivated forgetting*! As you reframe your thoughts the memory of 'needing' a drink will fade.

Like any habit of thought, repetition of 'good' or positive optimistic thoughts will take hold and become a permanent pattern. How, if our anger is constantly getting in the way, can we think 'good' thoughts?

By patiently replacing each thought, consciously, with another! – How? – By being Honest. Open. Willing.

Looking 'Behind' Anger

By self inquiry – H.O.W. with introspection and self talk regarding what feelings really 'lie beneath' this powerful surge of emotion – we can work through anger. There is a difference between irrational anger and rational anger. Putting this basic emotion in its proper perspective will help us deal with our anger in a positive rather than negative way.

Start by admitting 'I'm angry'. Then deal with each 'layer' of feelings, continually asking yourself why you feel that way.

Ask yourself:

'Is this Person, Place, Thing pushing my buttons, leading my thoughts automatically down memory lane?'

'Who, what, when does this unconsciously remind me of?'

'Who or what am I really angry with?'

Introspection often requires us to 'look behind' and 'go beyond' feelings of comfortable self-absorption. H.O.W. helps us identify any self-pity, self-righteousness, and judgemental or blaming attitude. Negative emotions/feelings ultimately keep us stuck in our anger, running the same scene over and over again in our mind. Old thought patterns allow the most convenient self-schema to feed our anger. Self-analysis allows us to discard any previous programming (external or internal), and truthful self-examination can dissolve feelings of anger which are nothing to do with the Here and Now.

Finding the 'root cause' of our anger obviously takes time, something we don't immediately have at the moment we feel our anger rising! That's when spirituality can comfort and restore our equilibrium. One good thought can stop negative feelings escalating.

With practice certain 'similar' situations with People, Places, Things will automatically push our stop button rather than pushing us to our old boiling point of tension. Simply learning to stop for a moment before we steam in can prevent rational anger turning into a full-blown rendition of what's wrong in the entire Universe! (Funny, but true.) In fact learning to laugh at our self, seeing the lighter side of a situation, stepping back for a moment (literally, sometimes) can instantly put the brakes on anger. 'Here we go again … Hmmm … Let's change my usual script here and now …' Learning to talk about our honest feelings opens the way for discussion. (That's of course if our perceptions are not being distorted. Never argue with a false chemical!)

Note: Be aware of humour to 'cover up' feelings and emotions. Though a great asset in life in general, sarcasm, quips, witty repartee, may not be funny if another person's feelings are being made light of! (The joker mask – see Masks we Wear at the end of the book)

Some of us erupt quickly, some simmer, some take it off the boil and internalise the whole lot. Not a healthy option. Repressed emotions just lead to increased internal tension. We need to learn Anger Management skills, which essentially require us to look within. By discovering a 'root cause' or acknowledging we are simply angry by nature of habit (nature being the habitual self-schema), we can do something positive to change our self.

Root causes may include a whole host of negative emotions: look at the *Feelings Word Vocabulary* at the end of this book: with which words from the Sad, Angry, Scared, Confused columns do you identify? Note how each word leads us to think of another, inter-connecting along our Path of Thought Process.

If asked to use one word to sum up these underlying feelings, the emotion which lies at the heart of many is fear. Fear is toxic, it can taint and poison all other thoughts and feelings. A feeling of helplessness or powerlessness can be changed by the Power of True Spirit within.

Look at the Happy column. The basic underlying emotion is love. Love, the opposite of anger, can dissipate fear. Finding compassion and understanding will automatically switch on the Sprinkler System. Discontent within can be treated with the power of love, for our True Self, others and the world in which we live. Tuning on, tuning in or plugging in to the divine 'unseen' source of love can make our heart happy.

A basic desire for good allows assertion of positive rational anger. Though do be careful: justification can lead to a desire for retribution. Taking false ego out of anger and placing goodness and love in its place precipitates a healthy humility to accept things as they are for the good of all involved. Contentment, peacefulness and the greatest expression of love – forgiveness – comes from our personal power over negative emotions with the most powerful word: acceptance. If peace is our heart's desire remember: the 'root' to our heart is the calming of anger. Faith, hope, the work of our imagination (belief to accept the unseen) and connecting our heart to our head achieves this.

Accepting we often drag along the past with unforgiveness, as well as projecting our fears into the future, that we can only truly positively deal with our anger towards People, Places, Things while living in reality, in the present, is the new way to be, now!

We can balance what we experience in the now by looking at the bigger picture. Is being angry worth losing our internal harmony and possibly our sobriety? We can agree to disagree and retain our inner equilibrium!

Restoring Balance and Harmony

Transformation includes discipline and order, balance and harmony. The information – events and feelings which influence and are part of Sensory Perception – you have received before all this new information, has 'programmed' you into a certain way of thinking. Disinformation will be hooked into your Autonomic Nervous System. Like the proverbial Pavlov experiment of 'conditioning', we can so easily teach our self from external and internal information, ways to automatically respond . . . even if the outcome is continually negative! Those of us stuck in the Prison of Addiction know that 'insane' behaviour only too well. As you will learn in the next chapter, this automatic negative thinking is a 'scheme' of our mind from our addict self. We simply keep pushing the 'wrong' buttons! Doing the same old things, with the same old thoughts, expecting a different outcome. Conversely, optimism, when married with the expectation from prayer, brings 'nice' rewards.

If we stick to the right path, pushing the right buttons, our thoughts will change. The power of prayer and connecting to the 'good' or God within us gives us endless opportunities to accept life's gifts. If we include truth and thankfulness in daily 'experiments' – 'How am I going to choose to feel today?'; 'What am I going to choose to do?'; 'Why am I thinking that way?' – on our New Path, being 'in time' and 'in tune' with our spiritual right choice self, becomes like breathing ... something we do naturally! (Just remember, prayer is often answered in ways not of our choice but in ways which are best for all and in God's time, not ours.)

The balance between optimism and pessimism is perhaps something we learn. At its root may be whether we were shown the example of reaching out to others with love and trust, or taught early on to withdraw. Seeing or looking for the 'good' in all People, Places and Things is the true meaning of being spiritual. If we give of our self we may not immediately receive 'rewards' in credit! But the feelings we receive when we know we've done 'right' or 'good' are always there for a rainy day. A stock of Emotional Muscle never goes amiss. Joy comes in the giving: we should not give expecting to receive in return.

Whatever habit – glass half full or glass half empty – and disharmony you find yourself in, stop it! Acknowledge it is a habit and challenge it. Remember: *strong emotions make strong memories*. Hormones like adrenaline wash over the amygdala. In moments of joy or sadness, pleasure or fear (back to our ancient flight/fight response), our neuron dendrites 'shift'. Most daily events are quickly forgotten. **The events which provoke an emotional response are written in neurological ink.** (See end of Therapies for suggestion on 'rubbing out' this 'ink')

Restoring balance to our emotions, learning to express our anger, fear etc., in a healthy, understandable way (for others) takes time and effort. That craving for 'being understood' is like an addiction in itself. So can 'being a victim' or 'attracting negativity'. On balance these destructive ideas, concepts, beliefs – perceptions – about our self are simply thought 'ink' in our brain! That's not to say we can't scribble over them making new patterns – 'rubbing out' the old, writing a different 'story' or 'scheme' is part of the wonders of transformation: a renewal of the mind.

Balance is the ability to create a multidimensional personality: to balance our true spiritual self with our earthly needs, wants and desires. To create harmony between our self, others and our environment.

To achieve harmony we need to let go of old ideas, beliefs and practices that brought imbalance, disharmony and disorder to our lives. Harmony fluctuates, it is never static – 'things' always change . . .

As we grow spiritually, accepting changes which are out of our control, we learn to see problems as challenges if we focus on the experience and lesson to be learnt to help our Emotional Muscles grow.

We re-balance our self naturally.

If we are thrown off balance and resort to a mood-altering drug for relief, we will never achieve that natural harmony and peace within. 'There is always a price to be paid for weakness when you could have been strong.'

Many of us will be aware, even in the early days of our 'using', the experience, the feeling of instant reward, the emotional 'fix', is something we 'love', drinking larger quantities, more often, than others. It is interesting to note that those of us who like to do things in excess – the so called 'addictive personality' – may also portray 'perfectionist' traits. This is a form of 'being in control' of People, Places, Things. Or so we'd like to think!

As our lack of control over our use of a substance progresses we may pay even more attention to detail – worrying about the top on a toothpaste tube, but being unable to confront the larger issues in life! Of course, even those of us who are 'perfectionists' relinquish care and control over anything as our control over everything dissolves with the over-use of a substance.

The 'perfectionist' will often switch from one 'addiction' to another. While in active addiction of a substance we may pick up and put down hobbies, exercise, projects etc. in quick succession: 'I'm going to learn how to . . .'; 'This is my new thing.' We will buy all 'the equipment', go to classes, show all the initial enthusiasm – until we either lose motivation through our substance use or think we're never going to be the best, so what's the point?

As we learn how to balance our self we must remain aware of, and be conscious of, our 'perfectionist' tendencies. It is all too easy on our New Path, even if it's doing things that are 'good' for us, to become obsessed with doing them! Particularly exercise, which gives us a chemical 'rush'.

Remember: *balance and harmony at all times, to limit our stress.* If we feel we need to 'fix' or 'finish' everything at once we can put our self under pressure and create tension – exactly what we mustn't do! Incidentally, sorting out old bills, finishing that DIY etc., can be extremely daunting in early recovery. Get as much support and help as you possibly can, doing one job at a time.

Don't try to completely change everything all at once! Unresolved issues, including those in relationships, may be concluded in time . . . or may not be. The Serenity Prayer should be remembered at all times.

This disease exists in sobriety in our thinking.

Be ever mindful that you can flash back into old ways of being. Old patterns of thought will fade but never be erased completely. Many an alcoholic or addict stops their drug of choice but doesn't change their way of thinking. Our thoughts create our behaviour.

If we don't change the way we think, our persona, our actions in everyday life will remain the same.

Others may say: 'Yeah. They're not drinking. But they're so miserable!'; 'They're not using, but they're no different. Things haven't changed.'; 'Their behaviour hasn't really changed, they're just not drinking.'; 'They're still an alcoholic/addict at heart.'

Our 'aholics' or addictive tendencies come in different shapes and sizes: shopaholic, workaholic, sexaholic, exercise addict, diet addict etc. etc. The degree to which we allow these to infiltrate our thoughts determines their destruction on our lives and 'recovery'. We may simply have to admit to another 'addiction' and deal with it accordingly!

One mention here of possibly the addiction not mentioned so far, in detail: *nicotine*. This is one of the main 'killers' in society, as well as cases of obesity and heart disease. Nicotine 'addiction' would fill another few chapters, so suffice to say here: addiction to nicotine is not purely chemical. While there are changes in our brain and body chemistry, smoking is also learned behaviour. Nicotine differs from such drugs as alcohol, heroin, cocaine etc., in as much as, most obviously, it doesn't cause intoxication. This is not the centre of the problem. Dependence, the inability to stop because its use is so habitual and hard-wired into our patterns of thought and associative memory, is at the core of smoking.

The core issue as to whether tobacco and nicotine is addictive is one which for obvious reasons the industry itself disputes. Scientific consensus is that 'The issue over dependence is the loss of control over use. The drug controls you . . . you don't control the drug.'

Specifically: you're not able to stop using it when you decide to. You use the drug despite clear evidence that it is harming you. There are clear withdrawal symptoms – including, in the case of nicotine, depressed mood, insomnia, irritability and difficulty concentrating. According to these criteria there's no doubt that nicotine produces addiction.

Nicotine, an obscure chemical from a tobacco plant is, by an accident of nature, able to bind to the neurotransmitter acetylcholine. The normal function of the receptors for this transmitter of chemical information is one of our brain's most important tools: to coordinate the activities of many other kinds of receptors, acting to 'fine tune' the sensitivity of a wide range of behaviours. Nicotine alters the release of many other neurotransmitters in the Gap, including dopamine and serotonin.

Final note on smoking tobacco: if you smoke and drink the two often go hand in hand. Give them up together. If you don't, be careful if you address smoking at a later date. The tension possibly created causes its own disharmony – make sure you have 'good sobriety' to tackle those thought patterns! Get as much help and support from professionals as you can.

Conclusion

The basic nature of addiction, or doing anything to excess, may be seen as the inability to stop regardless of the consequences. Human beings are 'addictive' by nature and our survival instincts dictate the necessity for certain rewards: food for hunger, drink for thirst, love and friendship for our species continuation and sense of purpose and fulfilment of mind and body. It is when what we put in the Gap is information biologically distorted by our D.O.C. that a habit may become a destructive addiction – progressing until such time as we decide to stop.

Filling our self and our lives with bigger, better things can be part and parcel of twenty-first-century life. Often we forget what really matters. Our quest to quench an inner thirst, an appetite for more can lead us down the wrong path. We can so easily lose our self on our journey through life. 'Getting to the top' or simply surviving often takes its toll on our inner harmony. When we lose our balance and fall it may be a long way down. Reaching our 'rock bottom' after losing our 'sanity' and all we hold dear to our heart, for the sake of a false 'love', is sometimes what it takes for us to admit and surrender: it controls us. There is no alternative but abstinence/death when dealing with 'it' to stop 'its' destruction.

Many of us resort to false chemicals to help us cope with our feelings. It is fair to say not all of those will directly lead to our death. But the anguish and heartache for all those involved by distorted perceptions affect millions of People, Places, Things. Our craving to experience feeling 'good' about our self, others and the world in which we live so often leads us on a path of ego-driven disregard for any 'goodness' in life itself.

The confidence 'it' once gave us eats away all goodness, from the inside out. Our self-confidence may be destroyed to the point at which we simply can't imagine being any other way – the basis of craving is the root of all suffering.

The disease of addiction can be arrested, if we:

1. Stop using our drug of choice
2. Change our thinking

If you crave for a different way of being,
To regain your self-confidence and self-worth.
If you're sick and tired of being sick and tired,
If you want to regain an appetite for life itself

Remember this:

Destructive addiction can be viewed as a disease of appetite.
A hunger, a feeling of never having enough, never feeling satisfied or content.
A thirst, a craving for something to fill us up, that emptiness inside.
A desire, a want, a need, to fill that Gap within . . .

By using mood-altering drugs and Things we deny that very part of us which can fulfil our craving – our own True Spirit.

10 Survival Kit for the Here and Now

'Let there be light.'

Genesis (1:3)

Survival Kit for the Here and Now

Keeping our sobriety is about commitment to change. Actively living our sobriety in spite of all that life throws at us may seem impossible to those just starting on their New Path. It is not. Millions of us are living proof! If we could we would all shout to you: 'You can do it!'

There can never be reason enough to pick up. Any excuse will simply not 'solve' the 'problem'. The solution lies in sobriety.

This truth will never change:

There is no compromise with this disease. Abstinence is not an alternative: it is an absolute necessity.

Surrender and accept this truth.

We are powerless over alcohol and other mood-altering drugs, and our lives become unmanageable.

Once we admit the truth we need help to maintain sobriety. We come to believe our own true spirit, or a power greater than our self can help us regain control of our lives.

Prepare and Plan – Prioritising Peace

Triggers will come. Of what intensity, duration and frequency you cannot determine. But with determination, and a few simple tools in your survival kit, you can build Emotional Muscle, 'feel the burn' and come through to win the day!

External and internal 'high risk' situations are obviously best avoided totally at the beginning of sobriety: pubs, clubs, dealers' venues, using friends, any old 'haunts' of our 'habit'. Resentment, anger, self-pity, blaming, dishonesty: anything potentially emotionally upsetting should be actively dismissed. 'Should' and 'dismissed' are in our control once we learn to master our mind! In the early days, before we learn how to detach the emotional content from a situation, it is simply best to keep our mouth shut and remove our self!

Obvious 'high risk' situations include any items of 'using' in our home (or work). Have a thorough spring clean. Move things around, if you can – don't sit in the same chair with the same glass/mug (even if it is full of orange juice or tea now!). Don't leave any trace of triggers. Place something 'positive' in or on the places you'd 'use' (a photo, a book, an affirmation, anything which holds 'good' memories or intentions). Some people like to 'cleanse' their home with sage, incense sticks, lavender oil in a burner, or various 'smelly candles'. At all times remember the importance of sensory perception. If our home 'feels' welcoming it will aid our relaxation. Think about colours, music, keeping things tidy (without being obsessive!), preparing food our self (a take-away kebab is not the smell nor nourishment we need!). Sort out your clothes. Take pride in your appearance. Cleanliness of body and mind goes a long way to helping us feel better! And with all the money we save it's OK to treat our self occasionally. (With an item of positivity that is!)

Of course, when others join 'our space' the equilibrium can change in an instant. Most 'others' can compromise on certain changes for our 'recovery' well-being – if they are given time to adjust to the new us! However, we must never force our New Path or New Way of Thinking on another. Accept some things may never change. Even if we cannot make the tiniest of spaces 'ours' – externally – we always have our internal environment to call exclusively our own: 'recovery' is ours, for our self.

Above all else: we are 100% responsible for our own thoughts and actions.

Back-up – Being Realistic

Particularly at first! And be aware for ever more as this **disease exists in sobriety** – it doesn't go away – we must always be mindful and realistic, remembering our Tension Thermometer. We never know when something or someone will 'ruffle our feathers', 'push our buttons' or 'twang our triggers'. Always have at least three phone numbers on you at all times, which you can call to at least start breathing 'normally' again! Never, ever, ever think you are alone. If you believe in God, he is always in. 24/7. Put God in the Gap. Send His chemical messages through the system. If you cannot find any form of spiritual thought (even though we're wired for spirituality, this does occasionally happen) – think of your neuronets: picture each stuck thought at a synapse, imagine that unwanted feeling as an emotional blob – stuck! Picture it as an 'entity' – you can give it a name: the demon, evil, Ted the Tormentor, Violet the Victim, Izzy Isolate, Slick the Suck in – whatever 'moves' your emotion, whatever shifts one dendrite to another!

Carry a 'symbol' of your recovery. Carry it with you until negative reactions become positive responses, naturally. Some people carry an item with them of significant meaning, to hold or press or simply look at, which either reminds them of the consequences of 'just one', or reinforces a need to remain sober: a simple tiny pebble can become a 'gratitude stone' to remind us things aren't all bad, all of the time ... and if they are, well that's another reason not to pick up. Things are always infinitely worse if we do. All that extra guilt and shame and regret and anger, etc.!

Some even wear an elastic band round their wrist, to snap them back to reality. One excellent approach can be to wear a symbol of faith. Clutching a Cross, Star of David, Moon and Star, Om or Aum, Ankh, Yin Yang, a Buddhist Wheel, Mandala or Chakra symbol, Celtic, African, Rasta or Shamanic symbol, a symbol for Allah, or a Chai (the list could go on, apologies for those not mentioned!) – and saying your own special prayer is far preferable.

The intention behind a symbol is to have something of material substance to 'hold on to', helping us focus our attention away from negative thought. Of course, the feeling given comes from the non-material – spirit – either as a direct reminder of someone who was, or of the essence that is. We humans sometimes need a thing, a tangible item, to grasp. Though spirit lies within and *comfort can be gained from a single thought of the spiritual nature of being*, our chosen One or source of light, sometimes we just need to touch a symbol for inspiration and encouragement.

Write down a list of things to do in an emergency. It should include making use of 'spare time'. Craving i.e. Need for Relief, can be as a result of, or symptom of, boredom. There are plenty of 'extra hours', as mentioned previously, when we stop. Sometimes we just don't know what to do to fill all those empty hours we so easily lost while existing outside reality. No 'scoring' to be done. No trips to the pub or off-licence. No lying comatose in front of the TV, or nursing yet another hangover in bed! What are we to do?

The answer requires effort on our part. Enormous effort, sometimes, especially if we're back at work and all we want to do is 'chill out' when we get home. Once we had our 'mate' to 'talk to' and 'relax with', now we may feel lost, anxious, agitated, wishing we could have 'just one' to settle us down. But we can't. Simple as that. Accept it.

Filling time doesn't have to be demanding. Finding something which interests us can be an exciting journey of its own. A 'hobby' to stimulate those brain cells. Any of the alternative therapies listed later on. There is a whole world of information just waiting to be delved into. Discover new likes and dislikes. Keep an open mind. Try anything at least three times before you rule it out. Go to classes, the library, meetings – a new friend may just be thinking 'I can't stand this' just like you – but unless you get out there, doing different, sober things, you'll never meet them!

Look upon time as an opportunity for self-discovery. Read. Watch nature programmes (it's amazing what you'll learn about adapting!). Learn from documentaries. Get your brain in gear! The greatest outlet for boredom is creativity. Make something. Draw. Write. Paint a wall. It doesn't matter if you simply doodle stick men, can't spell or drip paint (as long as you tidy up). The important outcome will be your engaging and expansion of your mind. If you find yourself getting frustrated, try again another time or accept that it's not for you and try something else. Gardening.

Cooking. There are always places to find inexpensive bits and pieces to do things with. Indulge your child within! In all of us there lies some aspect and ability to do, make, create. It doesn't matter if no one else sees it or likes it, or even if they ridicule it – creation is an achievement: it makes us feel good.

This age of technology gives us easy access to information. Computers can tell us things, machines can make things, but *only we humans can create emotions and thoughts by bringing our imaginations to life*. So, your poem doesn't rhyme. The vase leaks. The spaghetti was too al-dente. That was a prize petunia, not a weed. You created it! With your mind you brought an idea to life: from internal reality to external existence – that's spiritual in itself!

Be your own Sobriety Coach

Any therapy, activity, distraction, which redirects our thoughts. Anything that engages self-observation, self-expression, self-acceptance. It is our self which needs to find, discover new tools for our New Path, to manage thoughts, feelings, attitudes, beliefs and behaviours. Have a concrete strategy ready and waiting for that trigger. **Enable your self to live on life's terms.**

Results come from self-awareness. Being focused. Mindful. Paying attention to People. Places. Things. The sensory information we're receiving in reality. Perseverance to change thoughts. Recovery is about making different choices. The 'placidity' or 'flexibility' of our brain (in most cases) allows us to change even the most ingrained patterns of thoughts. Simply by repetition of new thoughts.

It is our head, not our legs which takes us for a drink!

Our mind, with its rational desire to understand, to control, can easily lead us down the wrong path. Opinions and viewpoints are often mistaken for the truth. Our self-concepts say: this is how it is. Once we learn to accept that our perceptions are merely part of our personal thought process, not part of the truth as a unified whole existence, we open our mind to the possibility of different perspectives.

Nothing exists by itself. Everything is interwoven in the great scheme of things. Our personal bundle of thoughts are only of our making: we have a choice to make our own New Way of Thinking.

When the thinking mind (the rational) takes over, we limit our self. By allowing the spiritual (which creates) to grow, we stop avoiding 'what is' (in our thoughts) and learn to be present in the here and now.

Hope, from dreams of transformation, of changing our life into something better, must be given 'wings'. To transcend our limiting thoughts and fly above the confines of our human existence is something we found easy to do by taking our D.O.C. Learning how to 'escape' from 'reality' without the aid of a false chemical, demands effort. A different prescription.

There is no 'quick fix' in recovery. If we want it, however, and we are prepared to go to any lengths to change our attitudes, ideas, beliefs and behaviour, doing no harm to others in the process, we will succeed.

Learning to say 'No!' in the moment to moment of the realities in life, to those People, Places, Things which are detrimental to our sense of self, is something not only those of us in 'recovery' could do with! Discovering who we are, in essence; taking away the masks and false faces; the pre-conceived dogmas and debilitating concepts of being 'right'; the ability to look at oneself in the mirror and like what you see inside that reflection; the self-acceptance which allows self-esteem without false ego or dependence on others' acceptance; pride in oneself without the 'I'm better than you' attitude; the loss of self-conscious striving which excludes us, often, from the enjoyment of life itself; unburdening our self from the false security of old unwanted thoughts and behaviour – to ask yourself: 'Who am I?' and work diligently on making changes, amending those traits of personality which serve no purpose for our better state of being – is actually a gift of sobriety that many others could do with discovering!

To transform our self from a hopeless, helpless, sorry state of being, dejected, rejected, desperate and desolate, physically, emotionally, mentally and spiritually drained, to a state of being with internal peace, which comes from leading a good, sober, life, can quite simply feel miraculous!

Many in recovery see life differently. A second chance. A precious gift. We have to. We have often experienced our own personal hell. We have no wish to return. We have no option but to choose a different path. One which may seem harder or longer, at first. Unless we put in the determination and effort required we just won't make it.

The darkness of doubt, to which we can also be addicted, can be illuminated by light if we just reach out and flick the switch! When we reach our rock bottom, in our heart, the only way is up – if want we to change. When we 'get it' we wouldn't swap this feeling for anything else under the sun! Once we identify with more than our thoughts we wake up to a spiritual consciousness much vaster than merely plodding along through with the flow ...

By learning to say 'No!', by becoming accountable to our self and others we become collectively responsible for changing the world in which we live: naturally, without the use of a single mood-altering distorted-perception-making substance. Our need for more, of never having enough, is replaced with 'I am content'. 'It is enough.'

'I am' is an affirmation of positivity. Being at ease within. Not afraid of 'not knowing' or not being 'enough' or not 'having' enough, including control over People, Places, Things.

States of mind come and go. At best our thoughts can direct us on our New Path. Just being, acknowledging 'all things are intrinsically one' can point us, as an explanation, in the direction of the truth. Feeling the understanding of those words can lead us into contentment, knowing we are both spirit and matter. Perfect in our ability to adapt with human imperfections. Perfect in spirit, which we can call upon at any time.

Abandoning our D.O.C. is only the beginning. We need a concrete base on which to build our future. Learning to challenge old distorted ways of thinking often needs specific tools or strategies, a guide or manual of instructions to work with, particularly during the first few weeks/months of sobriety.

This Too Shall Pass

An ending and your beginning. Now is the time to pull yourself together in mind/body/spirit. Don't wait for the 'I haven't done that – yet . . .' thought. Get to the doctors and tell him/her of your intention to stop. You may need some pharmacological help whilst your body adjusts from the chemical Yo-Yo Effects of withdrawal.

If you choose the tree of life rather than the tree of death, remember the following:

It is our head, not our legs that takes us for a drink! This is a disease which tells us it's not a disease. External/internal tension may 'push us' to that biological boiling point of 'stinking thinking' and our ego/personality/addict self will whisper in our ear 'Go on . . . you weren't that bad . . . you have will-power, just one's OK . . . you can beat "it" . . . you're not powerless!'

Knowledge + Action = Success.

Flick the switch

Let the 'light-bulb' of the truth shine within. Live in reality. Be mindful and self aware. Don't give in! Below are a few suggestions to help you re-wire and reframe your life.

Don't pick up that 'just one'. Tell an unwanted thought of using: NO chance! Remember, destructive addiction is an incurable, progressive, often fatal disease. Put your sobriety first, above all transient thoughts – this too shall pass. Use the Serenity Prayer; put God in the Gap.

Remain aware of People, Places, Things that may cause trigger thoughts. Keep an open mind: search for an alternative way of thinking, an 'opposite'. Do first things first. Don't confuse thought with 'if', 'but', 'should', 'could'. Repeat 24/7: 'I am 100% responsible for my own thoughts and actions.' Live in the now. Not in the past.

H.A.L.T. It is our freedom of choice we lose by picking up that first one. Listen: connect your heart to your head. Learn to hear the truth. Continually expand yourself. Our New Path is a process, not a destination. Look after yourself: physically, emotionally, spiritually. Be positive. Discard negativity. Create a new, internal reality. Remember we are not alone. Nurture faith, trust and hope. Be mindful of the difference between want, desire, need and acceptance. Bring your dreams to life with determination and effort. Don't fear needed change; there are endless possibilities when we're sober. Retain an attitude of gratitude.

Lose the 'ego'. Retain humility. We are only 'one' away from where we left off. Be thankful. Treasure sobriety above all else. See obstacles as challenges to build Emotional Muscle. See the glass half full, not half empty. Count your blessings, not your misfortunes. 'Talk is cheap': actions speak louder than words. Keep you own counsel. Mind your own business. Share and help when appropriate. Respect others. They may return the compliment. If not, let it be, accept. Practise self-restraint in all things. The quick fix is short lived. Anticipation of a greater reward – doing the right thing – is lasting. Accept life as it unfolds, and others as they are.

Remember: **we can only change our self.**

Share your joy as well as your pain. Celebrate being human with real emotions. Share of yourself but retain yourself. Keep your integrity. Nurture love for yourself. We cannot give what we haven't got. Find forgiveness, for yourself and others. Let go and let God. Forgiveness frees us.

Thinking Tips for our New Way

Don't allow 'victimhood' to be an excuse to use. Take control of your thinking. Stay sober for yourself. Share successful sobriety with others. Beware of boredom. Don't allow fear and insecurities to breed when alone. Don't deliberately isolate yourself. But learn to enjoy your own company. Accept offers of help. Reach out and ask for help. Make time and use time for introspection: get to know the true you. Beware of procrastination. Life happens while we are thinking about it. Negativity keeps us stuck. Optimism propels us forward. Release feelings of shame. Re-connect to others. Work through guilt and humiliation. Set goals: but practise non-attachment to results. Remember: addiction is often looking for 'fulfilment' in the wrong places. Beware of cross-addiction with People, Places, Things. Be present in the Now. Breathing, posture, stretching, can release emotional baggage. Eat properly. Exercise. Drink plenty of water and reduce caffeine consumption. Beware of the Pink Cloud. Happy stressors can also be triggers. Add your own New Way of Thinking tips to this list!

Abandon your D.O.C. Concentrate on the disease you have in sobriety. Our D.O.C. is the problem. Sobriety is the solution.

Above all else never forget:

1. We are powerless.
2. Our lives became unmanageable.
3. We have to look above humanity for help to displace our D.O.C. with thoughts and feelings of equal importance and emotional satisfaction for our needs. Inner peace surpasses all else.
4. When we enter into the truth we enter into spirituality.
5. Right thoughts, right actions, right speech. Acknowledgement of something 'other than' our self. The source. Good or God. Pure consciousness of self without the ego. Willingness to change. All facilitate recovery on our New Path.
6. Live life and love being alive in reality.
7. There is only one you. You are precious.

What Now?

'Pulling our self together' in mind/body/spirit is a process. But we have to start somewhere!

The physical and mental aspects may be helped with rational thinking and various alternative 'tools' for transformation: these are briefly described next, to end this book and perhaps at least one will help you on your own journey of discovery. **Own your recovery.**

Spirituality often comes more as a way of being, as a result of doing and thinking in a different way. Don't worry if you don't 'get it' immediately. Time heals. Transformation takes time. We are often impatient by nature. Allow time to 'grow into' your new self. Love and respect the process.

There is one obstacle which not even love can overcome, one thing which will prevent any insight or understanding of all you have read becoming the catalyst for your own transformation: denial.

Denial wastes precious time: 'the precious present'. Give yourself the present of time. Don't wait to tell yourself the truth. If you were given a winning lottery ticket you'd be excited at the prospect of spending the money! The knowledge contained within you, now, is far more exciting – you have the power to change your life! To spend time living and loving in reality! Grasp it, take control, do it now!

Stop denial: start transformation.

Living in a false reality with our D.O.C. has to stop, first, before we can move on. If there is any doubt or denial about the need to change, willingness will be impossible without honesty, and more 'research' may be needed until we finally admit the truth.

Research: we keep buying into false information. Test 'it' out, time and again. Moan, if you must: 'Why me?', 'Why did I pick the wrong numbers?' We think we're losing something. In fact: we're only 'losing to find', 'giving in to gain' and 'surrendering to win'. Mistakes, wrong choices, are only reprehensible if we keep on making them: when we know the truth. The disorder of destructive addiction will progress. The cycle will continue: until you choose to buy into recovery. Treat yourself with a renewal of your mind.

First things first: acknowledge the past. Your addiction, its progression and consequent effects on yourself and others. The storyboard of your life is important. To know where we are within our self, we sometimes have to recount our steps and look at where we've been. Willingness to change requires a willingness to accept and admit those things that need changing. The story so far will almost definitely seem vastly different to you than it does to others. Blame, being a 'victim', distorted thinking and false information, false perceptions, can easily keep us in denial, about many things.

a. People. Places. Things: reasons for the 'problem'. Denial: 'I'm not that bad.' 'I'm managing' ... with help of my D.O.C. 'It's not got me. I'm different.'
b. Listen to how it was from others' perspective. Claim your own 'baggage'. We may not intend to cause harm, but we do. Mistakes can be rectified once we're self-aware.

The loss of a) because of b) can cause immense inner turmoil. Fear of change can easily feed our denial.

c. The trouble tunnel: often filled with shame. Fear. Questions. Guilt. Sadness. Anger. Blame. Work your way through.

We may look for protection or an accomplice to hold our hand in the tunnel: Why me? What if? Excuses, rationalisation, minimising, justification – 'I'll change if they change'. Raw denial: shock, disbelief – 'How did this happen?'; 'I'm not an addict/ alcoholic.' Pretending won't make the truth go away.

d. A New Way of Thinking and positive action. Self inquiry, self acceptance: a New Path to inner peace. Remain self-aware. Mindful of the truth, in all things.

Be particularly aware of denial: 'I'm not; I don't' may just be our old self-scheming addict voice, trying to win us back in any way possible. Don't give in and don't give up!

Grow up, grow into yourself, take responsibility, take action: transform.

11 Therapies

'The Kingdom of Heaven is within you.'

Jesus Christ

Therapies

We often need help to find our feet on our New Path. Learning how to place old unwanted thoughts in the cerebral transmission trash can is a possible process if we choose to change.

As stated previously, living in reality often changes our perception of the past. If there are still underlying psychological issues, problems we just can't get our head round on our own, after achieving good sobriety, we may need 'expert' help. Choose a therapist with great care. Someone who has a proper understanding of destructive addiction.

Getting better is different from feeling better. We may feel better by going over and over the past, but changing our way of thinking ultimately means letting go of Past stuff and baggage! Find someone to help you separate negative patterns of thought and behaviour created by this disease, and those issues either inherent in our true nature or arising in our New Way of Being.

Separate the problem of addiction from other problems. Remember: we cannot deal with any emotional baggage until we live in reality. Our D.O.C. is not the solution.

Types of Therapy

To simplify matters consider three main categories:

Psychological therapies.

Biomedical therapies.

Complementary therapies.

Psychological Therapies

Counselling or Therapy?

The two terms are perhaps interchangeable. The experience of each can differ. By definition, counselling is the systematic guidance offered by social workers, doctors, health professionals etc. Problem areas might include: educational/career planning, marital problems, situational stress. Available at schools, colleges, universities, vocational rehabilitation agencies, counselling agencies, work places, community mental health centres and private facilities. Major goals include: improving coping skills and overall functioning, increasing the person's ability to make rational decisions, providing support; often used to help in times of crisis.

By definition, therapy is the treatment of physical, mental and social disorders or disease. Usually deals with more serious or long-term problems. Major goals include: increased understanding of self and relationships, exploration of past experiences to gain insight. Therapy may follow counselling. Practitioners found in counselling agencies, hospitals, community health centres and private practice offices.

There are five main types of *psychological therapy:*

1 Psychoanalysis. Finding the 'root cause'. May help uncovering buried thoughts, unconscious and repressed impulses and conflicts, childhood memories and life experiences, and may expand our awareness of personality traits. There are numerous schools of thought, different theories and techniques used in psychoanalysis. Many practitioners include the use of the psychodynamic schools of psychotherapy, sometimes psychodrama and others which focus on the link between the mind and body. Long term psychotherapy may not be advantageous to our Letting Go.

Brief therapy or strategic therapy is short term and solution focused.

2. Humanistic or supportive therapy focuses on the present and future, not the past. Therapists will 'actively listen'. May help, but beware of 'reflective' listening. We often need to be challenged, not only listened to.
3. Behaviour therapies don't worry about finding the root cause of symptoms, concentrating instead on the outcome of our 'condition'. Counter-conditioning treats symptoms as learned and that can therefore be unlearned. There are two types of counter-conditioning: systematic desensitisation – get into a relaxed state and confront your fears; and adverse conditioning e.g. drugs which make us feel sick if we drink – this should not be taken lightly as there can be dire consequences if we drink on top of such drugs.
4. Cognitive therapies. Our thinking colours our feelings. Cognition (thinking) therapy, replaces depressing thinking patterns with better ones. There are many different types. The most commonly known is C.B.T. when behaviour therapy is included in cognitive therapy. Many require active participation in the form of 'doing things' to help the process of changing thought patterns, such as 'homework': keeping a diary of feelings etc., working through set levels of 'tools' with which to form new ideas and concepts about our self. C.B.T. is often a relatively short programme. It is up to us to live what we learn.
5. Group and family therapies. These treat the family as a system. Addiction is a family affair in many respects. The consequences, the 'ripple effect', of our disorder can reach far and wide. Each member has their own baggage and their own recovery process to go through sometimes. Their own issues may pertain as to their role or place in the family system.

Depending on the level of maturity – the real consequences not only individual perceptions of such – and the willingness to accept, admit, and participate in change, relationships can actively flourish with a new-found honesty and the realisation that we weren't mad or bad or weak-willed, but we have a serious biological disorder, directly linked to People, Places, Things. Family dynamics may change dramatically when we're sober. Sobriety allows us to look objectively at how we can make things better. This freedom of choice may seem selfish sometimes. Each member will have their own issues which change as we change.

Group work, learning how others deal with family issues etc., can be extremely comforting. Knowing we're not alone is therapy in itself. AA (Alcoholics Anonymous) may not suit everyone, but it remains a constant place of refuge for identification and companionship when no one else understands.

Note: Nothing will change if we resort to picking up because People, Places, Things don't change! Trust takes time.

Old ways of thinking will creep into our behaviour sometimes, even though we're sober. This frightens others. Their own thought patterns will take time to adjust. Realise that children, especially young ones, may either show signs of having been affected or not: to what degree or what level our deterioration – mental or physical – has occurred, sometimes only time will tell. Be patient: understand your pain often became their pain. Accepting the 'damage' we created helps us repair relationships. However, with the best will in the world, we can only ever change our self. Time may heal. Or it may not. Letting go of unhealthy adult relationships; waiting, watching over and helping children to work though their own emotions; setting boundaries for our self and others, is all part and parcel of true recovery. It is appropriate to mention here a little on the emotive subject regarding the ripple effect of addiction from a personal perspective.

Personal Note: The 'damaging' ripple effects of addiction include not only the obvious drunken outbursts or physical expression of distorted thinking (violence). The inability to communicate through altered moods and 'changed' perceptions often makes relationships in general difficult; confusing in the least and impossible at the worst.

How this effect impacts on those around differs with the level of 'extremity' of changed moods and behaviour, depending also upon the social (including financial) environment and other external influences surrounding the 'family unit'. Factors such as age (child, adolescent, adult), the support network within the immediate/extended family system or outside of the 'unit' (school, work, etc.), cultural influence and religious background/inference, all help determine the psychological effects of living with addiction to a substance (or any other 'problem', illness or chronic 'disorder').

The experience of such is another subject which fills volumes. There are organisations to help those who feel their personalities or self-schemas were moulded by another's behaviour. Therapy rooms are frequented by those who see their own behaviour as a direct result/influenced by, another's actions. Whilst there is no denying the impact can be mild – moderate – extreme on one's own psyche, and in respect of children may be a 'cause' or contributing factor for their own behaviour 'problem' (from being withdrawn at one end of the scale to being disruptive/aggressive themselves at the other); there comes a time in adulthood when we have to take responsibility for our own thoughts and actions.

Observing the use of alcohol, etc., in adolescence, if readily available/portrayed as a way of 'relaxing', seeming the 'norm' of 'life', may encourage rather than discourage (i.e. in contrast to if there is no emphasis/role model/substance around). It is generally peer pressure and outside influences (including media etc.), together with the pressure of adolescence itself which have a greater influence on personal substance use.

Let's face it: we drink/use initially because we like the Party Effect! Not because our mum/dad/family member 'taught' us. (In fact, the experience of watching another's demise through excessive use should, if anything, put us off.)

I speak from experience. Promising never to make the same mistakes. But the Party Effect Progressed to Destructive Addiction. This was due to **My** Life Style. **My** Way of Thinking. **My** Substance over-use. **Not** another's. No one from the past poured it down my throat! In no way am I discounting the psychological 'disturbance' (many of my own self-schemas are rooted in past experiences during childhood and adolescence), and for those of us affected by physical violence the trauma can leave us with disturbing memories requiring much 'internal' work on our part (letting go).

The point of view, from my own understanding in recovery, is that we are ultimately 100% responsible for our self. Not being 'a victim', not 'blaming' others, pushes us to examine our self in the Now, rather than perpetually 'examine' others' past behaviour. This is both scary and liberating at the same time. Discovering we have the Freedom of Thought to choose how we respond/react to life in the present, rather than automatically, from the past, allows us to discover who *we* really are – not just part of the 'effects' of another's addiction.

In the words of Robert J. Ackerman, PhD (co-founder of the National Association for Children of Alcoholics): 'We need to differentiate between what is situational and what is development, or potentially pathological.'

So often 'negative labels' are attached to an individual's identity. Roles such as 'hero, scapegoat, lost child or mascot' (Nathan Ackerman) ignore the positive or healthy attitudes (behaviours) found in children of alchoholics.

However, we do have the ability to adapt. Indeed 'resilience is part of the genetic makeup of humans and ... is the norm rather than the exception' (Masten, 2001). But as Robert Ackerman points out: 'Problems can occur ... when a person leaves the negative environment and continues with the learned adjustment behaviours, even though they might be in a healthy environment.'

Biomedical Therapies

Drug therapy. Anti-psychotics lower dopamine levels. Anti-anxiety drugs (Valium etc.) depress the Central Nervous System. Anti-depressants (SSRIs like Prozac etc.) increase levels of serotonin. Lithium may be used for bipolar disorder. Be guided by your doctor. The obvious aim is not to substitute one drug for another. But sometimes we have to have a little pharmacological help.

Complementary Therapies

The list of things to do as an alternative to using our D.O.C. is endless. Any practice or therapy which considers our mind/body as a whole may be called holistic: harmony, health, healing, balance, personify a holistic approach.

Complementary medicine and therapies are gaining increased endorsement. The benefits of meditation etc. are now getting recognition as science uncovers the complexities of the human brain! Books extolling the virtue of spirituality in nursing;

homeopathy; yoga etc. are no longer refuted. Full scientific proof is not necessary: 'the proof of the pudding is in the eating' – results speak for themselves.

These are a few suggestions. Some integrate the third aspect for our self: the spiritual. Each may set you on a path of discovery, new friends, new experiences, a New Way of Being within yourself. Some require more practice that others. Don't expect too much from yourself in the early months: a simple walk can replenish our mind/body/spirit!

Mind/Body Connection

1. Exercise – vital to our physical and mental well-being. Find an interest suitable to start you off. Check with your doctor if you're uncertain about your level of fitness or capability. Easy does it if you haven't been active for a long time! Anything rhythmic or which needs concentration, gentle or more demanding, e.g. swimming, tennis, golf – but be careful of stress levels by being too competitive!
2. Mind/body intervention. Complementary therapies cover a variety of techniques designed to enhance the mind's capacity to affect bodily function and symptoms. These include aromatherapy, hypnosis/autosuggestion, meditation and yoga, etc. Energy therapies include reiki, shiatsu, breathwork, Emotional Freedom Technique etc. There are also massage and manipulative therapies including: acupuncture, Tui na, Alexander technique, cranial-sacral massage etc.

For those who have trouble sitting quietly, various movements – martial arts such as T'ai chi, Qi gong or karate – can focus and calm the mind, enhancing feelings of self-confidence and self-worth.

For those who prefer to sit quietly, try biofeedback, which gives immediate feedback on the level of tension via sensors which measure the activity of your sweat glands. *Journey to Wild Divine* is a biofeedback video software which requires relaxation and meditation to solve its puzzles or games. Three fingers, attached by sensors, measure heart rate and skin conductivity. Learning to regulate heart rate by conscious effort of thought helps develop meditative skills and gain greater control of unconscious bodily pressures. It is very successful for migraine headaches and hypertension.

Use anything which reduces tension and anxiety to bring a sense of control in stress – provoking situations that strengthen our long-term resistance and resilience to stress, improving mental concentration, mental stability and relaxation: meditative breathing, chanting and movement techniques, imagery and visualisation, art therapy, gardening or knitting, biking or hiking ... interest, motivation and practice are the keys to success.

Be resourceful and diverse: acts of consciousness generate self-esteem. Complementary therapies can help us get in touch with our inner self. They provide a form of expression for feelings that cannot be easily identified or put into words. Whether working out in the gym, participating in a Pilates class, or quietly meditating while fishing; discovering new forms of enjoyment, learning new skills, overcoming challenges, stretching our mind and body, all helps us thrive in recovery.

Help your Heart: Physically and Metaphysically

Exercise your heart so that you are out of breath, breathing hard for at least five minutes, at least once a day. Jogging, even in the same place, will achieve this. But it's far better to go outside, for two reasons: body (heart, physical) and mind (heart, spiritual). Being out and about opens up our spatial intelligence, rather than being confined and isolated; allowing us to be part of humanity, living in the world but not part of its chaos; and there is beauty to be found anywhere and everywhere in the world, things to fill us with awe and wonder, the sheer joy of being alive!

Even on a crowded pavement you can spot a tiny green shoot pushing its way through the concrete; even a dull, grey sky holds the mysteries of the universe; an intricate spider's web; a smile, nod or word from a passer-by; put them together and what do you see? Determination, hope, a reminder of freedom rather than the trap of addiction, and human connection, love in its simplest form.

Love and Laughter

Probably the best medicine and complementary therapy of all! Connecting, sharing, having fun, all these and much, much more are part of the reality of life. Metaphysically, 'plugging in' to life itself will make us feel good: a happy, healthy heart!

Two Specials Please!

Two complementary therapies are being widely recognised and used in many different contexts of recovery from all different types of illnesses – mental or physical – yoga and meditation. Both help return us to homeostasis.

Yoga

Yoga has been shown to significantly reduce depression and because the practice of yoga asana (physical postures) involve an awareness of the breath, it heightens mind/body awareness and encourages us to be present in the moment in a way few activities do. Yoga asanas stimulate the pineal and pituitary glands which in turn stimulate the endocrine, metabolic, digestive, circulatory and lymphatic systems: cleansing our body, relaxing our mind.

Pranayam (deep breathing) oxygenates our body approximately 80% better than regular breathing and stimulates the Parasympathetic Nervous System: positive neurochemicals, serotonin and other endorphins. It also stimulates adrenal glands that secrete adrenaline and norepinephrine, the stimulating hormones. Yoga with meditation helps us free our self from the emotion of thoughts so they don't 'rule us'. Meditation decreases oxygen consumption, heart rate, respiratory rate and blood pressure; and increases the intensity of alpha and delta brainwaves – the opposite of the physiological changes that occur during stress.

During the 'gaps of silence', come moments of freedom from our 'Helicopter Head,' the blissful emotional state of just being, and sometimes, depending upon which new thought we choose to place in the Gap, a natural euphoric feeling of contentment!

Yoga has 4–8,000 years of history. It was first expounded in Hindu religious texts. Uniting mind/body/soul in the Cosmic One, is found in yogic explanation in the texts of Hinduism. Evolving as a spiritual practice it was understood as a transformation of the mind, a perquisite to attaining liberation from earthly bonds. Enlightenment by means of yoga:

1 A shift into meditative consciousness wherein self is perceived as the awareness that experiences the thoughts.
2 Emotional equilibrium or 'positiveness'. Metta meditation cultivates loving kindness, the perfect antidote to anger.

While yoga is a religion or a way of life to many, incorporating knowledge of the chakras for total well-being of energy flow throughout our body, some Western practice has little or nothing to do with spirituality. It is strictly an exercise regime, an overall programme of keeping physical and emotional well-being, a fitness practice for health of mind and body, with or without a spiritual goal of inner peace included.

Regardless of specific religious orientation any mind/body practice with spiritual awareness offers a deepening sense of self acceptance: a way of life by meditative teachings or simply learning how to breathe a stretch! Benefits of stretching include: increased circulation and decreasing muscle tension i.e. cramping tightness and pain (we've all had those!)

As a final note on yoga – there's one to suit any levels of motivation and commitment, including Ashtangar, Hatha, Raja and Chair yoga.

Meditation

An absolute must in its simplest form: learning how to still the mind. Contemplation, bringing the mind 'back home', connecting our heart to our head, being rather than doing, flicking the switch, using the sprinkler system etc., is vitally important in recovery. There are many forms of meditation. What degree or level of 'pure consciousness' you wish to attain depends upon your commitment. Don't be put off it if right now you can't even imagine sitting still, yet alone stilling your mind. Many of us pray just to have one moment of calm from our helicopter thoughts!

Like all things in life: progress not perfection.

A continual journey of discovery or 'just a minute' when needed, meditation is an invaluable tool for escaping to a peaceful place within.

Meditation is the practice of quieting stresses to the mind by the use of sitting and breathing techniques sometimes, but different meditative disciplines encompass a wide range of spiritual and/or psychological practices. Recognised as a component of Eastern religions, where it has been practised for over 5,000 years, many faiths have their own form, including: Hinduism, Buddhism, Christianity, Islam, Jainism, Judaism, Sikhism, Taoism (apologies for those not mentioned).

Physical 'postures' play a part, including: spine, hands, eyes (open, half closed, half open looking slightly downward, fully open), focus and gaze, cross-legged sitting (not always required), walking (mindful – walking is very relaxing), using beads, humming or chanting to help induce a meditative state. You can 'meditate' while washing up/ washing the car, muttering the Serenity Prayer, allowing acceptance to wash over anxious thoughts, creating a sense of calm.

Personal suggestion:

One of the easiest forms of meditation is to put God in the Gap in a particular prayer.

For example, take the well-known 'Lord's Prayer' which has comprehensive, univeral, ethical, personal, and social scope. It embodies every need the human heart has and every desire man craves from God.

Close your eyes and repeat the first few words:

'*Our Father who art in Heaven*'

Then say the first two words leaving a Gap in between:

'*Our … … … Father*'

Put God in the Gap.

Rest in the Gap. Rest your mind in the Gap. Rest your spirit within His love. Feel the peace and tranquility of a spiritual thought.

Rest in the silence, if only for a few seconds, and be still.

Still and quieten a Helicopter Head.

Rest in the Gap … with an awareness of self as spirit, rather than matter. At one with creation and the Creator.

This amazingly effective 'switch' for instant calm can be achieved with any Daily Prayer or Affirmation of Faith:

'Shema Yisrael Adonai Elohanu ... Adonai Ehad'

'Hail ... Mary'

Or use one word:

'Om ...'

'Allah ...'

Or use non-religious 'I ... am'. Thinking of ourself as pure in spirit, devoid of false ego, connected to a Higher Power.

Lord Tennyson asserted correctly: 'More things are wrought by prayer than this world dreams of.'

'K.A.T.' Knowledge – Awareness – Truth

The cultivation of mindfulness is essential to mental concentration, which is needed to achieve insight.

To be mindful = to fall awake to life.

We were born in a mindful state: meditation simply wakes us up to what we have forgotten! To be present in moment to moment awareness helps us to be present in the here and now. Not in yesterday's anger, or tomorrow's anxiety. But in the here and now accepting reality as it really is.

Paying attention to each event experienced in the present moment places emotions in their rightful context. Emotions are normal and an inevitable part of life. Breath concentration develops cognitive awareness and minimises distractibility. Thoughts are just thoughts rather than 'truths' we have about our self, others, and the world in which we live.

MiCBT

Mindfulness-integrated Cognitive Behaviour Therapy. The integration of skills developed with Mindfulness training and principles of C.B.T. The object of this therapy is not to avoid feelings, including rational negative emotions, but to increase our ability to cope with painful emotions, allowing us to move on to the next moment and the next feeling life experiences bring. Cognitive psychology helps us to see how our faulty thoughts (effects of the past) affect present perceptions. Mindfulness works in more subtle ways; non-judging, silently accepting and observing in this non judgmental way awakens us to truth.

To conclude meditation: there are many types and different ways of practice, incorporating one or both of these basic forms:

a Concentration meditation – holding attention on a particular object, with or without repetitive prayer, mantra etc.
b Mindfulness meditation – open focus, awareness, the here and now.

Ultimately any practice which helps us to 'watch our thoughts', to change our way of thinking (therefore our behaviour), is of benefit to our recovery. Becoming intentionally aware of our thoughts and actions in present reality, non-judgementally, with no demands: must, should, have to, got to; or 'if'.

The 'Prescription'/Therapies Conclusion

'Prescription': Written instructions (suggestions), directions, a recipe for remedy. Specifications for correction in defects of vision. Required or recommended structure, magnitude, efficacy (form, dose, strength) for a mixture of information and application of something to make us feel better: A Prescription for Life includes knowledge, wisdom, compassion, empathy, self-inquiry and acceptance of above all else, the Truth.

My Story Summary

This entire book contains certain truths to help you transform your life. Written from the heart, in the hope of touching that special, private place within yourself. You are not alone. We *can* overcome the complexities of addiction by absorbing and acting upon the right information. I've been there, done it and I've got several T-shirts in various sizes/colours, depending upon what level of eating/mood disorder I was experiencing. Extreme intake of substances make my survival a mystery.

My transformation seems like a miracle. One which you can achieve!

Many moons ago a therapist tried to explain that my thoughts were 'irrational'. Together with the concept of being 'insane' and having 'character defects' it's not surprising my addicted self denied every possible suggestion there was something wrong with me!

For nigh on twenty years, people and places never quite managed to explain exactly what was the matter.

Personal observation gave me warning signs. But we never admit 'it' has got us till we have to, do we? I was going to be different. Exactly what our clients say to me now! It's a comforting thought that no matter who, or where, or in what circumstances, human emotions are basically the same. We all feel. We all hurt. Some of us party too hard, find solace in our D.O.C. too often, cross that invisible line.

No one (initially) likes to admit inner truths. Dissecting yourself takes courage. Making changes takes strength. Transformation requires honesty. None of these are possible until we stop using our D.O.C. to escape reality.

False perceptions make 'rational' choice an impossibility. When people said: 'You don't see', they were right! I couldn't. I only saw my hopes and dreams disappearing down with my wine. Ten years of mega (prescribed) pain-killers, progressed this disease without my knowing. Yet I remained 'functional' in many respects. Dying inside I managed to maintain a semblance of coping along life's paths.

The morning I drank for relief was the day I started my true journey. I admitted 'it' had 'got me'. I was an alcoholic. With all the prescribed medicine for my back (having had three disc operations) I was a 'junkie' too. Apart from the Avoid Alcohol warning, no one explained the psychobiology of addiction, so I drank on top of co-proxamol, diazepan etc! Several centres later I was still 'missing' something. Sobriety of many months destroyed in an instant by stress. All the while I thought I had a drink problem!

Every explanation became a lie. Things were the problem. My D.O.C. seemed the only solution. I knew in my heart the 'weak-willed' woman wasn't me. But I didn't know why I really needed that drink! No one told me the truth of the matter.

How do you find a miracle? When all else is disintegrating around you? There is only one way. To look within.

Down on my knees I finally found the 'missing component'. With love and guidance from my spiritual mentor, now my partner in business and life, I discovered who I was meant to be. I re-discovered God. A wholeness came upon me. Spirit came back to matter.

Finding my True Self has been (and will continue to be, please God) an amazing, often excruciatingly emotional and hard journey. One I wouldn't change for anything.

I do not define my self as an alcoholic/addict

I am a recovering person. On a New Path.

I don't hide in or from my past. Neither do I regret it. It's part of who I became. I now choose to become more. (Regret is a negative emotion, a destructive indulgence!)

I feel sorrow for all the hurt I caused for myself and others. I live my 'amendments' as best I can.

Unaware ego has been replaced with mindful intention to consciously do no harm to myself, others and the world in which I live. Being human I still fail (sometimes miserably) to achieve this!

But I have found self-acceptance and forgiveness (for others, too). I no longer feel the desire to escape reality. I practice serenity. Life itself is enough. Flashbacks keep me on my toes. I'm grateful for every day of sobriety.

With the right information in the Gap I live in the present, look forward to the future and know I can change my thoughts, feelings and actions.

I've abandoned my D.O.C. I can still dance, love, laugh with wild abandon. I've survived, evolved. So can you!

Here's a ditty I've remembered since I was little. It serves me well, together with the Serenity Prayer, a few deeps breaths (smell the flowers – blow out the candle) self-inquiry, affirmation, optimism, effort and determination, and above all hope and faith in myself and God.

> One step in front of the other,
> One step in front of the other,
> As the little dog travelled from London to Dover . . .
> . . . When he came to a stile – jump! He went over!

Take the plunge: jump into life. Allow your true nature (your spiritual self) to be in the driving seat along your new journey.

As bad as things have been before, that's how good they can become – everything's the opposite! Surrendering ultimately gives us what we always wanted. To feel good.

Change: a Good Experience

Here at Affinity Lodge we are different to make a difference. Our programme has transformed the lives of many. This book and our DVD came into being on the insistence that we had to 'get it out there'. Each person is asked to take home a 'prescription': a cognitive behaviour therapy within a spiritual framework which they work with at home.

Receiving the right information, if we absorb its truths, can create a shift in conscious awareness. The 'emotional experience' – to shift those dendrites – comes from within.

Some of us 'get it' fairly quickly. Some need to do more 'research' to prove the Geometric Progression and Tolerant Terminals Trap (just one = where we left off). 'Getting it' is a much easier process if we accept the principle of pleasure is not an 'easy fix'. It requires doing the right things, thinking the right thoughts etc.

> Knowledge is the catalyst to experience the 'right' within. The truth. When we enter into the truth we enter into spirituality. It is our true nature or spiritual nature which gives us the 'experience' of feeling good within.

Our intolerant terminals will try to push us back to our D.O.C. in times of stress. Using the Mirror Image (do the opposite of what your addicted self is saying) and placing good in the Gap, can keep us on the right path.

Sometimes our 'nature' is run by our addictive self-schema. Our own true spiritual nature needs some guidance – a map or route to follow.

'You Little Schema' The 3-S Programme

The entire 3-S (spiritual self-schema) programme can be downloaded free at www.3-S.us.

The word schema, in cognitive psychology, is used to describe a mental process for efficiently processing and organising incoming information. Our self-system of thoughts and emotions, built over time, become automated cause/effect, response/reactive 'scripts'.

Like an actor, we use a 'script' in daily life. We may have learnt and rehearsed our 'lines' from childhood to the present moment. Multiple self-schemas, or several informative 'scripts' are often necessary. We wear different 'masks' or 'hats' and 'play' different 'roles' all the time. See the list of 'masks' at the end of the book for clues to yours. A woman may be many 'characters' in one day: a girlfriend, daughter, wife, lover, mother, co-worker, boss, confidante, 'chief cook and bottle-washer'. (You can add you own 'roles' for each gender.)

Problems arise when we allow a negative self-schema – or addict self-schema – to 'run the show'. Intolerance, narrow-mindedness, prejudice, sectarianism; habitual thought patterns leading to a stereotypical 'role'. We may label our self (I'm just hopeless . . .) or others (he's just . . .). We can become blinkered, unable to see the truth or 'read between the lines' of each habitual script.

The negative self-schema may: condone 'wrong'. Be biased, bigoted, dogmatic, illiberal, intolerant, uncharitable, authoritarian, dictatorial, repressive, rigid, pessimistic, unsympathetic, neglectful, nefarious, superficial, uncooperative, unwilling (i.e. refusing or denying the truth).

The most accessible, most easily triggered, most detailed and well rehearsed schema will 'automatically' be used in any given context. Habitually activated self-schemas intrude upon the true spiritual nature of our self.

Which driving force is reading which script?

A negative self-script and an addict self-script are a recipe for disaster. If we get on the highway of thoughts and drive without really knowing where we're going we can end up in the middle of nowhere – mindlessly going round in circles, getting off at any exit we 'feel' will lead us somewhere we 'think' we want to be! Feeling lost and insecure, frightened and alone, when we discover the place or thing we 'thought' of doesn't either exist or is not what we really wanted. Wrong exit. Wrong choice.

With no 'sat. nav.' to guide us, we turn to our memory map. If it's old, with unchanged signs and symbols, the directions we remember will be of little use. If we're impulsive, unaware of where we are, let alone of where we need to be, oblivious of the signs and symbols, the bigger picture or the complete map, we'll get easily frustrated, tense and stressed, turning off, going back and forth along the same old road expecting it to lead somewhere new! Stuck in traffic. Idiot drivers. 'Road works' and 'diversions'. Patience sorely tested. 'Road closed', panic! Need for Relief!

Internal guidance: a survival map

To 'get out' of the place we don't want to be or find the correct route to where we'd like to be requires knowledge and learning of a new script, a guidance system, a map which gives us the right information. This book has given you the information. The 3-S programme can help you develop and make corrections to your old internal self-scheming map of misinformation.

Like learning to read, a New Way of Thinking takes time and practice. Repetition. Repetition. Repetition. We don't usually find making time for our D.O.C. an inconvenience. Conscious thought, time to apply our self to our True Self, has to be made daily for the first two months. Thereafter we should need less 'manual' structure to work with, 'practically' living our new guide-rules.

The programme consists of 3 phases:

1. An awareness of habitual thought patterns – the self-schemas – which automatically 'drive' us. Automatic pilot and cruise control.
2. Help to construct (or strengthen) our spiritual self-schema.
3. Practice so 3-S becomes our predominant or habitual self-schema: Our New Path becomes wider, stronger and there, ready to turn onto when needed.

At each phase you are asked to:

Reflect: Self-reflection and self-observation. We begin to identify patterns of thought and roles we play.

Rehearse: Mental rehearsal, meditation and guided visualisation. Behaviour practice. Visualising our self – what do we see? Imagine an actor had to play the role of you – what character information would you need to give them?

Record: Keeping a simple diary helps immensely to 'see' our self and our ten 'perfections' or spiritual qualities: generosity, morality, renunciation, widsom, effort, tolerance, truth, strong determination, loving kindness and equanimity.

Phase One

Awareness of habitual paths.

1. Becoming aware of experiencing and expressing yourself in daily life.
2. Awareness of 'mindless' automatic thoughts, etc.
3. Awareness of consequences of habitual self-schemas.
4. Increased awareness – 'Stop that! That's not me!'
5. Check in: several times a day ask, 'Who's driving, where am I, where am I going?' Which self-schema is in charge? Note: The times we 'can't be bothered' guess who is in charge!
6. Weekend review.
7. Strengthen commitment to New Path.

Phase Two

Constructing a New Path

a. *Design* – a 'blue-print' with guidance and support systems.
b. *Skills and tools* for path construction.
c. *Clearing* the site – reducing automatic, habitually-activated self-schemas.
d. *Construction* of New Path.

Phase two (a) *design* has 5 steps:

1. Blue-print – 10 'perfections'
2. Cognitive scripts, behavioural action, new sequences to keep on New Path in daily life. Creating new cognitive skills – affirmations, mantras, metta (loving kindness) meditation.
3. Establishing guidance and support systems.
4. Using our five senses – sight, hearing, taste, smell, touch as cues-to-action.
5. Signs along the way to know we're on the right path and warning signs.

Phase two (b) *skills and tools*. Possibly 'things' everyone should take to heart, not just those in recovery! (Actually, definitely!) Taken from the spiritual teachings of Buddhism. These simple principles for leading, a 'good' rightful way of being provide the necessary skills and tools to re-frame a false script and re-connect a false personality (with negative thoughts and distorted attitudes) to our true nature.

There are *four noble truths* from which the noble eightfold path unfolds.

1. There is suffering.
2. There is a cause of suffering – craving.
3. There is the cessation of suffering.
4. There is a way leading to the cessation of suffering.

The noble eightfold path: essential for transformation.

The sooner we acknowledge we have to change our self and realise that means in every way possible, the easier and more complete our recovery can become. Obviously this is an ongoing process. We don't gain insight immediately (plenty of denials!) and there will always be an attitude of thought we can improve on! But there is no greater gift to gain than a sense of self-respect and the experience of self-esteem, which comes from following a path of goodness and self-respectability.

No one and no thing can give us healthy 'pride' in our self. Knowing we are doing everything possible, going to any lengths, to effect real, lasting change as the script of our life story continues, does! When we live in reality with acceptance, integrity, purpose, mindful of the following, we consciously become self-assertive and truly authentic in our true nature.

The 3-S programme helps us understand the noble eightfold path with these trainings in specific 'right' expressions of establishing our true spiritual self.

1. Morals practice and personal code of ethical behaviour: right speech, right action, right livelihood (occupation)
2. Meditation practice to train our mind to take the right path: right effort, right mindfulness, right concentration.
3. Wisdom. Developing insight into our true nature: right intention (or right thinking) right understanding (or right view).

Phase two (c) *clearing* the path. Mindfulness. In 5 steps:

1 Thought, emotion, action.
2 Thought stopping.
3 Purposeful interjection e.g. mirror image.
4 Choice points.
5 Object mindfulness.

Phase two (d) *construction* of New Path:

1 Reflection – 10 'perfections'.
2 Rehearse – visualisation.
3 Rehearse – practice and record.

Phase Three

Object: To transform addict self-schema to habitual spiritual self-schema. In 3 steps:

1 Increasing number of contexts for new self.
2 Assessment of progress.
3 Routine maintenance tasks.

10 'perfections'. See website 'worksheets'.

Brain State Conditioning™

There is an extremely exciting technology emerging, which although in its relative infancy has already helped thousands overcome various pathologies associated with stress or 'trauma'.

The term 'stress' is short for distress, a word evolved from Latin that means 'to draw or pull apart'. Using this, and the 'neurological ink' statement, I personally like to think of this technology as 'rubbing out' (not erasing completely) informational statements acquired by the brain through emotional experience.

This technology assists an individual in self-optimisation by balancing and harmonising their brain wave patterns. Brain State Conditioning™ is vastly different from standard neurofeedback models.

For information click on www.brainstatetech.com.

Here are a few statements to whet your appetite:

'The brain changes when it experiences a state, or new pathway created by its own neural-networks.'

'Every brain, like every person, is unique. Still, the consciousness of all people includes many realms – physical, mental, emotional, spiritual. All of these realms have been considered together as the basis for Brain State Conditioning™. Brain State Conditioning™ does not treat a symptom or diagnosis; it deals with the entire person. The founder, Lee Gerdes, has a background in math, physics, psychology, and theology – and has brought all these disciplines together in providing Brain State Conditioning™.'

'Lee Gerdes has done extensive research into the effects of trauma on the brain (i.e. emotional experience) and believes "there is a genetic propensity toward certain vulnerabilities for some of us".' He continues:

> I think of it as one leg of a 3-legged stool. Genetic propensity is one element in the puzzle here. Pay attention to this: it does not mean that we can't help those with PTSD (for example), due to their genetic propensity towards it – quite the contrary. Balance and harmonize the brain and PTSD (for example) may be dramatically diminished or simply disappear altogether.
>
> Our environment is the second leg of the stool. As humans we can alter our environment – especially if we have information that the environment we are in has consequences we did not previously understand. In the last few years I have learned that the incredible amount of information my brain receives every day causes me undue stress. Now I take time to be quiet – especially to sit still for a time, eliminating most of the media for news, and limiting TV dramatically – this creates a more peaceful environment. And to support myself in my environment, I also spend time listening to my body every day. If I don't do these things, my environment will put me at risk of brain imbalance. If I don't have regular waste elimination and/or if I don't eat healthy food and exercise, again my environment will put me at risk. However, I can alter and control my environment.
>
> Circumstance is the third leg of the stool, and is something we can do little about at times. If someone runs a red light and crashes into our car, BANG – we likely have just experienced trauma. There are lots of trauma possibilities, some of which seem to have little to do with our will. Any time the brain perceives (be it a correct or incorrect perception) that its life is being threatened, a trauma is the

result. And, as traumas stack up during our life journey, one more small trauma may be the proverbial straw that breaks the camel's back, and off we go into some kind of imbalance or chaos based on the neural-net which was created for the brain to protect itself.

Brain State Conditioning™ uses internal brainwave patterns, client self-assessment, and client input to create a brain balanced and harmonised for physical, mental, emotional, and spiritual optimisation. Note this statement includes 'client input'.

There is no 'quick-fix' in recovery. But from a recovering person's point of view any 'tools' to help, particularly in the early months when we are extremely vulnerable and susceptible to stress, flashbacks and negative thought patterns, anything which helps the process towards a New Way of Thinking has to be beneficial (providing it's not substituting one drug for another, although some pharmacological help is neccessary sometimes).

It is up to us to ABSTAIN, RE-ORGANISE our LIFE
RE-WIRE OUR THOUGHTS and our ACTIONS in order to
RE-FRAME/CONDITION our Brain State.

The Impulse to Cross the Gap

Those medically 'in the know' will note there is no mention of ions or detailed description of impulse movement within a nerve cell. The complex action-potential of positive ions, polarisation, repolarisation, depolarisation, and resting potential, is something the author feels it is unnecessary to fully understand for the purpose of this book. However, for those 'lay-persons' interested, I will give a very brief outline:

Action Potential

The nerve impulse is based chiefly on movement of positively charged sodium and potassium ions through the neuron's cell membrane. Impulses are 'created' along the membrane as a wave of depolarisation and repolarisation. When the membrane's polarity is reversed to become slightly positive an 'action-potential' of +30 millivolts results on the inside. With no impulse there are more positively charged ions outside the cell membrane and more negative ions inside. The membrane is polarised with the inside negative. The type of nerve dictates the speed of an impulse. Movement is much faster in sheathed (myelinated) axons, in which the action-potential jumps along successive sections from one node to the next.

Poetic License/Matching a Spiritual Thought to one of 'Matter'

When we use Good for our shield or sheath as protection against Evil (our D.O.C.), putting G–d in the Gap as a direct action, we create the potential for any *inside positivity* to shift *outside negativity*, decreasing negative impulses at the speed of thought. Successful recovery occurs from one day to the next!

Neurotransmitters etc. can trigger a new impulse or actively prevent the receiving neuron reaching its full action-potential.

Mood-altering substances act in our brain and inhibit our full potential. Just as 'Everything's the Opposite', these Messages of Information can trigger a New Way of Thinking!

Remember: One day at a time. We only have One Life.

List of Neurotransmitters

Scientists have now identified some 60 different molecules that meet the criteria for being regarded as neurotransmitters. See below for the best known.

Peptides are released by neurons as intercellular messengers. Many are also hormones released by non-neuronal cells. This large family of neurotransmitters, with over 50 known members, include: endorphin, enkephalin (opiod peptides), insulin, prolactin, gastrin, thyrotropin and glucagon.

Many peptides act more as neuromodulators than as neurotransmitters. Neuromodulators are substances that do not propogate nerve impulses directly, but instead affect the synthesis, breakdown, or reabsorption (reuptake) of neurotransmitters. Neuromodulators can also exert regulatory effects on many extra-synaptic receptors, rather than on synaptic sites exclusively.

Certain soluble gases also act as neurotransmitters. The most important member of this category is nitrogen monoxide.

Among the small molecules constituting the 'classical' neurotransmitters, are:

- acetylcholine
- serotonin
- catecholomines, including epinephrine
- norepinephrine and dopamine
- excitatory amino acids such as aspartate and glutamate (half of the synapes in the central nervous system are glutamatergic)
- inhibitory amino acids such as glycine and GABA (one-quarter to one-third of the synapses in the Central Nervous System are GABAergic)
- histamine

Food for Thought: Nutritional Gene Therapy

Written by Dr Peter Willis

Despite decades of research there is no firm agreement on the respective roles of nature and nurture in the development of the disease of addiction. Addictive behaviours are influenced by a mixture of genetic, social and psychological factors; the relative importance of which varies amongst both individuals and the substance of misuse. There is now significant evidence to suggest that nutrition plays a significant part both in the genetic predisposition to alcohol misuse as well as significantly hindering recovery.

The importance of correct nutrition is emphasised in all treatment programmes. The general assumption is that an improvement in physical well-being will assist in adherence to recovery programmes. A more specific role for nutrition in recovery has long been recognised and vitamin supplements are administered in order to correct for example the Wernicke-Korsakoff Syndrome (deficiency of Vitamin B1 is recognised as the cause of this severe alcoholic dementia). It is our contention that nutrition may have a more profound role both in the predisposition to develop addiction and the subsequent failure to maintain sobriety.

The respective roles of genetic and environmental factors in the aetiology of alcohol addiction have been the subject of considerable debate. Early epidemiological and genetic studies indicate that there was a genetic component particularly in the development of the more severe, type II alcohol biotype. Pioneering studies by Prof. Blum in the United States discovered a genetic variant in the dopamine DR2 receptor gene, known as the dopamine D2 A1 variant; carriers of this variant have significantly reduced levels of dopamine receptors. As dopamine is the brain's 'pleasure molecule' a reduction in its receptors leads to the seeking of subsequences for relief. It has been estimated that as many as 1 in 3 individuals may have a genetic make-up which predisposes to addiction. A major reason for addiction treatment failure and high relapse rates is reasoned to be the untreated deletion of neutransmitters. Prof. Blum termed correction of this depletion 'Nutritional Gene Therapy', literally a nutritional manipulation of the brain's molecules of emotion. When all of the transmitters are working in harmony at the nucleus accumbens, the brain's reward site, there is a sense of well-being and calm. Depletion of important transmitters like serotonin, dopamine, noradrenaline, GABA and endorphins results in a disturbance of the brain's Reward Circuit and subsequent need ro relief. For many individuals this relief is achieved the first time they consume alcohol. However, whilst this provides relief, excessive use of such substances results in further depletion of neurotransmitters and a consequent downward spiral into addiction.

In order to identify and treat patients with genetic variants in neurotransmitter systems DNA is extracted from cheek cells and appropriate therapy can then be instigated. It is not yet possible to manipulate the gene involved but instead depleted neurotransmitter stocks can be replenished by increasing the intake of the appropriate amino acid precursors. For example 5 hydroxytryptophan is the precursor for serotonin, L-phenylalanine for dopamine and noradrenaline, L glutamine for GABA. Administration of these substances has proven remarkably beneficial in the successful treatment of addictions, both reducing withdrawal symptoms and preventing relapse. Effective synthesis of neurotransmitters from amino acids is also dependent on the presence of appropriate vitamins, mineral and anti-oxidants. It must be stressed that whilst amino acids are naturally occurring substances, therapy must only be commenced under the supervision of a fully qualified practitioner.

Even though there is general acceptance of the disease nature of alcoholism, most treatment programmes do little to redress the biochemical imbalances that affect many suffers. Alcoholics have poor diets and many have both pancreatic and liver disease which contributes to the malabsorption of essential nutrients. They often, therefore, exhibit nutritional deficiencies particularly relating to B complex vitamins basic amino acids and minerals, such as zinc, magnesium and calcium. In addition a particularly prevalent finding is hypoglycaemia. Other common problems are sub-clinical hypothyroidism ('sluggish thyroid'), candida-related complex and significant food allergies. What is not generally realised is that the mortality statistics for dried-out alcoholics is little better than for those that continue to drink and, more alarmingly, a quarter of those deaths are from suicide. Many individuals who maintain sobriety do so under great duress, never achieving the peace and serenity they so desperately seek. It is our contention that undiagnosed biological changes play a significant role in this miserable outlook.

Joan Mathews Larson has recognised important differences in the biotype of alchohol addicts, which necessitate specific therapies. For example some alcohol addicts have been shown to have an abnormality in the metabolism of certain dietary essential fatty acids (EFAs). These EFAs are normally converted to Prostaglandin EI (PGEI) which plays an important role in the prevention of depression and hyperexcitability. Alcohol immediately lifts depresssion and creates feelings of well-being by activiting the brain's store of PGEI, but this supply soon becomes exhausted and the ability to lift depression ceases. This problem can be helped by administering Evening Primrose which contains gamma linolenic acid (GLA) which aids the conversion of ELAs to PGEI.

Probably the more typical alcoholic is the person who initially drinks for the 'Party Effect' and, because of social and environmental circumstances, becomes dependent on alcohol. In the early stages of the disease alcholol only provides a minor lift and the initial contact with alcohol makes them feel ill. The periods of pleasure and social confidence become progressively shorter and more and more alcohol has to be taken in order to function at all. At this stage many alcoholics simply drink to avoid symptoms of withdrawal. Behaviour is often loud, abusive and aggressive. Later these people often drink heavily to stimulate the release of natural opioids, suffer quite severe hangovers and become depressed and agitated when alcohol is withdrawn. Biochemical repair for alcoholics depends on two things: the freeing of the body of alcohol and related substances like caffeine, nicotine and refined sugars and replenishing the body's depleted substances.

One particularly important nutritional problem that is frequently overlooked is that of sugar sensitivity and hypoglycaemia. Simple sugars have opioids-like properties to which some individuals are particularly sensitive. Sugar promotes the release of beta-endorphins and boosts serotonin levels which alleviates the symptoms of irritability, cravings, mood swings, irrational reactions to minor stress and sleep disturbance that are almost taken for granted in recovery. It is often said that people at AA meetings have a cup of sweet coffee (sugar + caffeine) and a cigarette (nicotine) in one hand and two Mars Bars (sugar + chocolate) in the other. The problem with excess sugar consumption is that the quick fix of sugar increases blood glucose levels triggering the output of insulin which facilitates uptake of sugar by cells and a dramatic fall of sugar levels causing hypoglycaemia. John Tinera M.D. goes so far as to state that, 'by far the most important part of the physiological treatment of alcoholics is the complete restriction of easily absorbed carbohydrates'. In fact as many as 90 per cent of alcoholics have been found to be hypoglycaemic. Wild swings in blood sugar lead to wild swings in behaviour eventually leading to depression and relapse. Fruthermore the body's response to this hypoglycaemic stress is to increase adrenaline secretion, prompting the body to convert stores of glycogen to glucose. High adrenaline levels cause anxiety, panic attacks, mood swings and aggression. This eventually results in adrenal burn-out and feelings of exhaustion. It is self-evident that short-term relief from sugar and caffeine can easily 'prime the pump' which results in relapse into taking relief from alcohol. Much of the craving for sugar can be reduced by taking Vitamin B3 (Niacin) and Chromium. Also glutamine provides an alternate source of energy for the brain. Magnesium helps to stabilise blood sugar and Vitamin B5 (Pantothenic acid) reverses adrenal burn-out. Hypoglycaemia also depletes stores of Vitamin C. A drastic dietary change away from sugar to complex carbohydrates is fundamental to recovery.

Once the metabolic deficiences are corrected an assessment is then made of the type of maintenance therapy required for each individual. Those clients with genetic abnormalities will need to receive nutrient supplements for life. It is hoped that the majority of clients will be able to maintain neurotransmitter levels and hence well-being by primarily diet alone. At its simplest a high protein diet will be rich in neurotransmitter-enhancing amino acids. High fat foods such as olive oil, yoghurt, cheese and omega 3-rich foods will boost neurological function. The all-important task of stabilising blood sugar and counteracting cravings will be achieved with intake of complex carbohydrates, nuts, beans, vegetables and low-sugar containing fruits.

It can be seen that nutrition plays a vital role in the development of the disease of alcoholism. The nutritional manipulation of the molecules of emotion is an important missing link in successful addiction treatment. Alcohol has wide-ranging metabolic effects in addition to its direct action on the brain and, if untreated, these biochemical changes contribute significantly to the inability of alcoholics to fully recover despite maintaining sobriety. It is hoped that accurate assessment of the client's biochemical profile will enable repair of these damaging effects and correction of genetic predispositions to the disease of alcoholism. This does not mean that other therapies are abandoned. On the contrary, once good nutrition has been established and the individual is calm and free from cravings, attention can then be directed towards the spiritual, cognitive, psychological and neurophysiological therapies that will transform their lives and promote successful recovery.

And on that note of neuronal information, as *The Secret Disease of Addiction* comes to a close with 'Letting Go of The Past', may this author add:

We started this journey looking at the brain. The term dendrite comes from the Greek word 'dendron' which means a tree.

Which tree will you choose?

The Tree of Life?

I did. So have many thousands of others ...

It is possible!

Freedom

I lived in fear
Where I thought
No light shone.

Trapped
In my own
Existence.

Till I felt
The Spirit
Within.

Freedom!

Now I have
What was always

Missing
Now I have peace.

Every day may be
What I think . . .

Whatever befalls
I have no need to drink.

What I found is nothing new
The answer to sobriety
Is inside me and part of you.

That inner peace of being
So precious, so complete
Nothing can compete –

Choose to use?
If I'm not sure
I just remember what I'd lose.

12 Letting go

'Peace begins with a smile.'

Mother Theresa

'Things' happen. Things, if we allow them to, can change our perception, our thoughts and feelings, about our self, others and the world in which we live.

The Law of Associative Memory links together past and present thoughts.

So, if we have 'bad' memories they can keep rearing up in the present. Somewhere behind bad memories often lies *fear*:

- Fear 'things' will repeat themselves
- Fear of the emotional attachments and response
- Fear of confrontation
- Fear of forgiveness
- Fear of fear itself!

Fear keeps us stuck in the present if we continually 'drag it up' from the past. If we don't let go of past bad memories 'things' can hold us back through fear, and we may become bitter and resentful, living in the past of old hurts. Unable to live fully in the present.

When dealing with memories it is essential to pay attention. By becoming aware of negative 'harmful' to our self emotions, we can, through letting go of the past, and healing 'old wounds', replace fear with the positive emotion: hope.

Hope sees the invisible, feels the intangible, and achieves the impossible.

Stress can 'feed' fear. We can feel 'out of control' to 'control our emotions'. And, if we use a mood-altering drug to 'relieve' that stress, we only succeed in limiting our ability to cope with fear. We have little chance of letting go of past negative emotions.

We may use mood-altering drugs to escape the preconceptions (from others) and fears from our past, to make us feel like someone we're not. Until we search for our true identity, not being frightened to project or confront what we really feel, even coming to terms with the darker side of our self, we cannot truly 'fill in' the 'blank spaces'. Our basic human need to be loved and accepted by first and foremost our self, for who we really are.

While 'using' we remain 'stuck'. Trapped by distorted thinking. Fear can grow uncontrollably.

When we live in reality, however, we can begin to choose. What we remember and how we emotionally respond.

Our aim of recovery is to return to our True Self, who we were meant to be, choosing thoughts which help us to let go and grow emotionally.

Fear is part of life. Part of our survival instincts. Acknowledging it and dealing with it demystifies it. We do not have to be frightened of fear! Attending to fear without losing our emotional balance is a simple, powerful skill which grows with use. Ask 'Why?' when you're frightened. Separate the 'story' around those 'fear thoughts' and 'imaginings' from reality.

Think about that, imaginings breed fear.

Fear is not without a purpose, it can propel us into positive action. Remember, we are not fear itself. We are multidimensional emotional beings. Put 'fear' in its proper place, never letting it 'fill you' and render you seemingly helpless. Fear can only paralyse if we allow it to.

In all 'things' and at all times remain aware – and we can remain consciously aware if we are 'clean and sober'.

We are 100% responsible for our own thoughts and actions. We ultimately have no control over others.

This is essential to remember if we are dealing with the past.

When we live in reality we have the ability to choose our perceptions, of the past and the present, not those of others. Therefore, if they choose to remain with exactly the same thoughts, attitude and behaviour towards us, even when we're not drinking, then that is their choice. There is nothing we can do about that. We must, in recovery, remain motivated, focused and committed on our New Path, continuing to do the 'right' things, even if those around us appear to be making the 'wrong' choices, even if they seem to be consciously 'stuck' in the past.

Our recovery is not their responsibility, it is solely ours.

When we change our perceptions of others, truly accepting others, we can view whatever 'things' happen in the perspective of reality.

Note: In respect of personal relationships, the dynamics of each will change as we change. Anything new can be 'scary', creating uncertainty or fear. Sometimes this uncertainty creates fear within others. Recovery allows us the opportunity to really examine our self, and others may never feel the need to do the same. We have to accept that. Work at new dynamics to make that relationship work, or accept the reality that 'things' may never 'be made right' and move on.

Time is a great healer. Having said that, our recovery is of the first and foremost importance. Never rush into letting go of a relationship, but, by the same token, never be frightened of letting go if it is destructive and detrimental to recovery.

Remember at all times: others are responsible for their own 'recovery'.

Everyone is entitled to their own opinion. We each have a choice whether to accept and 'take on board' another's. We can learn a great deal from others about our self. Others can 'hold up a mirror' to us, reflecting what we don't want to see. Providing there is no hidden agenda on the part of others, constructive criticism may help us to examine our personal beliefs and attitude. Acceptance of our 'faults' through others' eyes can 'open' our own, creating an opportunity for mutual growth.

Each experience we share with another can either help or hinder our recovery. Every 'bad experience' we 'work through' to find resolution, and mutual acceptance of each other's feelings, can build trust – something vitally missing when we're in the grips of a destructive addiction. Even seemingly 'hindrance', if we 'work through' it, is an opportunity to build Emotional Muscle, an ability to cope while living in reality, taking no mood-altering substance to alter, distort or change our experience. Some emotions are obviously harder to deal with than others. All the negative ones are often 'tied up' with memories of past events. The thoughts and emotional attachments to those thoughts from the past can colour and reflect upon our present thoughts, which can influence or bring 'fear of' the future.

Consider this: today is the tomorrow I worried about yesterday. Not good if we're on a New Path! So, it is important to let go of the past.

Easier said that done, you might think, but remember – **we are 100% responsible for our own thoughts.** We can choose not to continually reflect upon the past, bringing it into the present, allowing it to disturb our future.

How do we do this? How do we let go of the past? Just as we change, consciously, our thoughts and behaviour from when we were drinking. It is a process. Sometimes we have to ask our self questions:

'What am I gaining from holding on to the past?'

'What am I expecting to happen?'

'What exactly do I want?'

If any of the answers demand retribution, punishment or vengeance, for others' thoughts and actions from the past, then we are on a slippery path.

We are responsible for our own thoughts and actions now, in the present. In an ideal world communication between all persons would remain open, honest and willing, but that does not happen very often, or it is not even possible if that person is no longer around. And if behind the answers lies hidden agendas, control, being the victim, unresolved anger, etc., acceptance of others and our self becomes impossible.

It is only once we accept things that we are able to move forward.

Acceptance requires a certain humility and surrender, acknowledgement that the past cannot be undone, and we have no power to change the past, only the power to change the present. To accept gracefully, in the respect that we no longer harbour thoughts of retribution, sets us free to forgive. By forgiving others we release our self from resentment, and a host of negative emotions which serve no true spiritual process or progress. By releasing the past we create 'space' in our thoughts: 'thought time' to progress with positive thoughts along our New Path. How can we have room for the new without letting go of the old?

Forgiveness is the first stop along the path of reconciliation.

To reconcile with others requires their acceptance. To accept past events if someone does not, or has died, requires us to find forgiveness for them, within our life now, to bring 'things' to an end.

Any beginning, on earth, has an end. Any ending provides a beginning; an opportunity to create something new. Working The Prescription gives us the tools of 'creation'.

Forgiving our self is a very important step along our New Path, and sometimes the hardest to achieve.

If we find by making changes or 'amendments', by truly 'turning over a new leaf', others remain stuck in the past and refuse to acknowledge our transformation, then it is doubly important to let go of trying to control others' thoughts and actions. Remain fixed on a New Path, accept the truth – we can only change our self. Only if we know in our heart, truthfully, we are not repeating the same old thoughts, creating the same old behaviour, will we find forgiveness within our self. We can find forgiveness for our self, and we must do so if we are to move on in recovery, even if others cannot find it in themselves for us.

Note: There is nothing so terrible that G–d will not forgive, if we humbly repent and change our ways. If we feel 'He can never forgive this' there is a kind of arrogance or 'control' from our addict self. If our personality presumes we are so special, so different, so unique, we are separate from the rest of humanity, separate from our spirit which remains pure in its essence of life. It is almost as if we place our human form next to G–d Himself. 'Why would He forgive me, even if I forgive others?'. Do we presume to be perfect? Above others?

Not even nature holds 'perfection'! No 'thing' is totally perfect, yet everything is made perfect in spirit.

We are no less and no more than creation itself. Transient, susceptible or 'open' to change, for no 'thing' remains the same; even when we're 'still' the earth is moving. Every 'thing' is temporal and perishable, evolving until its natural end, imperfect in its very nature and ability to grow and change, yet our spirit, of G–d's light, remains part of the truth, the divine, which alone is perfect. In whatever form we perceive a higher power, there resides the truth, acceptance and forgiveness.

Life itself is progress, not perfection!

We need to accept that we are powerless *only over our use of any mood-altering drug*, one is too many and a thousand never enough. *Not powerless to take responsibility for our True Self.* Allowing our spirit to balance our personality, to make a transformation of self by a renewal of our mind (and heart), like a butterfly emerging from a chrysalis, requires determination and strength to let go of what we no longer need.

We can let go of the past, no longer allowing it to 'infect' our future, to find forgiveness and peace in the present, by living in balance and harmony with our self, others and the world in which we live.

Accept the past, learn from it, make changes daily in order to move forward and grow.

Always keep in mind the Serenity Prayer, with or without the word G–d:

The Serenity Prayer

God grant me
Serenity to accept the things I cannot change,
Courage to change the things I can, and
Wisdom to know the difference.

It works every time, for every 'thing'. Whether we're waiting in a queue, or trying to forgive from the past!

If we believe in any type of creation of the universe, even the 'Big Bang' theory and quantum physics, it leads to the ultimate conclusion that we are part of everything, so respect and 'do unto others as you would wish them to do to you'! By accepting and respecting our self and others, by working The Prescription, re-evaluating our life with simple spiritually 'good' thoughts and actions, we grow in the right path, we gain self-confidence, self-worth, self-esteem; 'things' we so easily lose when living in a destructive addiction. Admitting our mistakes, that we are not 'perfect', is one of the roads to self-love. And only if we love our self can we truly love another, to say *'I need you because I love you'*, not *'I love you because I need you'*.

When we live in the reality of life there are endless possibilities to love our self and others, loving life itself! When we choose how we live, in the present, creating thoughts which help us grow, we grow emotionally, spiritually. When we take responsibility we grow up. Part of growing up is becoming emotionally responsible (something we cannot possibly achieve if we're 'using').

The earlier we started using mood-altering drugs on a regular basis to change our emotions, the more 'catching up' with emotional maturity we have to do. And the less 'reality' we have to 'fall back' on. Working The Prescription is vital.

In the proper order of things:

- Birth (dependency on others)
- Babyhood (learning from others)
- Adolescence (beginning to make our own choices)
- Adulthood (emotional, physical and mental responsibility)

We learn to cope with our self and 'difficult' emotions. By building Emotional Muscles.

Every time we 'go through' an emotional experience we store information, in our memory, in every cell of our body, of how that experience felt. There is current scientific research into the mind/body connection. Suffice to say here, and there are countless books on this subject, that there is undoubtedly a definite link between stored 'mind' information and 'body' disinformation or disease.

Back to the power of thought: hopefully when we do 'get through' difficult emotions we learn positive 'things', like the knowledge we're coping with life, growing up.

Emotional Muscles give us strength to say No! or 'walk against the crowd'. (and we feel so proud of our self when we do this in recovery and we don't 'pick up').

Back to hope, faith, perseverance and responsibility:

- Hope allows healing and forgiveness
- Faith lends a helping hand
- Perseverance helps us achieve success
- Responsibility keeps success in our own hands

Hope is an opportunity for spiritual and emotional growth. To accept hope into our lives requires no more than acknowledging what we do have, and being grateful, working with faith, that 'things' can and will improve if we persevere and take responsibility. Improving, not destroying, our quality of thought, being positive rather than negative, choosing the 'right' path, choosing the right growth of the Tree of Life

There are several emotions and thoughts which can prevent growth. Some we've discussed, others include: blame, self pity, the '*I am a victim' syndrome*, and one really big one – anger. Back to responsibility for our own thoughts! When we *accept*, with dignity, we gain 'flexibility' of thought. Remaining true to our self, in the now, yet finding diversity, allowing our self to look at 'things' another way. *We become less rigid in our perceptions. We are able to balance our self.*

By allowing our spirit to 'harmonise' our personality, and by not 'using', our spirit is able to return within our personality, enabling us to live life on life's terms (not our addict self's terms), giving us back our freedom to choose life's endless possibilities.

Choice is only possible if we don't 'pick up' that first 'one'. When we make the right, responsible, choice we retain our dignity, spiritually, physically and emotionally. When we live by the truth, in reality, our freedom of choice plays its part in our growth and transformation. To experience the greatest free-will choice, the choice to experience the knowledge of G–d in our life, the ultimate freedom of thought.

You may have noticed there's been no exploration of anger, yet. Well, such an intense emotion requires a mention of its own. And often anger can be one reason we start off in life with 'belief', then as 'things' happen we lose faith and become 'angry' with G–d. But,

He never leaves us, even if we abandon Him. And, once we abandon the destructive addiction, His love offers a haven in recovery. He is there 24/7 if we ask and allow Him in. We may turn away from religion, for various reasons, but true spirituality and knowledge of the divine, the truth of virtue and goodness in life, is part of life, the parts which keep us sane.

When we participate in life, living in reality, we are being spiritual. When we live according to the virtuous path we enter into spirituality.

'Actions speak louder than words.' Saying one thing, or thinking 'good thoughts' yet doing another, or even the exact opposite, is like lying – not a good virtue! Lying, to others and primarily ourself, is highly detrimental and destructive. '**Secrets keep us sick**', locked in a prison of deceit. **Only the truth will set us free!** If we cannot trust self, who else will trust us? If we lie to our self we are only fooling our self, feeding negative and destructive emotions. When we are stuck in a destructive addiction lying becomes 'second nature'. To protect our supply; the amount we consume; to 'cover our tracks' of more and more lies. With 'righteous' indignation we proclaim our 'truth' with no thought and no compassion towards any 'thing' or anyone, other than our self and our need for relief!

Anger and hate can become 'second nature' too. We may hate ourselves and others, getting angry with everything and everyone.

Tense, nervous, agitated, irritated, easily aggravated (remember: biochemically we reduce our ability to cope with stress when we take any mood-altering substance enough to create the disease of addiction).

In recovery, those old patterns of thought and behaviour have to be re-directed. *Take the being 'right' out of 'righteous'*. You're sort of left with us. Us being not only you to think of, but including others' perspectives and thoughts and feelings, finding compassion for another human being. Ask yourself 'Do I prefer being "right", or being at peace?' (knowing you've done the right thing). When we no longer desire retribution, when we drop prejudice and withhold judgement, we allow the spiritual energy of compassion to calm our anger and hate.

Anger and hate destroy you. When they combine into rage they form an overpowering and 'uncontrollable' emotion. We are often willing to persist 'against all odds', however it damages us, for revenge. Sometimes our efforts to cause 'damage', emotionally, to others, drains and debilitates us. We give away our power when we give in to 'evil' thoughts. But may not have the desired effect, externally. We are 100% responsible for our own thoughts; the intended recipient may not accept our opinion. (Careful what you think of others though, and what you 'put out there'. What we intend for others very often comes to us, and thoughts and words affect others internally.)

If we resort to physical revenge, well that can end with our self in another type of prison.

Revenge is always a false completion of conflict. There is no resolution or 'closure'. Forgiveness is the true closure of conflict, and the completion or resolution is for one self. **Forgiveness is not absolution, it is a way to set free, release or let go of anger, hate, bitterness and resentment.**

Some 'things' we must not necessarily forget. Forgetting may lead to repetition, but *we can 'forget' the 'emotional content'*, it's all in our responsibility of thought, our choice.

Releasing anger and hate, not towards another – externally; not towards our self – internally; but as a conscious act of dispersal or diffusion provides us with a tool to get to know who we are, and the ability to share our True Self with others. When we diffuse our anger by identifying our true feelings, and if we allow the experience of the emotion not to colour our judgement causing us to be judgemental, we can accept 'things' as they are.

Judgement is entirely different to being judgemental. We have to make 'judgements' sometimes, weighing up the 'pros and cons' to reach a decision. But we do not have to be 'judgemental'. That thought process only hinders our acceptance and our recovery.

Anger itself is not judgemental. There is no 'right' or 'wrong'. It is simply an emotion which, if acknowledged before it gets uncontrollable or unmanageable, if understood, does not become a serious problem to threaten our recovery. Simply becoming aware of anger allows us to choose how to express it. Once we own our own anger and see where it is coming from, we can act in a constructive rather than destructive way.

So, next time you start getting hot, you start tensing up, your heart starts beating faster, etc, STOP! And ask yourself:

'Where do the roots of my anger lie?'

Is it in:

- Hurt (past or present)
- Guilt or shame
- Fear
- Wanting to get your own way
- Feeling helpless
- Old repressed resentments
- Wanting an excuse to use
- Being reminded of past situations
- Wanting to blame/avoid responsibility
- Wanting to control people/situations
- Feeling a 'victim'
- Not wanting to face the truth.

By owning our anger, not projecting our frustrations onto others, not absorbing their anger, we are being honest. Honesty is the 'cornerstone', the first 'building block' of recovery. Nothing can be achieved without honesty.

Tips for getting anger 'STOPT':

S Serenity Prayer
T Talk about your feelings, realistically. Why are you angry? Where is it coming from?
O Try to be open and willing. Repressed anger only builds up.
P Don't presume you or others are perfect. We all make mistakes.
T Time out. If you're in a rage, wait until you're calmer before you try to communicate.

Suggestions for time out:

Let off steam physically. Go for a walk, run or hit a pillow! Sit still and contemplate exactly where these emotions are buried, still the mind by 'breath work' – inhale/exhale 'deliberately'. Write down your feelings. When we write we give our self a chance to think, choosing our words rather than verbally spewing them out.

Remember at all times, anger is not an excuse to relapse.

Finally, anger is a *powerful source of energy* if 'harnessed' and dealt with in a positive manner. When you feel that angry 'energy' in your body use it as motivation! 'I'm getting it finished, and getting my anger out!'. 'I am going to do it, and do it well!' Motivation is doing things, doing positive things which do us good. Doing good, no harm to our self or others, is one of the first principles in recovery and the essence of spirituality.

Note: we mentioned repressed anger. Any repressed emotion can be detrimental to our health. There is now emerging scientific evidence that every single cell in our body has a 'memory'. We know cells 'think', i.e. they receive all sorts of information from all the chemicals in our body – hormones, proteins, amino acids, etc., and pass on that information by 'talking' to other cells. That's how we grow and function! Like the way mood-altering drugs distort information and alter our perceptions, so too cell information can be altered by emotional experiences, to cause distortion in how that cell 'works'.

'Trauma' is particular to each individual. Like any other (positive) emotional experience, the degree or intensity of a negative emotion is perceived or felt 'personally', as an individual. What may be 'traumatic' or an intense experience for one individual may be of little significance to another. Experiences are 'relative' to those we've felt before.

This mind/body connection, where feelings are 'translated' by cells into actual physiological symptoms, is of the utmost help in healing of any kind.

The 'informational connective tissue' of neuropeptides (or 'emotional' cells) unites and co-ordinates all the cells, tissues, glands, organs and systems of the body. According to a well-known author and physician, Deepak Chopra, neuropeptides serve as a point of transformation between thoughts and bodily reactions, i.e. a *transformation of non-matter into matter*. In simple terms, the possibility that how we think, how cell 'memory' may alter or transform depending on 'emotional' content, can manifest itself in physical symptoms.

So, the opposite must be true: healing bodywork, the power of our five senses, the power of our thoughts, can create positive change in negative physical ailments or disease. More and more medical practitioners are acknowledging complementary methods to 'treat' and 'alleviate' physical symptoms, and there are books on the advantages of spirituality in nursing. The benefits of a 'holistic' approach to healing our mind – body – spirit is fast becoming not only accepted, but preferred.

Letting go ritual

To accept any loss, be it someone or something (namely, here, a mood-altering drug) we need to go through a natural process of grief.

To honour that process takes time. Learning and growing, spiritually, with 'Emotional Muscles' is part of the healing process.

Just as grief's opposite, joy, which is as transient as the waxing and waning of the moon, or the rising and setting of the sun, every emotion, like nature and evolution, has its time and place in our hearts and thoughts. A paradox exists between grief and joy. Grief we may try to push away, yet it stays until time heals. Joy we may try to cling on to, yet it can fly away to return at another time!

Both are experiences to be appreciated for what they are: feelings of being human. Both are natural 'processes' of emotion and progression through the natural order of 'things' in life.

When we connect with our mind – body – spirit we are creating the 'threads' which make up the 'fabric' of life.

There are numerous occasions in life when we acknowledge, celebrate or honour events in the natural order: birth, birthdays, marriage, death. Each special event is marked by ceremony or 'ritual' to give the occasion meaning. The purpose behind ritual is to show to all those involved the importance, the commitment or intention of the person whose 'event' it is.

Letting go and 'grieving' for the loss of our drug is truly a special occasion and should be marked as such. Many in recovery will remember the exact day they had their 'last' and celebrate each year with a 'birthday' of their New Self. To make our intention an event to celebrate our 'letting go' of our drug, there is a simple, but extremely powerful ritual we can experience. One that can 'shift' buried emotions and bring release of past experiences.

This ritual is as follows:

- Write a letter to your 'old friend', alcohol, or any other mood-altering drug
- Go through your life together
- How you 'fell in love'
- How you had good times
- How you 'fell out'
- How you hate it now, for what it's done
- How it has made you feel
- How you have reached a point when you never want it in your life again: it is destructive, vindictive, evil, 'foe not friend'.

Feel the meaning and intention behind the words.

If there are other issues you want to let go of (and as you write all sorts of memories will come up), include them all, let it all out! Secrets make us sick.

Rituals often require a witness. If there is anyone you trust in complete confidence, implicitly, read it to them. If not, read it out loud to yourself. This 'gets it out there', making our intention to let go of our substance or past, known to the future (with the Universal Power of the Present).

Then burn it, outside (carefully). Either dig a hole or use a non-flammable container, e.g. a metal bucket. As it burns, watch the smoke rise up. 'Everything came in fire and shall end in fire'; 'Ashes to ashes, dust to dust'. *Watch the drifting 'message of information', your intention for healing, rise up to the heavens, or the cosmos. Now the earth, the sky, every 'thing' knows you're letting go!*

Return inside and sit quietly. Reflect upon the importance of this emotional event. You have officially, in the eyes of all, let go of the hurt of the past, making known your intention for the future to be different. If we follow The Prescription our New Path will be one of peace.

Peace comes quietly, internally, when we externally live by our true spiritual nature.

Your thoughts have been brought forth, from the internal 'reality' to the external, for closure.

By putting pen to paper the 'demons' are no longer 'trapped' within your 'Helicopter Head'. You have released internal pain by intentionally, externally, ritually letting go.

If we accept 'things' and our experiences as they are, changing those 'things' which are harmful to our self or others, that we are in this earthly form to experience the magnificence of human emotion, that our True Self, our spirit, lies beyond the boundaries of earthly constraints, that there are endless possibilities if we are honest, open and willing, then we can begin to see our self as part of everything else. **We need not feel 'alone'. We recognise that by holding on to the past, we only harm our self.**

The 'struggles', the stress and tension, in life are simply events by which we spiritually grow. Until we shake off this mortal coil, the strands of information, the threads and fabric of life, and find external peace, let's enjoy the experience! **Let go and let G–d.**

Feelings Word Vocabulary

Level of intensity: Weak

Happy	Sad	Angry	Scared	Confused
Content	Sorry	Uptight	Reluctant	Bothered
Relaxed	Lost	Dismayed	Anxious	Undecided
Glad	Inadequate	Tolerant	Shy	Uncomfortable
Good	Bad	Resigned	Nervous	
Satisfied			Unsure	
Peaceful			Timid	
Calm			Concerned	
Tranquil			Perplexed	
Hopeful			Doubtful	
Enjoyable			Worried	
Pleased				
Relieved				

Level of intensity: Mild

Happy	Sad	Angry	Scared	Confused
Valued	Disappointed	Resentful	Tense	Awkward
Gratified	Upset	Disgruntled	Threatened	Puzzled
Encouraged	Inadequate	Smothered	Uneasy	Disorganised
Optimistic	Dismal	Frustrated	Defensive	Foggy
Joyful	Unappreciated	Stifled	Insecure	
Proud	Discouraged	Offended	Sceptical	
Cheerful	Ashamed	Controlled	Apprehensive	
Relieved	Distressed	Peeved	Suspicious	
Assured	Distant	Annoyed	Perturbed	
Determined	Disillusioned	Agitated		
Grateful	Lonely	Irritated		
Appreciated	Isolated			
Confident	Alienated			
Respectful	Abandoned			
Admired				
Accepted				

Level of intensity: Strong

Happy	Sad	Angry	Scared	Confused
Excited	Hopeless	Furious	Fearful	Bewildered
Elated	Sorrowful	Seething	Panicky	Trapped
Exuberant	Depressed	Enraged	Afraid	Troubled
Ecstatic	Wounded	Hostile	Shocked	Demobilised
Terrific	Hurt	Vengeful	Overwhelmed	Stagnant
Jubilant	Drained	Incensed	Startled	Ambivalent
Alive	Defeated	Abused	Intimidated	
Energised	Exhausted	Hateful	Desperate	
Enthusiastic	Helpless	Sabotaged	Frantic	
Loved	Crushed	Betrayed	Terrified	
	Worthless	Repulsed	Vulnerable	
	Dejected	Jealous		
	Rejected	Pissed off		
	Empty	Bitter		
	Miserable			
	Distraught			

The Masks we Wear

To Avoid Feelings or Displace Uncomfortable Emotions

With which statements/behaviour do you identify in some way?

Statement	Behaviour
'I hate the world/the world hates me'	Physical or verbal abuse towards
– **Acting Out** internal disruption.	People (including our self) and Things
'Its OK. Leave it!' – **Avoidance**, difficulty communicating/expressing our feelings.	When we withdraw from others, 'swallow' our emotions (or not, with anorexia), 'bottle-up' emotions (downing one to drown them).
'Not now!' – **Avoidance** with **Procrastination** and Postponement.	Playing for time, the 'waiting game', perpetually putting things off.
'Let's have lunch' (I can 'pick your brains')	'False faces' to get what we want.
– **Charmer/Manipulator.**	Doing things in order to receive. Conditional.
'I'm right! I know best!' It's my way or no way!	When we take over, dominate, seeing things as 'black or white' with no acceptance of 'grey'.
'Don't know, don't want to know.'	Discarding/belittling People, Places, Things instantly. Making
– **Closed Mindedness.** Includes showing **Contempt** before 'investigation'.	assumptions without knowledge, understanding or interest.
Being Dogmatic without any reasoning.	Inability to see 'the matter behind the matter'.
'That's it – I'm off!' – **Escaping.** 'Too-hot-to-handle' shut down/lock out of feelings.	Hates confrontation. Slams doors/ phone down, walks away. Often in panic/fear of dealing with rising tension/emotions.

'I deserve the best, 'cause I'm the best, the Greatest. All shall be mine!' – Inflated **Ego**, Grandiose **Attitude**, pretentious, affected, bombastic, arrogant.	Placing our self above others. Ideas of grandeur being 'special' or 'different'. No need for humilty or gratitude, little acceptance of 'lesser' mortals! Feeling as if we are 'owed'.
'. . . can't stop . . . too much to do. . .' – **Busy Busy Bee**, but can't be still – Agitated, Aggravated, Tense, Nervous.	Fill our time with endless (sometimes unnecessary jobs). Things to do. *Doing* not *Being*. No time for contemplation/ introspection/feelings.
'Sure, I'll do that.' (Not in this lifetime.) – **Passive-Aggression.** Quietly boiling **Tension Thermometer.**	By *not* doing things we 'show' our anger, etc. Silently defiant. May include refusing to enter into discussion.
'The world's ending.' – **Awfulising** and **Dramatising.**	Making mountains out of molehills! Everything is or has to be bigger, better, **more** intense.
'That's OK. You forgot. Doesn't matter.' (Actually I'm heart-broken.) – **Minimising**. Includes **Ignoring** feelings.	When we tell our self and others. Things aren't as bad as they really are. Pretending Things don't 'hurt' our feelings.
'Just so, just right, it has to be . . . perfect!' – **Perfectionism** may lead to **Obsessive** Compulsion.	When we can't accept Things, including ourself and others that 'fall below' our 'standards'. Needing to constantly repeat to 'get it right'. Feeling something 'awful' will happen if we don't.
'Hah, hah! That's funny . . . Heard the one about . . . (only joking!)' – **Comedy Act**. Making quips, sarcastic remarks 'repartee' *par excellence*!	Making 'a joke' helps us avoid feeling uncomfortable. Deflecting emotions to escape acknowledging them. Can deflate/negate another's feelings.

'Mirror mirror on the side ... *Take it down so I can hide.'* – **Projection**. Includes choosing People often becoming **Co-Dependent.**	Far easier to find fault in others then look at ourself. Easier to blame or play the 'victim'. May include scheming, projecting our feelings onto another. 'I love you 'cause I need you.' Not 'I need you 'cause I love you.'
'I can explain that neuronal transmission.' – **Rationalisation.** Difficulty 'seeing' the unseen, or connecting with, acknowledging things we can't touch, explain, qualify.	With logical thinking we can rationalise our feelings (and others'). By not connecting our **Heart** we ignore our Spirit.
'I do it my way ... ' – **Self-Will**. Myself and I know what's best for me! May include unhealthy **Ego.**	We insist on doing Things our way, regardless of the consequences. Includes constantly 'researching' the 'just one' or Geometric Progression/Addiction Theory!
'It's not my fault!' –**Victim Thinking** Seeing our self as **Helpless. Blaming**, etc. No 'Letting Go'.	Using Past experiences to qualify our Present. Conveniently keeps us 'stuck' in old patterns of thought/behaviour. Believing we have no control – Things 'just happen' to us.
'I believe I'm seriously authentic.' – **Pseudo-Spiritual**. Over-**analysing**, using psychology to manipulate. Over-zealous beliefs discounting others' or using a 'cause' to actually cause harm.	Not walking the walk. Feelings/thoughts not expressed in words and actions. Dogmatic views on others' perception of what is 'real' and 'right'.
'None of the above apply to me!' – **The Addict Self**. Makes use of all the above. Drinking, using our D.O.C. is the **Ultimate Way to Avoid/Escape** our feelings and emotions.	We drink, eat (or not), sleep around, gamble, work/tidy up obsessively, shop, exercise (the list of 'aholics' goes on and on).

We can 'play' certain 'roles' or 'wear' certain 'masks' separately, or **Link, Attach and Associate** one with another.

And of course, the Secret Disease of Addiction – the distorted perceptions of altered information make any 'mask' 100 times more 'powerful'.

Until we *accept we are powerless* over our D.O.C. but *powerful when we abandon* the substance and *focus on the disease*; that we are 100% responsible for our own thoughts and actions; that avoiding/repressing feelings and emotions is not the solution; that by surrendering our D.O.C. we gain freedom to feel in reality, we may never be **aware** or **mindful** of these masks.

Relapse/Craving (need for relief) is born from our thoughts and Way of Being. Unconscious triggers come from 'just being our old self'. **Lifestyle** changes are born from **Brain States**. How can we find a New Way of Being with old 'statements' in our brain?

Recovery = A New Way of Thinking.

Addiction Begins and Ends in the Brain.

A Wish for You

May Angels watch over you
while you sleep

May God Bless you
and from harm keep

May your True Spirit awaken
to Life itself

May your New Journey be filled with
love, laughter, peace and health

LIVE IN THE LIGHT

Feedback from your own New Path can be helpful to others. Use our websites: I would love to hear your stories.

Jane Allen

Personal Favourites Reading List

Massive Myths with Simple Solutions: Dr Paul M. D'Amico
Together with his videos form a 'bible' of reference.

The Buddha's Teaching: Thich Nhat Hanh
Clear, poetic, immensely revealing and transforming. A must.

Awareness: Anthony De Mello
A guide to the spiritual life. Direction on coping with love, anger and fear.

I Am With You: Fr John Woolley
Divine 'thought for the day': help for today's needs. Peace and consolation. Essential 'plug-in' for wisdom, inspiration and comfort.

The Wisdom Way of Knowing: Cynthia Bourgeault
For understanding life's meaning.

Stress Reduction: Dawn Groves
A practical guide.

Change Your Thoughts, Change Your Life: Dr Wayne W. Dyer
81 verses for a 'New Way of Thinking'. Short essays on the Tao Te Ching (Lao-tzu). Works well with the 'Prescription': 'One a day keeps bad thoughts at bay!'

Full Catastrophe Living: Jon Kabat-Zinn
Perspectives on mindfulness.

Natural Highs: Patrick Holford and Dr Hyla Cass
Comprehensive alternatives to drugs and alcohol.

Families and How to Survive Them: Robin Skynner and John Cleese
Simple, down-to-earth explanation for those with relationship difficulties.

It's the Thought that Counts: David R. Hamilton, PhD
Research and evidence for the power of mind over matter.

Letting Go: Morrie Schwartz
Moving, inspiring, leaves a lasting impact.

The Diving Bell and The Butterfly: Jean-Dominique Bauby
A gift for the mind and spirit.

The Laws of Spirit: Dan Millman
A tale of transformation.

Jacob's Ladder: Noah Ben Shea
Wisdom for the heart's ascent.

Affluenza: Oliver James
'A sizzling reality check' exploring the virus spread by the demands of 21st-century living.

Leadership for an Age of Higher Consciousness:
Swami Krishnapada
For those who want to pursue their work from a more spiritual, humanistic and philosophical perspective. Relevant for all those seeking greater insight into leadership of the self. A must for the organised affairs of humankind.

What the Bleep Do We Know: www.thebleep.co.uk
DVD and handbook. Explores some of life's most fundamental questions. Highly enlightening, compelling revelations on the perception of reality.

Some Useful Websites

http://learn.genetics.utah.edu/units/addiction (University of Utah)

www.fi.edu (Franklin Institute)
Click on Resources for Science learning and search for Stress

http://thebrain.mcgill.ca (The brain from top to bottom)

www.nida.nih.gov (National Institute on Drug Abuse)

www.med.howard.edu/pharmacology (Introduction to neuropharmacology – Howard University College of Medicine)
Click on Course Material – Handouts – Introduction to Neuropharmacology

http://webspace.ship.edu/cgboer/limbicsystem.html (Shippensburg University)

THESE SLIDES ARE TAKEN FROM THE ACCOMPANYING DVD

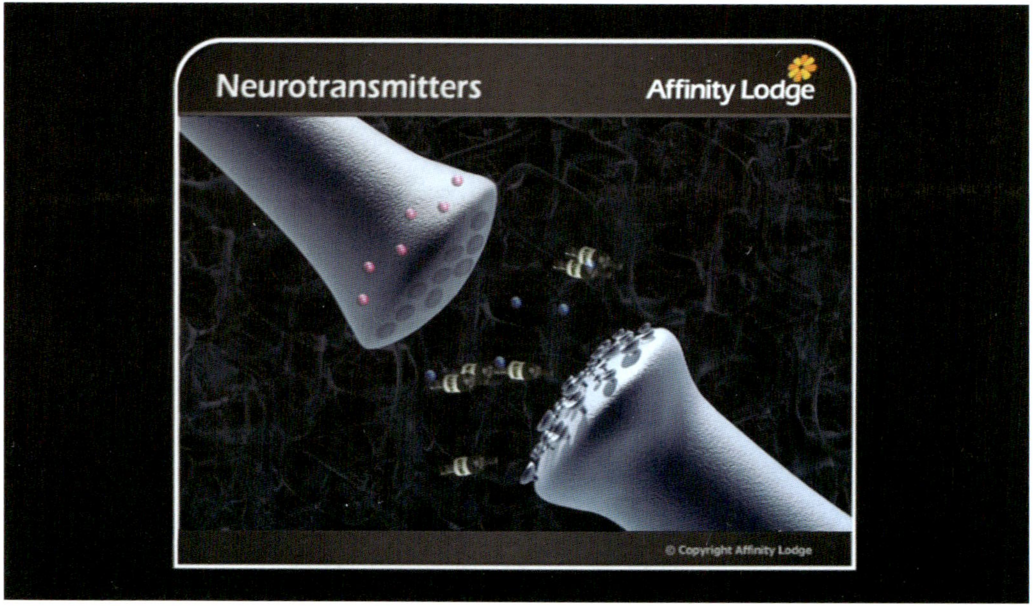

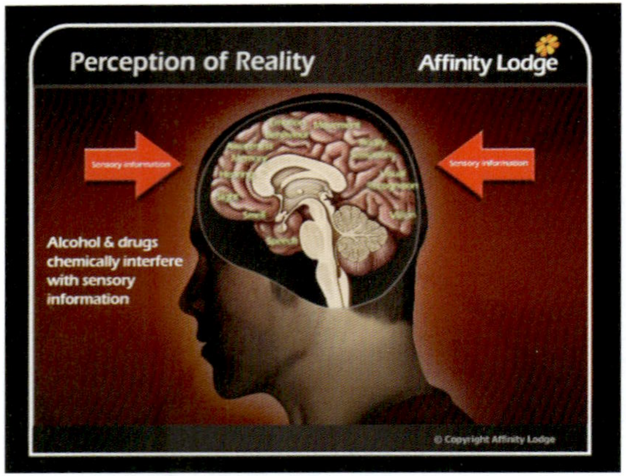
Perception of Reality
Affinity Lodge
Sensory information
Sensory information
Alcohol & drugs chemically interfere with sensory information
© Copyright Affinity Lodge

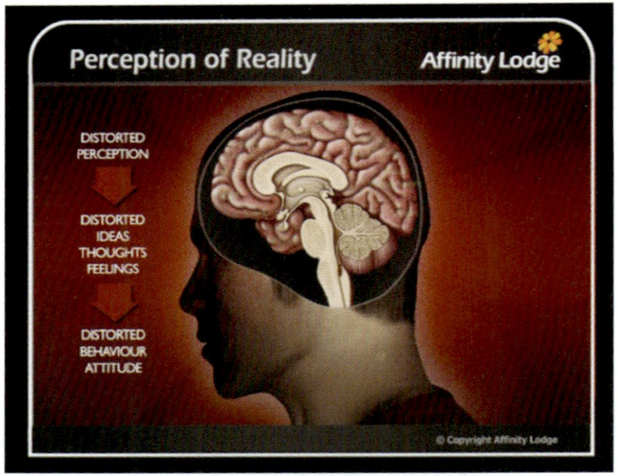
Perception of Reality
Affinity Lodge
DISTORTED PERCEPTION
DISTORTED IDEAS THOUGHTS FEELINGS
DISTORTED BEHAVIOUR ATTITUDE
© Copyright Affinity Lodge

Yo - Yo Effect
Affinity Lodge
EUPHORIA
Release of excitatory chemicals
Leading to Tolerance or Overdose
Depressing effects of alcohol
DEPRESSION
© Copyright Affinity Lodge

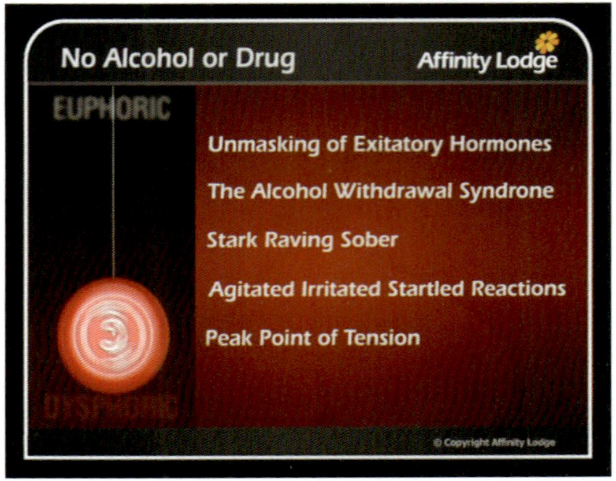
No Alcohol or Drug
Affinity Lodge
EUPHORIC
Unmasking of Exitatory Hormones
The Alcohol Withdrawal Syndrone
Stark Raving Sober
Agitated Irritated Startled Reactions
Peak Point of Tension
© Copyright Affinity Lodge

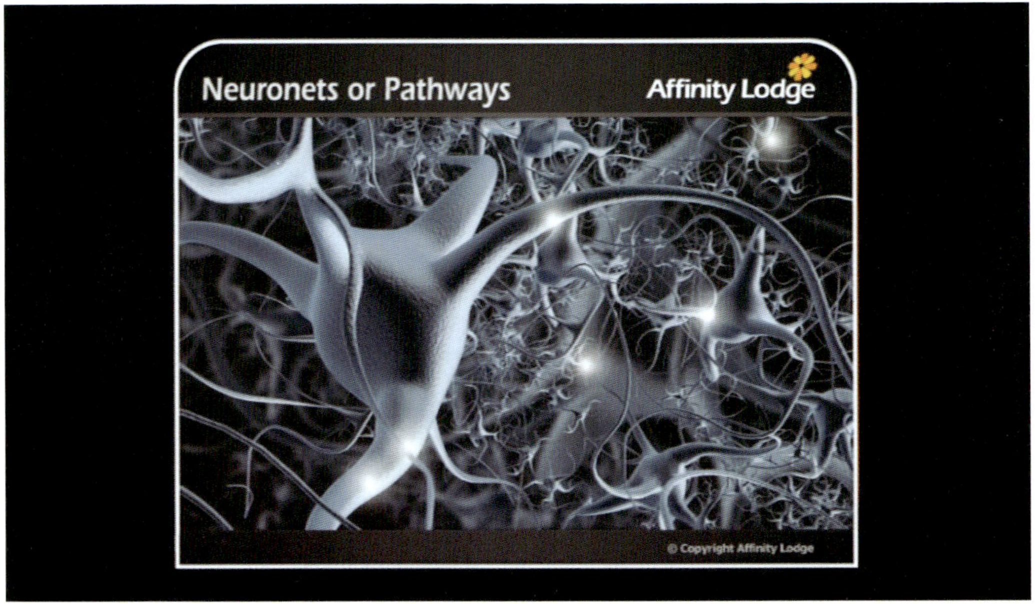
Neuronets or Pathways
Affinity Lodge
© Copyright Affinity Lodge

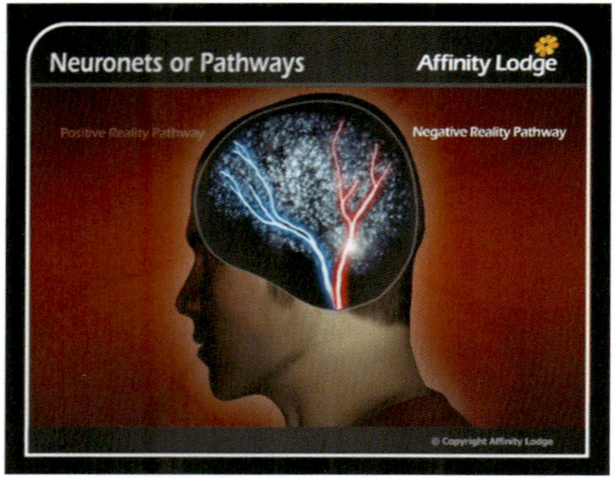
Neuronets or Pathways
Affinity Lodge
Positive Reality Pathway
Negative Reality Pathway
© Copyright Affinity Lodge

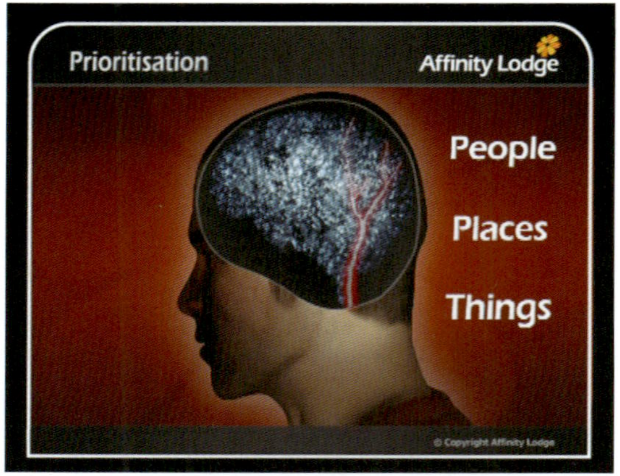
Prioritisation
Affinity Lodge
People
Places
Things
© Copyright Affinity Lodge

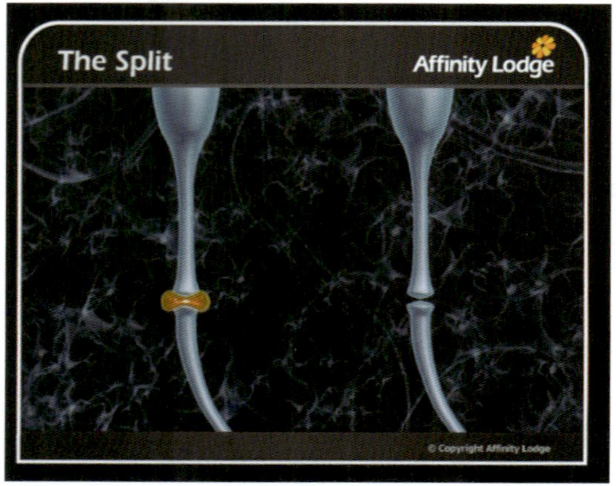
The Split
Affinity Lodge
© Copyright Affinity Lodge

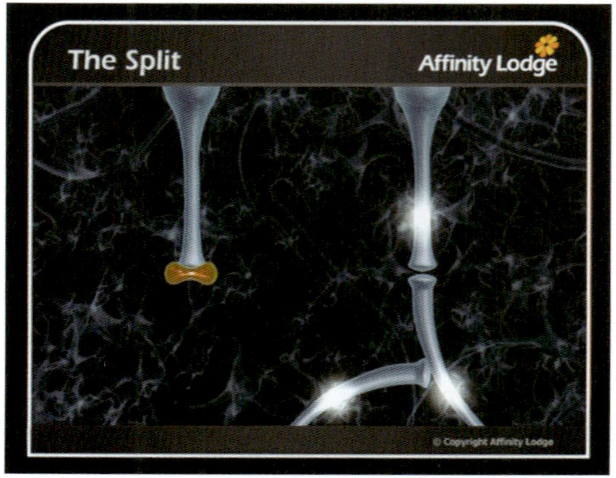
The Split
Affinity Lodge
© Copyright Affinity Lodge

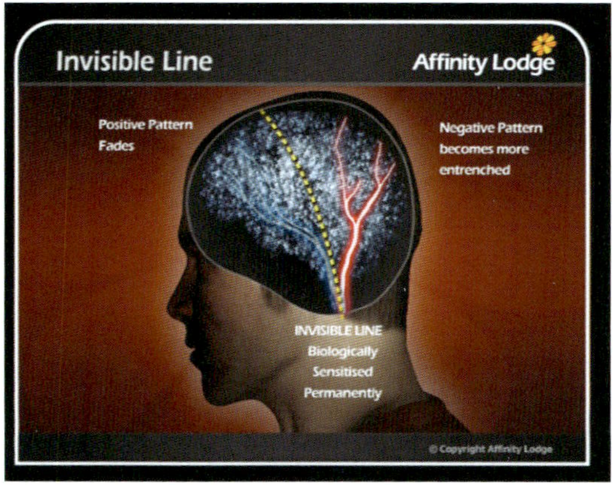
Invisible Line
Affinity Lodge
Positive Pattern
Fades
Negative Pattern
becomes more
entrenched
INVISIBLE LINE
Biologically
Sensitised
Permanently
© Copyright Affinity Lodge

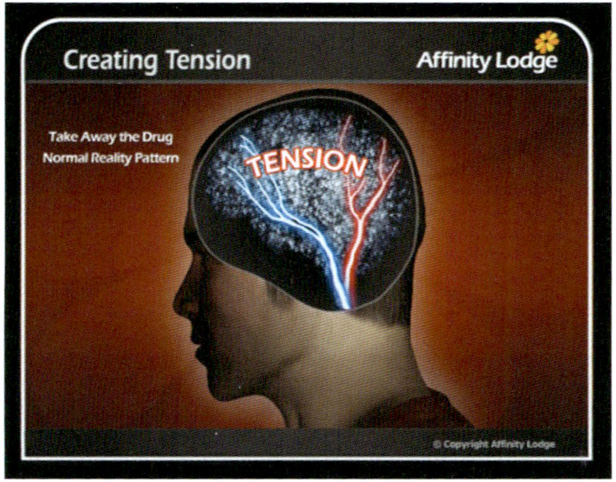
Creating Tension
Affinity Lodge
Take Away the Drug
Normal Reality Pattern
TENSION
© Copyright Affinity Lodge

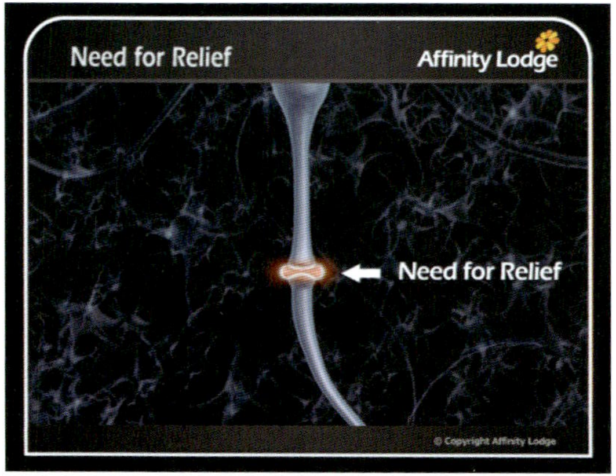
Need for Relief
Affinity Lodge
Need for Relief
© Copyright Affinity Lodge

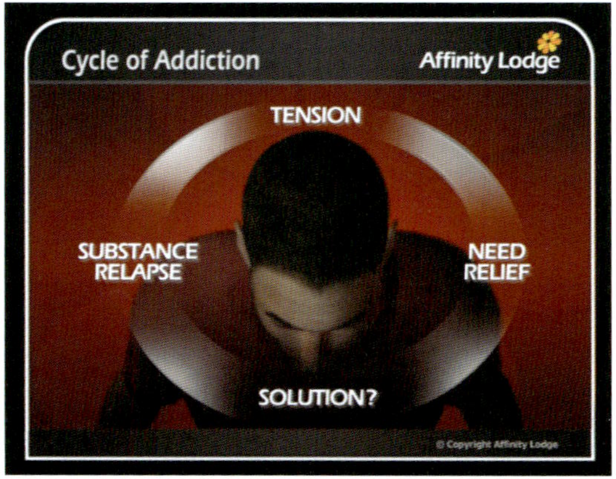
Cycle of Addiction
Affinity Lodge
TENSION
SUBSTANCE
RELAPSE
NEED
RELIEF
SOLUTION?
© Copyright Affinity Lodge

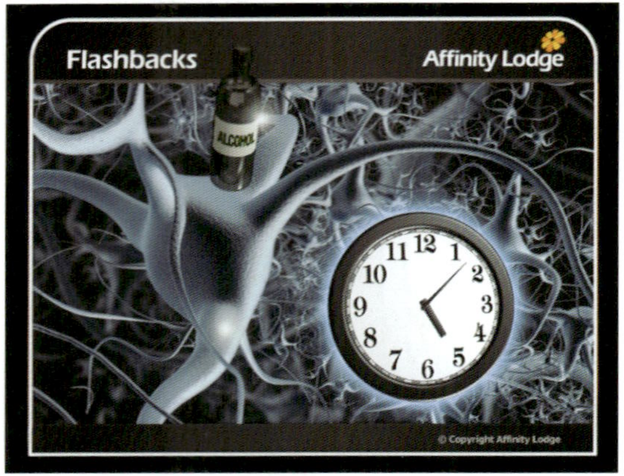
Flashbacks
Affinity Lodge
ALCOHOL
© Copyright Affinity Lodge

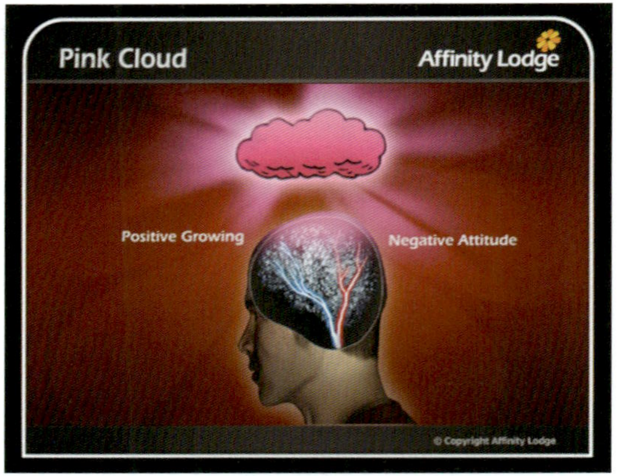
Pink Cloud
Affinity Lodge
Positive Growing
Negative Attitude
© Copyright Affinity Lodge

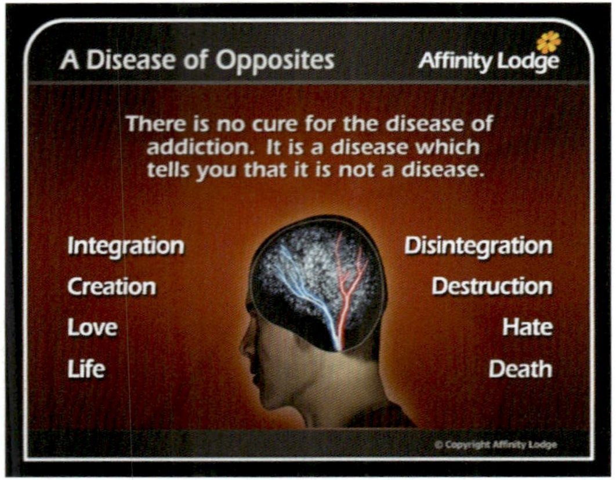
A Disease of Opposites
Affinity Lodge
There is no cure for the disease of addiction. It is a disease which tells you that it is not a disease.
Integration
Creation
Love
Life
Disintegration
Destruction
Hate
Death
© Copyright Affinity Lodge

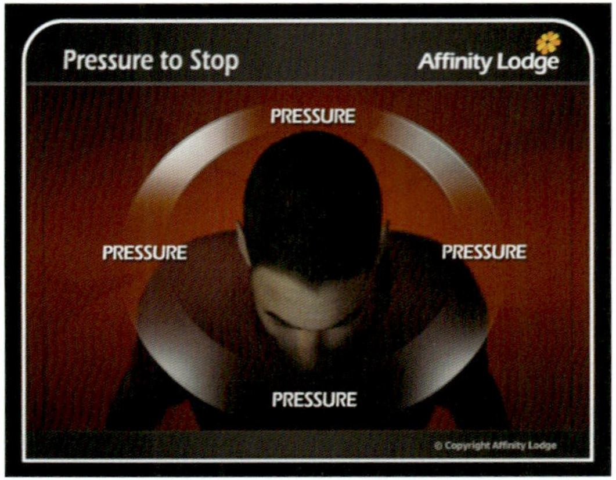
Pressure to Stop
Affinity Lodge
PRESSURE
PRESSURE
PRESSURE
PRESSURE
© Copyright Affinity Lodge

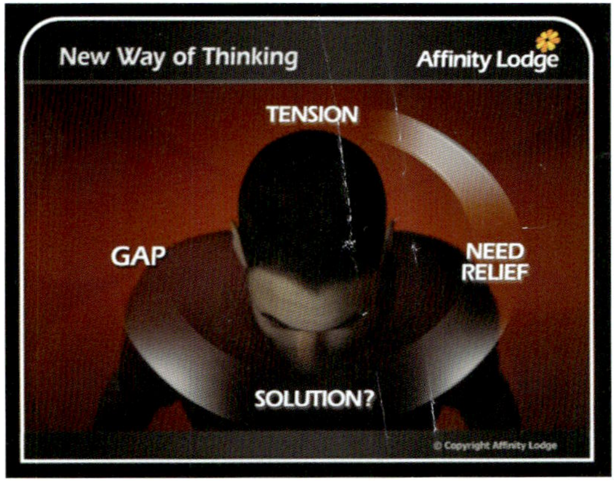
New Way of Thinking
Affinity Lodge
TENSION
GAP
NEED RELIEF
SOLUTION?
© Copyright Affinity Lodge

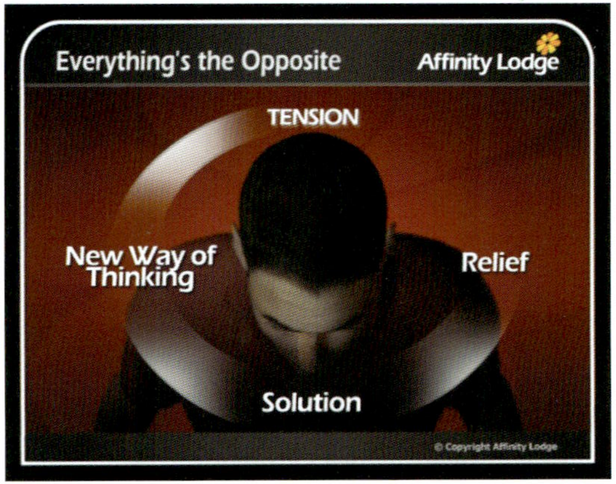
Everything's the Opposite
Affinity Lodge
TENSION
New Way of Thinking
Relief
Solution
© Copyright Affinity Lodge

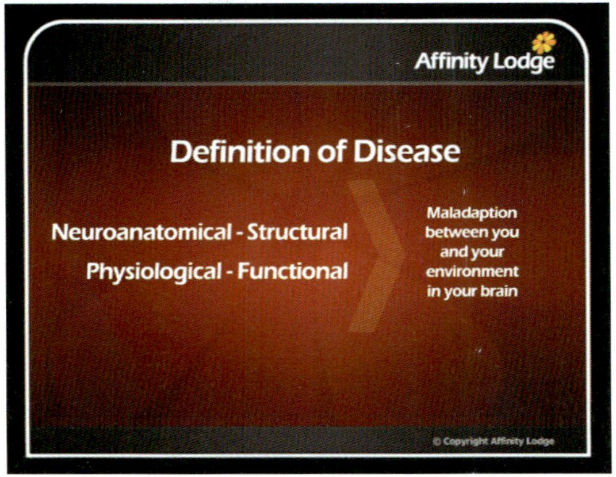
Affinity Lodge
Definition of Disease
Neuroanatomical - Structural
Physiological - Functional
Maladaption between you and your environment in your brain
© Copyright Affinity Lodge

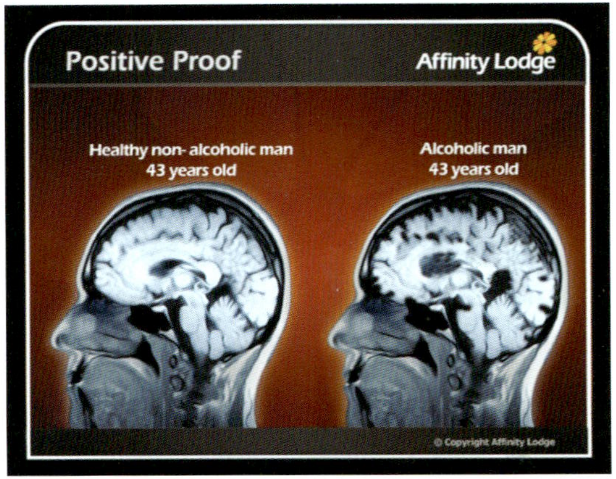
Positive Proof
Affinity Lodge
Healthy non- alcoholic man
43 years old
Alcoholic man
43 years old
© Copyright Affinity Lodge

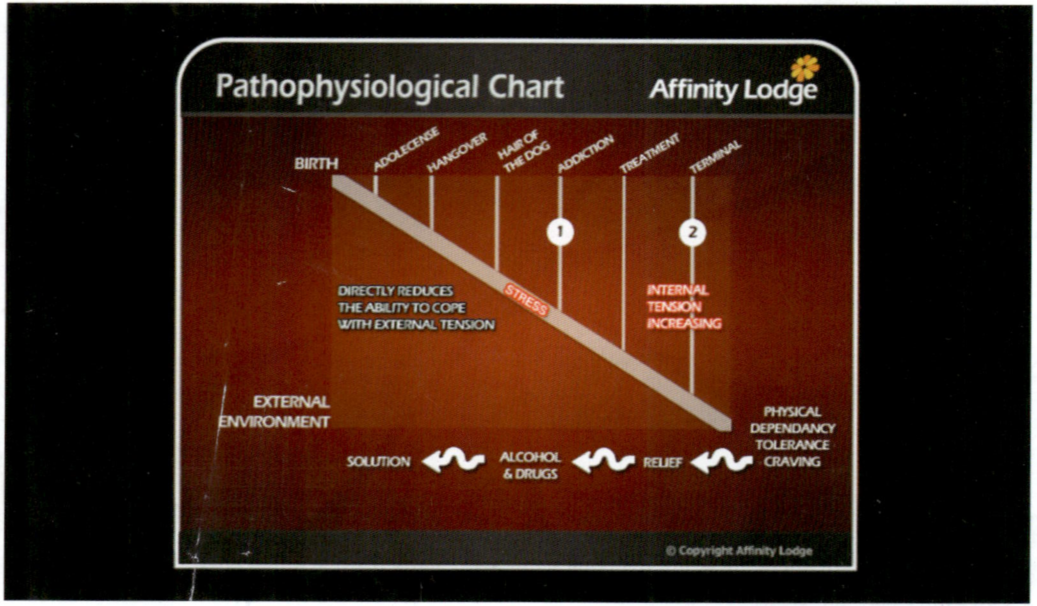
Pathophysiological Chart
Affinity Lodge
BIRTH
ADOLECENSE
HANGOVER
HAIR OF THE DOG
ADDICTION
TREATMENT
TERMINAL
1
2
DIRECTLY REDUCES THE ABILITY TO COPE WITH EXTERNAL TENSION
STRESS
INTERNAL TENSION INCREASING
EXTERNAL ENVIRONMENT
PHYSICAL DEPENDANCY TOLERANCE CRAVING
SOLUTION
ALCOHOL & DRUGS
RELIEF
© Copyright Affinity Lodge